WESTERN MARYLAND NEWSPAPER ABSTRACTS

1806-1810

Compilation of Items Taken from Microfilm Copies of
Newspapers of Hagerstown and Frederick, Maryland

Volume 3

F. Edward Wright

HERITAGE BOOKS
2006

HERITAGE BOOKS

AN IMPRINT OF HERITAGE BOOKS, INC.

Books, CDs, and more—Worldwide

For our listing of thousands of titles see our website
at
www.HeritageBooks.com

Published 2006 by
HERITAGE BOOKS, INC.
Publishing Division
65 East Main Street
Westminster, Maryland 21157-5026

International Standard Book Number: 978-1-58549-009-1

Introduction

This is the third in a series of abstracts covering the newspapers of Western Maryland. For the period covered by this volume the only known newspapers for Western Maryland were published in the county seats of Frederick and Washington Counties. Most of these items were abstracted from a microfilm copies held by the Maryland Historical Society, representing newspaper collections of Harvard University, New York Public Library, New York State Library, Maryland Historical Society, Philadelphia Library Company and the New York Historical Society. The microfilm copy of the (Hagerstown) Maryland Herald is held by the George Peabody Library, Baltimore.

The Maryland Herald and Elizabeth-Town Advertiser began with the issue of June 8, 1797. Its name became The Maryland Herald and Hager's Town Weekly Advertiser in 1804. During the period covered by this work it was published by Thomas Grieves. Another newspaper was established in Hagerstown in 1809 - the Hagers-Town Gazette. It was published by William Brown from May 16, 1809 until circa June 15, 1813. The (Hagerstown) Westliche Correspondenz was established in June, 1795, by Johann Gruber and continued, apparently with some interruptions, until 1820.

There were at least seven newspapers in existence in Frederick-town during much of the period of these abstracts, 1806-1810. They were Bartgis's Federal Gazette; Frederick-Town Herald; (Fredericktown) Hornet; (Frederick-town) Independent American Volunteer, (Fredericktown) Freiheitsbothe, (Fredericktown) General Staatsbothe; and the Republican Advocate.

Matthias E. Bartgis was involved in the publication of several newspapers of Frederick County. His English and German Printing Office was located at the corner of Market and Patrick Streets, Frederick-Town. Bartgis's Federal Gazette continued from 1800 until 1820. It passed through several name changes; among the names were Bartgis's Republican Gazette and General Advertiser, The Republican Gazette and General Advertiser and Bartgis's Republican Gazette and General Advertiser, and similar titles. The Hornet was introduced to the public on June 22, 1802 by Matthias Bartgis, later taken over by William B. Underwood. Succeeding the Hornet for a while was The Independent American Volunteer, also published by William B. Underwood beginning with its first issue on July 8, 1807. After Underwood's resignation, Jan 6, 1808, the paper was published at the office of the Republican Gazette, by Matthias Bartgis. The last issue located is that of December 28, 1808. The Hornet renewed publication under Bartgis with the issued dated February 1, 1809. Bartgis also published the German newspaper, (Fredericktown) General Staatsbothe from 1810 to 1813. (No copies were available to this compiler; only one copy is known to be in existence.)

(Frdericktown) Republican Advocate was established December 6, 1802 by John B. Colvin who announced his retirement in December 12, 1806 issue. Shortly thereafter Silas Engles took over and continued its operation until the last issue dated December 15, 1808.

The Frederick-Town Herald was established with its first issue on June 19, 1802, printed by John P. Thompson and continued by him until after 1820.

Aside from General Staatsbothe there was another German newspaper printed at Fredericktown during this period. This was Freiheitsbothe, published by Charles T. Melsheimer. The only known issue, April 14, 1810, is held by the American Antiquarian Society.

At the beginning of each issue is a trigraph signifying the name of the newspaper.

FHB - Frederick-Town Herald (copies of microfilm are held by Md. Hist. Society, Baltimore, and the George Peabody, Baltimore)
EAM - The Maryland Herald and Elizabeth-Town (or Hagers-town) Advertiser
HGM - Hagers-town Gazette (microfilm held held by the Md. Hist. Society
RGM - (Frederick-town) Bartgis's Republican Gazette (microfilm held by the Md. Hist. Society
RGL - (Frederick-town) Bartgis's Republican Gazette (copies held by the Library of Congress)
FHM - (Frederick) Hornet (microflm held by the Md. Hist. Society)
RAM - (Frederick) Republican Advocate (microfilm held by Md. Hist. Society)
IAM - (Frederick) Independent American Volunteer (microfilm held by Md. Hist. Society)

The following abbreviations were used.

a. - acres
AA - Anne Arundel
adj - adjoining
adm or admr - administrator or
    administratrix of the estate
agnst - against
Balt - Baltimore
co - county
dau - daughter
decd - deceased
dwlg - dwelling
est - estate
exec - executor or executrix
Fred - Frederick
ft - feet
inch - inches

inst - instant (this month)
Mtg or Montg - Montgomery
nr - near
occ - occupied
pers - personal
Phila - Philadelphia
PG - Prince George's
prop - property
pt - part
res - resided or residence
stry - story
ult - ultimo (last; used in
    reference to last month)
Wash - Washington
yrs - years

Comments and questions are welcomed.

F. Edward Wright
13405 Collingwood Terrace
Silver Spring, Maryland 20904

Frederick-Town Herald

1. FHB Frederick-Town Herald, Printed by John P. Thomson - Price $2.00 per
Annum, No. 30, Saturday, Jan 4 1806/A List of tracts and list of land in
Allegany Co, held by persons not res of said co: Charles Boyles; Michael
Boyer; William Bell, Williamson's Discovery; William Bell, John Steinmetz
and Thomas Jones, Clifton, Sportsman's Fields; William Baker; John Burnham;
Bailey E. Clark; George Cook - Bottom; James Cook; Peter Casnave's heirs;
John Doyle; John Fitzhugh - pt of Eden's Paradise regained; Philip Greybell;
Solomon Geer; James Greenleaf - pt of Spruce Spring, Durham; Robert Gover;
Elias and John W. Glenn; Levi Hughs; Adam Hope; Robert Hughs - Locust Ridge
Resurveyed; Bennett Jarrett; Thomas Johnson - Promised Land, Thomas and Ann,
Peace and Plenty, Pt of Spruce Spring; Thomas Johnson & James Greenleaf;
Henry Kuhn; Henry Kemp and Lawrence Brengle - Sugar Camp, Partnership;
Randolph B. Latimer - Savage Ridge, Buck Ridge, Glade Farm; James Miller;
Peter Mantz; Samuel Norwood - Norwood's Farm; John Orme - pt Orme's Mill
Seat, Felicity; Richard I. Orme - Lovely; Rezin Offert; John Pollard; Robert
Peter, jun - The Mark Amended; John Ritchie - Pott's Adventure; Constitution
Vale, Addition to Hunting Ground, Rich Glades, Potatoe Garden, Elk Lick;
Christopher Richmond; John Randle; John Ross; John Schley; John H. Stone -
Addition to Hotel; Gustavus Scott's heirs - Orme's Attention, Chesnut Grove,
Now or Never, Hard Struggle; John Stoddert - Pt Granery; John Thompson;
Edward Wright; Philip L. Webster; Abraham Vanbibber - Diadem, Orme's
Delight; Orme's Choice, The General's Wish, Friendship, Elk Garden, Orme's
Discovery; James West, Jun; William Woods; John Wilmot, jun.; William Brown
- pt Flowery Meads; Joseph James - pt Road Lick, Sugar Camp; William Stidger
- pt Alleghany; William Lovell - Brodhag's Coal-mine; Harmanus Allricks -
Half lot 28 in Cumberland; William King; Jacob Myers - 1/3 Tan-yard formerly
Geo. Pains; John McPherson - Lot in Cumberland; John Myers - Cumberland;
Conrad Muma - Cumberland; Thomas Orme - Cumberland; Thomas Price's heirs;
Robert Selby's heirs - Brodhag's Addition to Cumberland; Francis Thomas -
Cumberland; John Watts - Cumberland; Simon Housar - Flintstone Gap; Jerom
Plummer's heirs - Locust Flats, pt Great Friendship, Whit-oak Hollow; John
C. Jones - Clear Meadow, Horse Pasture; William M. Manydier - Chance;
Russell's heirs - Rabbit Range; Samuel Ridgley - pt of Richard's Discovery
Amended. Lands are to be sold if county tax not paid to Levi Hilleary by 2
June next, Aquila A. Brown, Clark, Allegany Co/Chancery sale of real est of
Robert Chesley, of St. Mary's Co, decd, his late res by name of Pork Hall on
St. Mary's river, 600 a./Persons forewarned from taking stone and other
injuries on property adj Catoctin mountain - Richard Templin, B. Johnson, W.
M. Beall/Sale of tract on Little Monocacy nr mouth of Big Monocacy, 200 a. -
Thomas Talbott, living on the premises/Sale at dwlg hse of late John Waters,
decd, Mtg Co, on Potomac River, above the Sugar Lands, on a place of Robert
Peters, within two miles of Samuel H. Wheeler's, 9 negroes, horses, colts,
cattle, hogs and ship, still of 125 gallons, plantation utensils, 150
barrels of corn - Sarah Waters, admr

2. FHB Jan 11 1806/Married Tues last by Rev Nicholas Zocchey, R. B. Taney,
Esq. to Miss Anne P. C. Key/Mtg of Visitors of Frederick Academy/Sale of
tract in Fred Co nr Potomac river, pt of Merryland Tract, 575 a. - Leonard
Jamison living on Carrolls manor, about 6 miles from Fred. Town/V.
Vincendiere forwarns persons from dealing with any of his slaves without his
permission

1

Frederick-Town Herald

3. FHB Jan 18 1806/Married at Lancaster on 10 ult by Rev Clarkson, Jacob Landes of this co to Miss Margaret Skiles of the former place/Married 7 inst by Rev Jascinsky, Isaac Strider of Virginia to Miss Sarah Steiner of Fred. Town/Died Mon last Jacob Birely, husband, parent/Payment required on each share of stock in Balt and Fred town Turnpike Road Company; persons res in or nr Fred. Town make payment to John M'Pherson, or Georg Baer, jun.; persons res in or nr Hagers Town, make payment to Thomas Sprigg, Esq - J. Lewis Wampler, Sec'r

4. FHB Jan 25 1806/Death of Alexander Contee Hanson, Chancellor of Maryland, 16 inst, in 57th yr of his age (long obit)/Died in this town, also of apoplectic fit, Fri 17 inst, Mrs. Priscilla Scott, in 60th yr of her age /Married Sun eve last by Rev Daniel Wagner, John Diehl, to Mrs. Phebe Fout/Corn for sale - 700 barrels, Otho H. W. Luckett, Nolands Ferry/Henry Koontz, jun. admr of Anthony Sim/Thomas N. Harwood and Polly Harwood, admr of Thomas Noland, junr, to sell his pers est, including 11-12 negroes /Christian Hull, admr, to sell at late res of Margaret Hill, on Carroll's Manor, negroes, horses, cattle, sheep, hogs, wheat, rye, corn, farming utensils, household furniture

5. FHB Feb 1 1806/Dissolution of partnership of Henry Ruth and William Addams, the bus. to be carried on by William Addams & George Wagner, Fred. Town/Mill and 50 a. for sale, on road from Harper's Ferry to Fred. Town - Jesse Matthews/Jacob Hummer cautions agnst taking assignment of bond given to Matthew Campbell

6. FHB Feb 8 1806/Lottery to raise steeple on which to place the town clock; managers: John Schley, Abraham Shriver, Grafton Duvall, Michael Hauser, Philip Rohr, Henry Koontz, jun., George Baer, jun., Fred. Town/7000 a. for sale in Virginia adj lands of Benjamin Harrison, jun, lying on the left hand fork of Big Sandy Creek, a Branch of the Ohio - William Hodgson, Alexandria, D. C./Basil Brown, admr, to sell by order Orphan's Court, of Anne Arundel Co, pers est of Richard Marriott/Election of Balt and Reister's -Town Turnpike Road Company; Commissioners: William Owings, Solomon Etting, David Williamson, Edward Johnson, John Cromwell

7. FHB Feb 15 1806/Seeking someone to fill vacancy of late master of the Merryland Tract school/Hse and lots for sale in Liberty Town where Andrew Etzler formerly kept tavern; hse is 2 stry high, with 3 rooms; apply to Upton Hammond, living on the premises/Thomas Patterson wishing to remove to the western country, offers for sale the plantation whereon he now lives, 158 a., 2 1/2 miles of Fred. Town/A tan-yard at Occoquan to exposed at public sale, undivided half interest, sold in consequence of the death of Robert Lindsay, one of the former proprietors - George W. Lindsay, Surviving Partner, or to Braddock Richmond, admrs of Robert Lindsay, decd/William C. Hobbs candidate for sheriff/Solomon Stackel, living in Fred. Town, offers reward for apprentice boy, bound to the cordwaining bus. named Anthony Klein/Lottery for purchasing an engine with hose for the better security of property in this town; managers: Henry Steiner, Francis Mantz, Henry Bontz, George Creager, sen., Lewis Weltshimer, Charles Shell, Jacob Medtard, Geo. Adam Ebert, Peter Burckhardt

2

8. FHB Feb 22 1806/Chancery sale of pt of real est of Adam Cramer, decd, to discharge his debts, on river Monococy, 183 a. - John Schley, Trustee/George R. Leiper, Piscataway, offers reward for negro man, Tom, 30 yrs old, 5 ft 9-10 inch; has relations nr Winchester, Va, and Wash City/Auction sale of prop of late Abraham Van Bibber, called Paradise, 300 a., dwlg hse and mill, 1 mile from turnpike gate on York road; apply to Mr. Aisquith on the premises - Andrew Van Bibber, Washington Van Bibber, Trustees/To rent hse and lot in Buckey's-town, formerly prop of Philip Sengstack, decd - George Buckey; also hse in Patrick st, Fred. Town, opp widow Stoner

9. FHB Mar 1 1806/Tobias Butler candidate for sheriff/Robert L. Annan, William Long admr of Solomon Kephart/Thomas Karr cautions agnst taking assignment of note given to George Devilbiss/Grist and saw mill to be rented on Owing's creek nr Creagers Town - Frederick Eichelberger, living on the premises/Hse for rent in Tramel's town, Fred Co, where John Whiteneck formerly kept tavern; hse is 2 stry with four rooms on lower floor, corn hse, stables, distillery with two stills, one of 119 gallons and the other 59; apply to Samuel Albaugh on the premises or the subscriber, John Whiteneck, living about 3 miles from Woodsborough/Noted horses for sale from Virginia; if not sold they will stand to cover mares in this town and at William Cookerly's, innkeeper, on the York road; enquire of Henry Brish, innkeeper, Fred. Town

10. FHB Mar 8 1806/Summer seat adj Fred. Town to be sold, 11 a. - Conrad Doll /Whereas it appears that by letters received from Jacob Gomber, formerly of this county (now living on Wills creek, state of Ohio) that he did, on or about 4 Oct 1805, inclose a bond in a letter directed to the subscriber, drawn in favor of said Gomber, and accepted by Abraham Shriver and Andrew Hedges, of this co, the amount being $600; said letter and bond have not come to the hands of subscriber, James Robertson, Fred. Town/Married Tues eve last by Rev George Bower, William Ross, Esq. of York, Pa, to Miss Catherine W. Johnson, dau of Col. Baker Johnson of Fred. Town/Died Tues last at the age of 85 yrs, Mrs. Alice Fleming/600-700 a. for sale in Jefferson Co, Va, 4 miles from Charlestown - Thomas Fairfax

11. FHB Mar 15 1806/Died at Boonsborough on Wed 5 inst, Mrs. Elizabeth Mitchel, dau of George Scott, Esq., of that place, lost to an only child, an affectionate father and other near relations/Died Tues last, Mrs. Mary Hymer, native of Germany, aged 103 yrs, could read the smallest print without the aid of spectacles/Nicholas Brengel gives warning to persons tresspassing on his prop/Solomon Davis, exec of Colonel Solomon Simpson, to sell at the store of John Kelly, in Mtg Co, tract called Elisabeth, 123 a., 4 miles from Conrads ferry; also 4/7 of undivided tract of 100 a. on main road from mouth of Monocacy to Geo. Town whereon John Kelly now lives; and other tracts (named)/Sale by court order of 199 a. being Resurvey on pt of the Resurvey on Bennett's Resolution, formerly prop of Elias Lefever, decd, 11 miles from Fred. Town on road to Graceham; Commissioners: Henry Leatherman, Henry Kuhn, Matthias Shrup, Conrad Shaffer/Conrad Shaffer will sell a new waggon and 6 horses, 2 negro men and other/William G. Lowe, Newark, Del, offers for sale a tract in Fred Co, nr Graceham and adj lands of Nathaniel Livers and Capt Kuhn, being pt of tract Content; also land adj Thomas Ogle (Owings creek) and George Devilbiss/Thomas Peter, Geo. Town, to sell tract

Woodstock, in Mtg Co, nr mouth of Monocacy, late the prop of Gen. Washington, decd, 519 a./Tanyard for sale in Shepherd's Town, Va - John Kearsley /John Eury, living nr the Linganore meeting hse, has taken up two stray cows

12. FHB Mar 22 1806/Died Tues 11 inst in 43d yr of her age, Mrs. Eleanor Briscoe, consort of John Briscoe, esq. of Jefferson Co, Va, after a painful and lingering illness, leaving an almost unconsolable husband with eight children; interred in family burying ground; funeral sermon delivered by Rev. Collins; she was dau and only child of Alexander Magruder, formerly a res of Fred Co, Md/Jeremiah Tarlton will offer for sale on Carrol's Manor, nr Buckeys, horses, cattle, sheep, hogs, and other/Jacob Baltzell will sell corner lot, 2nd and market sts and hse and lot in Patrick St/Sale of land and negroes, where he now lives Alexander Boteler, Wash Co, 250 a., on road from Harper's Ferry to Hagers Town/To rent stand for store and dwlg hse in Market St, next door below Jacob Steiner's, formerly occ by Mr. Herstons; also brick hse in Market St next door to Conrad Shaffer's, now in tenure of Mrs. Colegate - Henry Bantz

13. FHB Mar 29 1806/Wm. Goldsborough offers for sale a tract, 120 a., 3 miles from Fred. Town, has good mill seat/Sale of tract called Stepney in Anne Arundel Co, 835 a. - Robert C. Stone, Port Tobacco/Married Sun eve last by Rev Daniel Wagner, Michael Buckey to Miss Kitty Pyfer dau of Philip Pyfer, all of Fred. Town/Died Mon 17inst after a lingering illness, James Henderson, sen. of this co, in 74th yr, kind husband and affectionate father, good master/R. B. Taney, Fred. Town, offers reward for missing cow /Denis Dunlevy exec of Louis Charles Sebastian St. Martin de Bellevue, late of Fred Co

14. FHB Apr 5 1806/Died Mon last, at an advanced age, Mrs. Price, of this place/James Whiffing has opened a House of Entertainment in New Market /Elizabeth Birely exec of Frederick Birely/The highest price will be given for tanner's bark, at bus. conducted by Frederick Birely, decd, continued as usual by Lewis Birely

15. FHB Apr 12 1806/Peter Troutman cautions persons from taking an assignment on notes given to James Watt, of Loudon Co, Va/Sale in pursuant to will of John Buckey, of household and kitchen furniture, blacksmith's tools & 6 slaves and real prop, noted Tavern Stand, within 6 miles of Fred. Town - E. Buckey, exec of John Buckey/Chancery sale made by John Schley of real est of Adam Cramer to be approved (case of William Campbell vs Apolonia, John, Amos and David Cramer)/Chancery case, Benjamin Blackford and others vs Frederick Masoner and others; whereas George Masoner died intestate and without issue, seized of real est in Fred Co which descended to defendant Frederick Masoner his brother and two sisters

16. FHB Apr 19 1806/Married Tues eve last by Rev Daniel Wagner, William Thomas to Miss Catharine Hauser/Married same eve by same, Jacob Cronise to Miss Catherine Funderburg/Leonard Jamison admr of Henry Jamison/James Robertson has removed into store lately occ by Charles Herstons, in Market St, between Francis Mantz's and Jacob Steiner, opp Mr. Miller's tavern; has handsome and cheap assortment of dry goods

17. FHB Apr 26 1806/Wanted two boys to the printing bus. in the English and German - Jacob D. Dietrick, Hagers Town/Dissolution of partnership of John Hughes and James Hughes; James Hughes will continue the grocery, liquor, flour and commission bus as usual/Doctor John Fischer has removed from Patrick St into Market st into the hse lately occ by Mrs. Colegate, next door to Conrad Shafer's tavern and opp Adam Keller's/For sale by Francis Mantz: Dr. Rawson's Anti-Bilious and Stomachic Bitters, Dr. Rawson's genuine Itch or Beautifying Ointment, Dr. Rawson's celebrated worm powders, etc. /Chancery sale by Roger Perry of interest of Thomas Beall of Samuel and Samuel B. Beall in the prop included and specified in a bond of conveyance given by Nathan Gregg and Robert Gregg to said Samuel B. Beall

18. FHB May 3 1806/James Moynihan has been nominated master of the intro- ductory School of the Fred Co Academy/William Willson, Clarksburg, Mtg Co, exec of John Clark/P. Thomas, offers reward for mulatto Abraham or Abraham Chase, 22, about 5 ft 9-10 inch, having stolen a pass from Thomas Clark, a coloured freeman/To sell land belonging to est of Wm. Deakins, jun., decd, Va - Leonard M. Deakins, John Hoye, Geo. Town/Samuel Clarke, has removed to lower end of Patrick st opp Dr. Duvall's where he will carry on the dying of wool, cotton, linen and silk in web or skein

19. FHB May 10 1806/Died Mon morn last in this town, Mrs. Beall consort of Upton Beall, Esq. of Mtg Court House/Riding Chair for sale, with a top - Nicholas Snethen, Mount Airey, between Libery and Mr. Owing's saw mill on Linganore/Persons indebted to Jeremiah Tarlton on account of late sales of prop before his removal to Kentucky should leave claims in hands of John Hanson Thomas/George Creager, Jun, candidate for sheriff/Elizabeth Dawson and Samuel Dawson exec of Nicholas Dawson

20. FHB May 17 1806/Merryman Stevenson, Westminister, Fred Co, candidate for sheriff

21. FHB May 24 1806/Married Sat eve last, by Rev Daniel Wagner, John Fritchie to Miss Barbara Hauer/Married Tues eve by same Henry Steiner to Miss Rachel Murray/New store - Nicholas Clopper, Fred. Town, has just opened in the store hse of John Hoffman, nr the N.E. corner of Patrick and Market sts, dry goods and groceries, glass, etc./Middleton Smith candidate for sheriff/George Price and Joseph S. Smith, admr of Thomas Price, to sell negroes, horses, hogs, milch cow, &c./Chancery sale by George Baer, trustee for sale of real est of Nicholas Hauer/Henry Clary, Linganore, offers reward for missing horse

22. FHB May 31 1806/George C. Sedwick, Taylor, has opened a shop in Hyatt's -town/Died Sun eve last at her son-in-law's, John Ritchie, after a long and well spent life, Mrs. Anna Barnhold/Boulting cloths just received - Kennedy & Ragan, Hagers Town/James Pearce, living nr Liberty Town, Fred Co, offers reward for negro man named Damond, 19-20, 5 ft 7-8 inch, purchased at sher- iff's sale in Fred. Town, formerly prop of Fielder Gant near that town; it is supposed that he will attempt to go to Charlestown, on the Ohio river, where the wife of the late John Gant lives

23. FHB Jun 7 1806/Married Tues eve last, by Rev P. Davidson, John White to Miss Mary Stewart, both of this co/William C. Hobbs candidate for sheriff/W. T. Lewis to sell the Fredonian mills in Campbell Co, Va

24. FHB Jun 14 1806/Addams & Wagner, Hardware, including clock and watch-makers tools/James Hawkins, living in Clarksburg, Mtg Co, offers reward for apprentice to the tayloring bus., John Bradford, 5 ft, 15, slender made; had on a superfine broad cloth coat, white mersailles vest, blue pantaloons with sundry other clothing

25. FHB Jun 21 1806/Roger Perry, Trustee, to sell lots in Westernport at the mouth of George's Creek, Allegany Co, where Able Sarjeant kept store, lot adj, lot whereon is erected a framed hse, late the prop of Able Sarjeant and sold at the suit of Abraham Faw

26. FHB Jun 28 1806/Married Sun eve last by Rev Daniel Wagner, John Rigney to Miss Sophia Heisley/Died on eve of 23 inst, Mrs. Elizabeth Cook, relict of Captain George Cook, whose remains were on Wed deposited in the Episc Church yard of this town/Benjamin Ogle, Fred. Town, has for sale next door to Mrs. Kimboll's, a general assortment of Cast Iron/Mary Sear exec of Israel Sear, Mtg Co, decd

27. FHB Jul 5 1806/John K. Smith and Harriot Williams adm of Elisha O. Williams, late of the District of Columbia, decd, who owned tract in Mtg Co, and lots in Montgomery Courthouse; apply to Leonard H. Johns

28. FHB Jul 12 1806/Edward Salmon forwarns persons from trespasing on his prop/John Patterson, living about 11 miles from Fred. Town and 1 mile from Creagerstown, offers reward for missing horse/George G. Tyler, near Hay Market, Prince William Co, Va, offers reward for two negro men, Jilson and George

29. FHB Jul 19 1806/F. Pool adm of Capt. Luke Pool, to sell his pers est

30. FHB Jul 26 1806/Died last week at Dover, Delaware, Revd Richard Whatcoat, one of the Bishops of the Meth Episc Church/Thomas Patterson to sell horses, cows, sheep, hogs, ten plate stove, several hogsheads, &c. at his res within 2 1/2 miles of Fred. Town/Elizabeth Dawson and Samuel Dawson, exec of Nicholas Dawson, to sell 14-15 negroes/Matthew Smith offers for cash at his store no. 3 North Liberty St, Queens Ware, Balt/P. Thomas, offers reward for steers missing from his farm adj the Catoctin mountain, 4 miles from Fred. Town/Joseph Clagett, living nr Montgomery Court hse, offers reward for mulatto man named Harry, midding broad face, about 5 ft 7-8 inch, 22

31. FHB Aug 2 1806/James K. Benson wishes to buy 7-8 negroes; apply to George Miller, Fred. Town/John L. Harding, offers reward for dark mulatto Moses, commonly called Lanham, who ranway from his farm in Fred Co; he was raised nr Piscataway, PG Co, by a family of the Lanhams, sold to late James Marshall of Fred Co, decd, by a Mr. Burriss, now living at the Eastern Branch bridge, who has a brother and two sisters of his at this time; he is about 30, nearly 6 ft, stout, active, fond of liquors/John Bryan, Wash Co,

10 miles from Hagers Town, 5 miles from Williamsport, offers reward for negro men, Perry and Glasgow, brothers, one about 23 and other about 25, chunky, about 5 ft 7 inch

32. FHB Aug 9 1806/Conrad Shaffer, Innkeeper, still keeps tavern, at the sign of the Fountian Inn, Market St/James F. Forker wants four young men to teach in a line of schools from Pipe Creek to the Lingan Chapel; apply to Messrs. Abraham Jones, Liberty-town; William Gibson, New market or to the printer/Farm for sale, 119 a. on Bennett's creek - Jarum Plummer, Joshua Plummer

33. FHB Aug 16 1806/Cash for wheat at Bruce's mill, Pipe Creek, by John Scott/Abraham Albaugh candidate for sheriff/Leonard Jamison, admr of Henry Hamison, to receive payment at Abraham Easterday's tavern, on Catoctin creek, on notes due from sale of pers est of decd/John Henderson, George Henderson, exec of James Henderson

34. FHB Aug 23 1806/Dissolution of partnership of John Hoffman and Thomas Baltzell/Elias Harding, living within 7 miles of Fred. Town, offers reward for negro man Moses, 24, about 5 ft 6-7 inch, raised by Richard Wootten of Mtg Co, who lived formerly in PG Co/Thomas Glisson, living nr Moorefield, Hardy Co, Va, offers reward for negro Joe, 5 ft 8-9 inch, 22-23, remarkable long feet

35. FHB Aug 30 1806/Benj. Maynard and Brice Maynard exec of Thomas Maynard, to sell pers prop/Will be sold by order of Fred Co Court, dwlg plantation of late John Karr, decd, 8 miles from Fred. Town on road to Emmittsburg, called Seven Bitts United, 196 1/2 a., encombered with widow's dower; commission-ers: Nicolas Holtz, Michael Myers, Andrew Hedges/Roger Brooke candidate for Gen Assembly/Tract for sale, 3 miles from Middletown, 131 a. - Thomas Oare, one the premises/Two lots in Leesburg for sale; also 309 1/4 a. nr Blue Ridge, and other - Stephen Donaldson, Arcadia, Loudon Co, Va

36. FHB Sep 6 1806/Married Thurs 21 ult, at Columbia Court House, Georgia, by Rev John Marshall, George W. Dent to Miss Ann Hutcheson, both of Charles Co, Md/Nathan Harris, res nr Liberty-town, Fred Co, offers reward for three negroes, Basil, about 30, 5 ft; Milfred, about 17, 4 ft 10 inch; Sam 15 about 4 ft 2-3 inch/Boundaries of election districts for third congressional district described/John Ritchie candidate for sheriff/Mr. V. Guillou to commence his Dancing School

37. FHB Sep 13 1806/Goshen Farms for rent in Mtg Co - R. M. Boyer, Geo. Town, D. C./Purchasers of prop at sale of late Anthony Sim are informed their notes are due - Henry Koontz, Jun., admr of A. Sim/Fred. Town Races to be run - Ben. Stallings, Conrad Shaifer

38. FHB Sep 20 1806/Ann Campbell adm of George Campbell, St. Mary's Co /Richard Brooke candidate for Gen Assembly/Jacob G. Smith, Balt, to apply to Balt Co Court for benefit of insolvency/Jacob Garty, Liberty-Town, cautions whereas his wife Nancy Garty, has refused to live with him, he is determined to pay no debts of her contracting/Leonard Jamison admr of John Jamison

39. FHB Sep 27 1806/Tanyard for sale in Clarksburg, Mtg Co - Joseph Burnsides, living on the premises

40. FHB Oct 4 1806/Repsonse to handbill published by Tobias Butler "in which the whole federal party were set at defiance in the most scornful tone." Statement by Ben. Blackford in which he mentions William Head, Baker Johnson, George Creager and Edward Moorhead

41. FHB Oct 11 1806/Justinian Mayberry, overseer of poor house, states that a man admitted into the poor house of Fred Co, name unknown, by birth a German, by trade a hatter, died Wed 8 inst/A miller wanted - John Scott, at Bruce's mill, Big Pipecreek/Warrented boulting cloths of every size - George Baer, Junr/22 negroes to be sold, pers est of John Holmes and Mary Holmes, decd - M. Browning, admr D.B.N., Clarksburg

42. FHB Oct 18 1806/No additional items

43. FHB Oct 25 1806/James Knight has just received at his store in New Market a supply of goods/Samuel R. Hobbs requests persons settle their accounts with him

44. FHB Nov 1 1806/Married Sun eve last by Rev Daniel Wagner, Augustus Gra... of Fred. Town to Miss Martha Cock, dau of Capt S. Cock of Fred Co /Married Mon eve by same, Doctor John Ott to Miss Ann Ritchie, dau of Abner Ritchie, all of Geo. Town/Died Mon last at Rocky Fountain, Miss Ann Chioeolon, niece of Major Henry Darnall, after long suffering under the most severe bodily afflictions/Dissolution of partnership in the line of Stages from Fred. Town to Lancaster: William Scott, Joshua Hallar, Joseph Hallar /James Stephens, living on Carroll's manor, offers reward for 6 head of cattle missing, which he drove from St. Mary's Co last fall/Lewis Stephens, living nr Stephensburg, Fred Co, VA, offers reward for missing horses/Samuel Popham, living on Linganore, about 1 mile from Steele's mill, has taken up a stray mare

45. FHB Nov 8 1806/Overseer wanted by Edward Owings, living on Lancaster road, 5 miles from Fred. Town/Elias Thrasher, Eli Thrasher, exec of Thomas Thrasher, to sell 12 slaves of est of decd/Ludwick Herbaugh, living in Herbaugh valley, on great road leading from Creagerstown to Waynesburg, to sell tract, 254 a./Henry Spalding exec of Philip Freich/James Baker, living in Fred Co, Va, nr Millwood, offers reward for negro Sam Doyle, around 6 ft, 35 yrs of age

46. FHB Nov 15 1806/James S. Hook, to sell at the Trap in Fred Co, 11 negroes/Nicholas W. Dorsey, living in Mtg Co, about 8 miles from Court hse, offers reward for negro fellow Jack, 5 ft 6-7 inch, 24-25/John Wolfenden has removed to Mr. Kephart's new buildings, Patrick St, between Messrs. Graham's and Bayly's, nr Mrs. Kimboll's tavern - Dry Goods, Hardward & Cutlery/Amelia Wolfenden has removed to new store in Patrick St where she is supplied with newest and most elegant fashions from Phila and Balt/Maria Catharine Metzger, exec of John Metzger

Frederick-Town Herald

47. FHB Nov 22 1806/Negro girl for sale - Richard L. Head/Overseer wanted -
Wm. Goldsborough/Undivided moiety of 2000 a. for sale now in the possession
of Denton Jacques, to be sold at hse of Daniel Harbine, at the Big Spring nr
the premises, in pursuance of chancellor of Md, in Wash Co; Mr. D. Jacques,
living at the furnace will shew the land - Launcelot Jacques, Trustee, Wash
Co

48. FHB Nov 29 1806/David Eater, living on road from Frederick to Liberty,
has taken up a stray mare

49. FHB Dec 6 1806/No additional items

50. FHB Dec 13 1806/Died Wed last, David Levy, innkeeper; left wife and
several small children/C. F. Kenter, Balt, to apply for relief of debts

51. FHB Dec 20 1806/Grist and Saw Mill for sale on Middle Bennett's creek,
about 10-11 miles from Fred. Town - Christopher Zeigler

52. FHB Dec 27 1806/William Stevenson to apply to Fred Co court for benefit
of insolvency/George Balters Detero has taken up 12 stray hogs which came to
his plantation nr Abraham Yesterday's tavern, 2 miles from the Trap/Richard
Bland Lee, nr Centreville, Fairfax Co, Va, has 8000 a. for sale within 12
miles of Fredericksburg, Va

53. FHB Jan 3 1807/Taxes due on pers prop in Allegany Co, names of person
listed - Aquilla Arell Browne, clerk/Commissioners of the tax for Fred Co
will meet - Ezra Mantz, clerk /New editor of Republican Advocate - Silas
Engles/Persons indebted to est of Matthias Buckey, decd, are requested to
make payment - Michael Buckey, admr

54. FHB Jan 10 1807/Reward by Elders of the Reformed congregation to person
who will discover to them who did shatter one of the windows in the hse of
Rev Daniel Wagner, by discharging a gun or pistol/Wheat wanted at Bloomsbury
Mills - Richard & Geo. Johnson/Brick houses to be let, now occ by John
Gwinn, Jun, of this City - Mary Mann, Annapolis/Thaddius White, living at
Clagett's Spring, Mtg Co, offers reward for stolen horse/Thomas Warfield
exec of Absalom Warfield/Baalis Coomes has taken up a stray cow/John James
wishing to remove to the Indiana territory, once more offers for sale, the
farm on Ben's Branch, 2 1/2 miles north east of New Market; apply to him or
to Maj. Daniel James adj same/Chancery sale of real est of Thomas Price,
decd - George Price, Trustee; also a parcel of wheat, rye and buckwheat -
George Price and Joseph Sim Smith admr of Thomas Price/Peter Hawkins, nr the
Sugar Loaf Mountain, Mtg Co, offers reward for negro fellow Jesse, about 32,
5 ft 3 inch

55. FHB Jan 17 1807/Letter to Federal Gazette, Williams-Port, describing
the route of the road determined by Commissioners, from Cumberland to state
of Ohio/Mill and farm for sale on south side of Monocacy, 3 1/2 miles from
Fred. Town - William Potts/John Dill has removed to hse lately occ by
Benjamin Ogle on Publick Alley and Church St, where he intends keeping
private entertaininment for man and horse/Drusilla Mobberly and Samuel P.

Richardson, nr Hyatt's Town, exec of Lewis Mobberly, to sell pers est of decd

56. FHB Jan 24 1807/Married Tues eve last by Rev Daniel Wagner, Doct. John Harrison of Wash City to Miss Elizabeth Hoffman dau of John Hoffman of this Co/Mary Ann Levy and Grafton Duvall, admr of David Levy/David Dudrow and Samuel Dudrow, exec, to sell farm of Jacob Dudrow, decd, adj Liberty town

57. FHB Jan 31 1807/Hse and lot to be sold in Shepherds town; apply to Jacob Getzendanner/Richard L. Head, living 5 miles from Fred. Town, offers reward for negro fellow Harry, about 5 ft 9 inch, 22, tolerable brick maker and rough carpenter, raised by Ignatius Disney nr Spurriers tavern/Sale of real est of Richard Cromwell, by order of Wash Co Court, tract on Conoco-cheague Creek, about 7 miles from Hagers Town: No. 1 - late res of Richard Cromwell, decd, 450 a.; No. 2 - at present in occupation of Oliver Cromwell, 350 a. and other tracts; Commissioners: Walter Boyd, Martin Kershner, Henry Ankony, Josiah Price, Wash Co

58. FHB Feb 7 1807/Sale of corner lot on Church St, hse adj Capt. John Adlum and other - John Hoffman, Fred. Town/Sale of tract, Eleven Brothers, 600 a. about 2 miles from mouth of Monocosy - Heirs of Edward Jones, Mtg Co /Sale by order of Orphan's Court of Fred Co of prop of Thomas J. Johnson, decd - John Grahame, admr/Philemon Griffith exec of Rachel Beall/Public sale of store goods where the subscriber now lives in New-town (Trap)_ and a tract of 60 a. within one mile of this place on same stream of water as Valentine Ebbert's mill; also hse where I now live - James Torrance

59. FHB Feb 14 1807/Lottery to build a school hse and purchase a fire engine; managers: Richard Anderson, Solomon Holland, Honore Martin, Upton Beall, Lewis Beall, Rockville/Daniel Burkhart to sell tavern stand, ferry and plantation lying on Balt Turnpike, 2 miles from Fred. Town/Pursuant to last will of William Farquhar, pt of land of James Farquhar to be sold - John Messler, David Rinehart, Pipe Creek, Trustees

60. FHB Feb 21 1807/Sale by order of Orphans Court of Adams Co, Pa, of prop belonging to Solomon Kephart, decd, messuage, grist mill, saw mill and 151 a. in Liberty township adj lands of John Spear, Samuel M'Nair; terms given by Robert L. Annan and William Long, admrs - James Duncan, Clerk/400 a. for sale on main road from Middle town to Shepherds town - Frederick Fox/Sale at late res of Elias Davis, decd, on Carroll's Manor, about 2 miles below Buckey's town, pers est of decd, including negroes - Christian Fogle, admr /Christian Fogle admr of Walter Davis/Baker Jamison, living on Merryland Tract has taken up two stray steers

61. FHB Feb 28 1807/James Knight intending to remove his store from New Market on 1 Apr next desires that all persons indebted to him settle their accounts/Thomas Johnson & Joseph Johnson, exec of Joseph Johnson to sell dwlg plantation of decd, 3 miles from Mrs. Craft's mill/Benjamin Biggs, Abraham Haff, Jun., John Ritchie, exec, pursuant to will of William Dern, decd, to sell negroes, stock and farming utensils; also farm, 258 1/2 a. /Philemon Griffith exec of Rachel Beall

62. FHB Mar 7 1807/E. Buckey exec of John Buckey, to sell tavern stand, smith shop, hse of stone and other/Sale of pers est of David Levy including two negroes, man aged 24 and woman aged 22, mahogany side-board with secretary drawer, full set of walnut dining tables with half rounds, beds and bedsteads with furniture, bureau, glass, brass andirons with shovel and tongs, ten plate and sheet iron stove, copper fish kettle with strainer and tinned, horse, billiard table with the necessary tackle - Mary Ann Levy and Grafton Duvall, admrs

63. FHB Mar 14 1807/Married Sun eve last, 8 inst, at William Herberts, nr Emmittsburg, by Rev Dubois, Ignatius Jamison to Miss Catharine Fenwick, dau of late John Fenwick of St. Mary's Co/James and Thomas Johnson, Jun., at Bush-creek Forge request persons to settle their accounts with them; call on George Johnson at Bloomsbury Forge; persons having accounts with them at Potomac Furnace and Mills are requested to call on Thomas Johnson, there for settlement/Tract within 2 miles of Fred. Town, 352 a., for sale, with stone dwlg hse, Switzer barn, still hse, good apple and peach orchard; apply to Henry Curfman, living nr the premises/Nicholas Meriweather, guardian, by order of orphans court of Anne Arundel Co, to sell negroes belonging to Matilda and Thomas Worthington, orphans of John/Elizabeth Charlton and John M. Beatty, admrs, to sell pers prop of John U. Charlton, decd/Tract for sale in Allegany Co 3 miles south of Brodhags old road, 12 miles west of Fort Cumberland, 120 a. of cleared land - Henry Wright/Sale of horse; apply to Henry S. Turner, Jefferson Co, nr Charlestown, Va; for terms apply to Capt. Charles Turley in Fairfax Co, nr Centreville, Va

64. FHB Mar 21 1807/Married Tues last by Rev George Bower, William Potts, merchant of Balt, to Miss Susan Campbell, dau of Capt. William Campbell, of this co/Married same eve, at Geo. Town by Rev Foxall, Charles Herstons, merchant, to Miss Elizabeth Anderson/Died Thurs morn last, Peter Ogle, son of Benjamin Ogle of this place/Baalis Coomes requests debtors to make payment/Nicholas D. Garrott to petition for benefit of act of insolvency /Roger Brooke admr of William Otto, sen/St. Mary's Co Orphan's Court orders that James Biscoe (of city of Balt), exec of Deborah Wolfstenholme, decd, to give note to creditors to exhibit claims

65. FHB Mar 28 1807/Married Thurs eve last by Rev Daniel Wagner, Jacob Rohr to Miss Elizabeth Hauer, dau of Daniel Hauer sen. all of this place/Chancery sale of real est of Dennis Ensey of Fred Co, decd, at the hse of John Ensey, living on the place, tract called Comes' Inheritance, 145 1/2 a. and tract of 40 a. called Ensey's Adventure, 4 miles below Liberty-town - Francis Brown Sappington/Sale of prop called Mount Pleasant Furnace in Metal township, Franklin Co, Pa; also Parkhead Forge nr the Potomac river, Wash Co, Md, 2300 a. - Benjamin Chambers, Joseph Chambers, William M. Brown, in Chambersburg, Pa/Rockbury Mills for rent on Linganore, 3 miles from New Market - Joseph W. Laurence/George J. Schley will rent his tavern stand in Market st, Fred. Town, now in tenure of George Miller, opp stores of Francis Mantz and James Robertson

66. FHB Apr 4 1807/Letter from Hagers Town states that there was a fracas at Baltzhoover's tavern the other day between a couple of democratic gentry about the merits of Mr. John Randolph; parties were the redoubtable Matthew

Lyon and Major Carroll of that vicinity. The Major pushed his arguments home with a blow on Matthews mouth, later fined $5.00/Negroes for sale - James Johnson, Jur./Hse for sale on Market St, nearly opp Col. M'Pherson; for terms apply to Col. Baker Johnson - John Johnson/Two story stone hse to be let, occ by widow Buckey - George Buckey/Sarah M'Cully admr of Robert M'Cully/John M'Allen, Taney-town, forwarns persons from taking assignment on bonds given to James Kerr with John Shert security

67. FHB Apr 11 1807/Married Tus eve last, by Rev Daniel Wagner, George Creager, sen., to Miss Mary Appler dau of Jacob Appler of this co/Apprentice wanted to boot and shoe making bus. by Solomon Steckel/Mahogany plank for sale - Henry Brice, Bowley's Wharf, Balt/Receiving ground rents on all lots in Creagerstown - Thomas Beatty, at his hse in said town

68. FHB Apr 18 1807/Sale of tract Ireland Eye, 100 a., at Major John Huston in Emmitsburg - I. Gist/Jacob & William Norris, Tea dealers and Grocers, No. 64 Market St, Balt/Fred Town and Winchester Mail stage, to start from hse of Mrs. Kimboll every Tues morn at 4 o'clock and arrive at John Brady's in Winchester Wed morning; passenger fare - $3.50 - William Scott/Aaron Offutt, living on new road from Barnsville to Rockville, offers reward for missing horse/Doctor Fendall, operator upon teeth, has just arrived in this town /James Carroll, City of Balt, offers reward for negro who ran away from his farm on Rhode River, Ann Arundel Co, named Gilbert, about 5 ft 10 inch, 35-40; has a wife belonging to William Johnson, who is now moving out to Kentucky with his family to settle in that country; he has a pass with the name of Peter Moore/John Fiffe, living in Mtg Co, nr John D. Medley's Tavern, offers reward for negro girl Milly, 16-17, has scar on right arm just below the elbow occasioned by the whip; a place about the size of a cent nearly bald which she says was occasioned by carrying water thereon; had on blue and white plaines petticoat and jacket, pair of country knit stockings, pair of tolerable good shoes; she has a father (Jack Locker), mother and connections that are free, living about the glass works of Fred Co, Md

69. FHB Apr 25 1807/Cash for wheat at William Potts' mill, 3 miles from Fred. Town by Graff & Beatty/William T. Lee admr of Henry Lee, St. Mary;s Co/Furniture for sale - John Livingston/James Biscoe, Balt, to sell pers prop of Deborah Wolstenholme, George Campbell and Anne Campbell, all decd, at late res of Deborah Wolstenholme of St. Mary's Co

70. FHB May 9 1807/No additional items

71. FHB May 16 1807/Tavern stand for sale at foot of Allegany, 5 miles from Fort Cumberland - Evan Gwynn/David Harry, Peter Hefleich, exec of John Protzman, Wash Co, decd/John Clark, having declined trading under the firm of Horton and Clark, now offers for sale at his store, No. 8, North Howard st, opp N. Huffey's tavern, assortment of groceries

72. FHB May 23 1807/Lost on road between Frederick and Mr. Late's smith shop, a subscription list of O'Neill's Universal Geography; leave at printer''s office or with George Cole, teacher on the Manor/Assortment of groceries - Nicholas Worthinton at his New Store in market St/Married Sun

last by Rev James Higgins, William Salmon to Miss Sarah Davis, both of this co/Married Thurs eve by Rev Daniel Wagner, Adam Zeiler to Miss Rebecca Levy, both of Fred. Town/Died Sat eve last, of a pulmonary complaint, in 45th year, John Wolfenden, merchant of this town/Grist and saw mill for sale on Middle Bennett's creek - Christopher Zeigler/Richard Wells, Emmittsburg, cautions agnst taking assignment on notes given to Alexander M'Kean and John M'Hugh/Tract for sale in Fayette Co, Pa, 70 a. on east side of Cheat river, 3 stry mill hse, and other - John M'Farland

73. FHB May 30 1807/Edward Salmon intends to petition to prove one of the boundaries of his pt of tract Addison's Choice/Osborn Sprigg, jun., Hampshire Co, Va, offers reward for negro slave Tom, who left him at Mr. Charles Carroll's nr Hagers Town on 21st inst/Joel Marsh intends to erect carding machine nr Mr. Deal's brewery in Fred. Town, for purpose of picking and carding wool into rolls/Henry M'Cleery, announces that he has been authorized to make any number of Buck and Arndt's washing machines, one of which is to be seen at his shop, Fred. Town/Elizabeth Luckett, Fred. Town, offers reward for negro man Jack, by trade a carpenter, in the service of John Brien, at Antietam Mills, when he ran away, 5 ft 9-10 inch; plays well on the violin

74. FHB Jun 6 1807/Married at Balt on Thurs the 28th ult, James Johnson, jun., Esq. of this co, to Miss Richards dau of the Rev Richards of Balt/To sell his dwlg hse in Patrick St - Nicholas Clopper; also cherry brandy bounce and rye whiskey/Thomas Hobbs, living within 3 miles of Liberty-town, offers reward for negro man Bill who calls himself William Scott, 30-40, 5 ft 8-9 inch sold last summer out of Fred. Town jail to Adam Freshour, who sold him to Thomas Hobbs; says he was raised at Norfolk, Va, and that he is free; was on his way to New York or Phila/John Martin, living in Toms Creek Hundred, Fred Co, offers reward for indented apprentice girl Matilda Dorff, about 13, about 4 ft 4-5 inch

75. FHB Jun 13 1807/Sarah Roberts and Richard Roberts admrs of John Roberts; exhibit claims to Richard Roberts in New Market/Sale of prop of Zachariah M'Kuben, in Mtg Co, 488 a., dwlg hse, mill house 38x42 feet, 3 stry high and other - Henry Howard, trustee

76. FHB Jun 20 1807/Jane Brayfield admr of Samuel Brayfield/John Glisan exec of Mary Mumford/Henry Brish, having disposed of his tavern stand in Market st, will sell furniture and other articles/William Cromwell offers reward for steers which strayed from his farm about 3 miles from Fred. Town

77. FHB Jun 27 1807/Nathan Browning, Clarksburg, has opened a House of Entertainment in Clarksburg, Mtg Co/Plantation for sale in Bethel township, Bedford Co, Pa, 390 a.; apply to John Johnson, merchant in Hancock-town - Joshua Johnson/Rachel Shipley wishing to retire from public bus., will rent tavern stand where she now lives, known by name of Fountain Inn; apply to her or to Thomas Shipley nr New market/Henry Darnall forbids dealings with any of his slaves without his permission

78. FHB Jul 4 1807/Journeyman bookbinder wanted - G. K. Harper, Chambersburg, Pa/Louis B. Apollo continues at his old stand in Patrick st where he

constantly keeps for sale butter and water crackers/Boarding hse in Market St - Elizabeth Buckey

79. FHB Jul 11 1807/Sale of tract, 65 a. 1/2 mile above Cumberland James Slicer, Allegany Co

80. FHB Jul 18 1807/Sale of 3 slaves agreeable to last will of Henry Rempsberg - Peter Kemp, exec/Sale of farm on Seneca, Mtg Co, 8 miles from Rockville, 422 a. - James Redman, Seneca, Mtg Co/Levi Phillips, Hyatt's-town, offers reward for stray cow

81. FHB Jul 25 1807/Died Tues last at an advanced age, George Baer, sen. of this co/Mr. Hays, Patrick st, nearly opp Dr. Bogan's will teach poor children gratis

82. FHB Aug 1 1807/Dissolution of partnership of James Horton and John Clark; James Horton has taken Dr. John M. Read into co-partnership in the Grocery and Flour Bus./George Carter, Oatlands, nr Leesburg, Va, offers reward for mulatto man Isaac, 5 ft 4-5 inch, 45; has driven my waggon several times to Baltimore and is very well acquainted in Alexandria/John Himes, Dayton, Ohio, offers reward for stolen gelding; the suspected person was bred nr Liberty town, Fred Co, Md, is a German, about 27, 5 ft 5 inch/Frederick Unkerfer certifies that Samuel Burgess, nr Liberty Town, brought a stray colt to be recorded

83. FHB Aug 8 1807/George Baer admr of George Baer, senr/Benjamin Biggs, Abraham Haff, John Ritchie exec of William Dern/Bennett Campbell, living on Bennett's creek, nr Cook's mill about 2 1/2 miles from Hyatt's Town, offers reward for stolen mare/William Dydenhover has rented Jacob Staley's Fulling Mill, 4 miles from Fred Town and intends to carry on the fulling and dying bus.; cloths will be received at Jacob Shriver's store, corner of Market and Patrick sts

84. FHB Aug 15 1807/Tanyard for sale in Shepherd'sTown, Va - Campbell & M'Knights, res on the premises/Samuel Slifer, living about 1 mile from Harley's Store, has taken up a stray steer/Henry Keefer has lost a red Morocco Pocket Book/Henry Kuhn certifies that Valentine Buckey has taken up a stray mare

85. FHB Aug 22 1807/Henry Boteler, Sen, living in Pleasant Valley, Wash Co, about 6 miles from Sharpsburg, offers reward for negro man Jerry, about 20, 5 ft 11 inch/Henry Stemble certifies that George Castle, Jun. has taken up a stray mare/James Hook certifies that Henry Swan, of lower Monocacy hundred has taken up a stray colt

86. FHB Aug 29 1807/Managers of the Balt and Fred Turnpike have engaged Mr. Herbaugh to superintend the erection of the bridge over Monocacy, to consist of five arches of 30 feet each/John Hughes, nr Frederick, has farm to rent, 1 mile from Noland's Ferry, 300 a.

87. FHB Sep 5 1807/Broke out of the poor hse Tues night last, Jacob Markel, who has been in a deranged state, about 25, 5 ft 8-9 inch; reward offered if delivered to Mr. Maybury at the poor hse, Fred Town

88. FHB Sep 12 1807/Hse for rent, presently occ by William Clements – Francis Mantz/Fred Town Races – Benjamin Stallings, Conrad Shaffer, William R. King/Ann Hilleary admr of Thomas Hilleary

89. FHB Sep 19 1807/Meeting of voters in 7th dist of Fred Co, at hse of Ludwick Wampler (Westminster); Jacob Powder apptd chairman and John Fisher secry/Benjamin Strong forewarns persons from taking assignment on note given to Alexander Montgomery

90. FHB Sep 26 1807/John Ritchie candidate for Gen Assembly/Sale of houses in Patrick St, 2 dors below Dr. Thomas's and adj J. Dorsey – Henry Baer /Joshua Howard to petition to open a public road from his mill on Sam's Creek to Westminster/Edward Owings forewarns persons from fishing or fowling on his enclosures/Samuel Thomas offers reward for negro man Sam, who sometimes calls himself Sampson of Sam Chace, 5 ft 7-8 inch, about 40, purchased about 12 yrs ago from Gustavus Scott, Esq. of city of Wash

91. FHB Oct 3 1807/Catharine Smith admr of John Smith/Jasper Cope, Trustee, for creditors of Philip Heynop, & Co, Daniel Heynop and John Heynop, to sell their right to tracts, pt of Monocosy manor, 125 a. in the tenure of Jacob Holtz; an undivided moiety of lot No. 12; and other parcels/Thomas Whitefoot gives notice that his wife, Elizabeth Whitefoot has eloped (Sun 27th inst) and forwarns persons from purchasing or bartering for a sorrel horse and a silver watch she took with her/Sale in Springfield, Hampshire Co, Va, at the dlwg hse of Rev John Lyle, decd, all real est of decd, two lots and houses

92. FHB Oct 10 1807/John Gebhart admr of Daniel Osborn, to sell prop of decd, negro woman and two children, horses, cows and hogs, waggon and gears and other/Charles Hammond to let saw mill and small farm at mouth of Linganore/Richard L. Head to sell negro fellow, about 22, tolerable brick maker and rough carpenter; apply to Richard L. Head, 5 miles from Fred. Town

93. FHB Oct 17 1807/Negroes for sale – James Johnson, Jun/Negro woman and two children for sale – John Allnutt, living on Bennetts creek, nr Hyatt's town/Jacob Staley and Daniel Biser, exec of Henry Staley, give notice that notes will become due on 4 Nov, on which day they will attend at Mr. Levy's tavern, in Middletown and Joseph Miller's mill/Joshua Jones, exec, Sams Creek, to sell plantation, agreeable to last will of Philip Boyer, late res of decd, 122 a., on road from Liberty-town to Andrew Worman's mill and in sight of what is commonly called Linganore Chapel/Greenbury Howard, Trustee, appt by Walter Friar, res in Kentucky, to sell tract whereon he formerly lived, in Mtg Co, 140 a., 4 miles from Clarksburg; Christian Leaman living thereon will shew the land/Maj. Roger Johnson has taken up two strays/Ann Robert and William Pole, admr of William Roberts, to sell pers prop of decd

94. FHB Oct 24 1807/Died 20th of last month, in Shepherds Town, Va, in 25th yr of her age, Mrs. Alcinda G. Green, consort of Allen Green of Mtg Co, Md; her illness was short; she left an infant, only five days old, husband and

relatives/New Store - William & John Baer, in the store hse formerly occ by
John Hoffman, Ladies' and Gentleman's wear, groceries, cutlery, crockery,
fresh teas/Thomas Warfield, exec, to sell tract pursuant to last will of
Absalom Warfield, Fred Co decd, 161 1/2 a.

95. FHB Oct 31 1807/Died Wed night last after an illness of several weeks,
Jacob Steiner, sen. From the very first of his confinement he was strongly
impressed with the idea that he should not recover/Charles Simpson offers
reward for horse stolen nr Liberty town

96. FHB Nov 7 1807/Died 1 ult, Mrs. Rebecca Willson, consort of Thomas
Willson and dau of William Murdock Beall, Esq. in the prime of live, leaving
her husband and parents, and 4 small children; funeral sermon given by Rev
Bower at the Episc church on Sun senight last/Warning to contractors and
undertakers of the Turnpike road, in and nr New Market, that if the labour-
ers and workman, under their direction, shall in future disturb the publick
peace and attempt to resist the civil officers in the discharge of their
duty, the military authority will be called upon/John Richmond requests
persons to settle their accounts/John Hughes intending to decline farming,
offers to rent his place, adj Fred. Town, 260 a. cleared land; apply to him
or to Levi Hughes nr Frederick

97. FHB Nov 14 1807/Persons who purchased prop at sale of Thomas I.
Johnson, decd, are to take notice that their notes are due/Died Thurs morn
at his farm nr this town, after a long illness and at a very advanced age,
Fielder Gant; funeral at Episc Church this day

98. FHB Nov 21 1807/Married Tues last, 17 inst, nr Creager's-town, by Rev
Dubois, Jospeh Minghiny, of Jefferson Co, Va, to Miss Mary Head; and James
Clark of same co to Miss Elizabeth Head, both daus of William Head of this
co/Richard Gaines wants 20 journeymen boot and shoemakers at his Lady's and
Gentlemen's Boot and Shoe manufactory, Bridge st, Geo. Town, D. C./Lancelot
Wade to sell negroes at the dwlg hse of John W. Young, nr Tremmells town

99. FHB Nov 28 1807/Died 20 inst in the 66th yr of her age, Mrs. Margaret
Schley, consort of Capt. George J. Schley of this place/Susanna Botelar adm
of Elias Botelar to sell sell wet and dry goods, a negro boy 12 yrs old,
milch cow, household and kitchen furniture

100. FHB Dec 5 1807/Married Thurs eve 26 ult by Rev Daniel Wagner, Joseph
Smith, paper-maker, of this co, to Miss Sybilla Doffler of Fred. Town/
Married Tues eve last by Rev David Martin, Samuel Phillips of this co, to
Mrs. Rebecca Lyles of this town/Married Thurs day eve last by Rev Daniel
Wagner, William Byerly, paper-maker, to Miss Charlotte Myer, both of this
co/Married same eve, by same, Jacob Berger to Miss Mary Kendall, both of
Fred. Town/Sale of Castings, stoves, mill irons, &c. - Evans &
Griffith/Jacob Brengel has taken up 3 stray cows

101. FHB Dec 12 1807/Married last Sun eve by Rev Daniel Wagner, Ezra Mantz,
to Miss Maria Ritchie dau of William Ritchie, Esq. of this place/Sheriff's
sale of right of Henry Hildebrand to tracts, Willson's Lott, pt of Resurvey
on Willson's Lott, pt of Fat Oxen, pt of Two Brothers, 106 a. in all, taken

at the suit of Derr use of Menkey, Brownings, Annon use of Bussard, Butts use of M'Pherson, Tabler and Getzendanner use of George Creager, and Hauser use of Evitt - George Creager, Jun. Sheriff/Joseph Stephen Hall to apply for benefit of insolvency law/Sale of negroes at the dwlg plantation of Miss Hoods, nr Annapolis - William Worthington, Sen., Acting for Miss Hoods

102. FHB Dec 19 1807/To be rented - stand for a blacksmith with dwlg hse - Henry Jackson for A. Shaaff/Meeting of stockholders of Balt and York Turnpike Road Company; commissioners: Joseph Thornburg, Thomas M'Elderry, Nicholas Merryman of Elijah, David M'Mechen/Blacksmith's shop to be rented on main road from mouth of Monococy to the Trap, nr Kemp's mill - Edward Thomas/Daniel Grant intending to remove to Balt, offers to rent plantation where he lives, in Allegany Co, 24 miles from Cumberland on Braddocks old road

103. FHB Dec 26 1807/Thomas N. Harwood to apply for benefit of insolvency law/Victor Guillou to open Dancing School for this season/Elias Harding of Walter, living within 7 miles of Fred. Town, has taken up two stray yearlings

104. FHB Jan 2 1808/No additional items

105. FHB Jan 9 1808/Commissioners to receive subscriptions for stock in an Insurance Company to be established in Balt: Abraham Shriver, George Baer, George Creager, Jun./James Vass, Falmouth, Va, offers reward for mulatto man Dick, 25, 5 ft 10 inch, accompanied by another mulatto Thornton, prop of Robert Henning, for the last two yrs hired to Wm. Bell, Tavern Keeper in this town

106. FHB Jan 16 1808/Sale by order of Orphan's court at former res of Hugh Reynolds decd, negroes, horses, cows, &c. - Joseph Fleming/James Buchanan, living 1/2 mile from Waynesburg, on road leading to Greencastle, offers reward for mare stolen of the stable of Andrew Armstrong, Wash City/Cod fish, shad, mackarel and herring - Benjamin & Eli Ogle

107. FHB Jan 23 1808/Died Sun 10 inst in 47th yr of his age, Rev Henry Willis, member of Meth Episc Church for 30 yrs/William R. King has lately opened a coffee hse, in addition to his hotel, in Fred. Town in hse formerly kept by Capt. Schley/John Ringland, Jun. has purchased the Tavern in Liberty, formerly prop of Richard Coale/Sale of 150 negroes at Anthony Tracey's hse in Mtg, with two miles of Messrs. Bowie and Hersey's Mill, Seneca - Thomas Peter & others, execs of Robert Peter/Chancery sale at hse of John Huston, in Emmittsburg, of real est of Christian Smith, decd, lots in the town of Emmittsburg, occ by widow of Christian Smith and 500 a. in South Mountain - Richard Brooke, Trustee

108. FHB Jan 30 1808/No additional items

109. FHB Feb 6 1808/William Lowe requests persons indebted to him to settle their accounts

110. FHB Feb 13 1808/Fire broke out Thurs morn last about 3 o'clock in back
buildings of Capt Schley of this place but discovered before serious damage
was done/Died at Taney town on 5 inst, in 75th yr of his age, Joseph M'Kaleb
/Ezra Mantz candidate for sheriff/William Han, Bedford Co, Pa, cautions persons from taking assignment on note given to John Swiser

111. FHB Feb 20 1808/Basil Dorsey forwarns persons in the town of New
Market, or elsewhere, from dealing with or selling anything to his slaves
/Negroes for sale at farm of Henry Smith, 8 miles from Fred. Town - Joseph
Smith/Thomas Noland forwarns persons from dealing with his slaves res in Md
or Va

112. FHB Feb 27 1808/Died Wed last in the 26th yr of her age, of a consumption, Miss Elizabeth Mantz, dau of Francis Mantz of this place/Chancery sale
of real est of Gustavus Scott, decd in Allegany Co (over 20,000 a.; tracts
are listed), Robert Perry, trustee/Mary M. Drury 1/2 mile from Buckey's-
town, will sell horses and cattle/Sale at the hse of William Springer in
Fred. Town for the creditors of William Springer, an insolvent debtor, store
goods; and at the hse of Benjamin Stallings in Fred. Town, a tract of land
lying in Nelson Co, Kentucky - W. C. Hobbs, Trustee

113. FHB Mar 5 1808/300 cords of tanner's bark wanted this spring by Isaac
& John Mantz/Rachel Shipley will rent her prop whereon she now lives, Fountain Inn, or The White House/Two distillers and 2000 bushels of corn wanted
- John S. Laurence, Valley Farm; deliver corn to Peter Shriner's mill, 3
miles below Liberty-town

114. FHB Mar 12 1808/Elected directors of the Branch of the farmer's Bank
established at this place: John Tyler, John M'Pherson, John Hoffman, Richard
Potts, Roger Nelson, George Baer, Henry Kuhn, John Grahame, Abraham Shriver/
William Hilleary and Benjamin West admrs of Henry Belwood, to sell a number
of decd negroes/Ann Willis, James M'Cannon, Francis Hollingsworth, exec of
Henry Willis, Fred Co decd, to sell tract of decd on Little Pipe Creek,
formerly occ by James Poulson, 198 a.; also 100 a. within 7 miles of city of
Balt/Garden Seeds - Francis Mantz

115. FHB Mar 19 1808/At meeting of Branch Bank Doct. John Tyler elected
pres, Thomas Shaw cashier, Lewis Green bookkeeper/George Trisler has just
received a large assortment of spring and summer goods/Joseph Aud will offer
for sale at the farm on which he res on Carroll's Manor, 1 1/2 miles from
Buckey's-Town, several horses, milch cows, cattle, hogs, wheat, rye and
corn/David Kephart has taken up a stray mare

116. FHB Mar 26 1808/Chancery sale at hse of Elie Phillips in Woodsbury, of
the real est of Christian Ebey, decd, farm of 303 a., 1 mile from Mr. Browning's Mill, one of the first farms in Fred Co - Joshua Delaplane, Trustee,
living on Pipe Creek/For sale 70-80 barrels of corn, bacon, waggon and
geers, &c. - Graff & Beatty/Peter Kemp exec of Henry Rempsberg

117. FHB Apr 2 1808/Chancery Case - Zephaniah Harrison agnst Henry, Sarah,
John, Andrew, Samuel and Elizabeth Alleson, and Samuel Duvall & Mary his
wife. Complainant seeking to obtain a conveyance to land, Burk Creek Hills,

pt Hazzard and Never Fear, pt Resurvey on Hobb's Purchase and land conveyed by Ullery Stuller to John Alleson, decd, in 1802. John and Andrew Alleson res out of the state/Proposals to be received by Leonard Herbaugh, res at the site for the bridge over Monocacy for furnishing various articles (listed)

118. FHB Apr 9 1808/Louis B. Apollo has removed to last alley in Haller's town next hse to William Clements, where he constantly keeps for sale, bread, cakes, beer, &c./David Slifer forwarns persons from fishing or trespassing on his premises

119. FHB Apr 16 1808/House of Entertainment - Benjamin Bean has removed from his late stand, nr Parkhead Forge to hse lately occ by Valentine Dye at the west end of Hancock-town, sign of the Green Tree

120. FHB Apr 23 1808/Died Mon last in 83d yr of his age, M. Samuel Miller, sen. of this place/Died Mon night, Henry White, in 19th yr of his age

121. FHB Apr 30 1808/Married Tues last, 26 inst, nr Creager's town by Rev Du Bois, Joseph Elder to Miss Lucy Head/Married same day by same, at Liberty Town, Captain Alexander C. Harrison of the United States Navy, to Miss Catharine Owings, all of Fred Co/Died Wed 20 inst, after a lingering illness, Benjamin Zimmerman, paper-maker, of this co/Died in Emmittsburg, Sat night last, in 18th yr of her age, Miss Elizabeth Livers, dau of Arnold Livers, late of Balt, decd/Sale at Buck creek Forge, horses, milch cows, hogs, waggon and gears, 30 a. of wheat and rye in the ground, 10 plate stoves, mahogany secretary, &c. - Joseph Arthur/George Devilbiss, about 3 miles from Liberty-town, offers reward for stolen horse

122. FHB May 7 1808/S. Silvester has rented the White House Tavern, 24 miles from Balt and same from Fred Town/Belleville land for sale, about 900 a. on the Ohio, in Wood Co, Va - David Putnam, Marietta

123. FHB May 14 1808/Married Tues eve last by Rev Daniel Wagner, Doctor Lewis Creager of Middletown, to Miss Susannah Hauer, dau of Daniel Hauer sen. of Fred. Town/William Dean has taken up a stray mare

124. FHB May 21 1808/Ely Babbs, Taylor, has commenced bus. in the town of Liberty, opp Mr. Keiler's tavern/Tench Ringgold, Wash Co, candidate for elector of Pres of the U.S./Carding machines for carding and rolling wool is now in complete operation at Joshua Delaplane's mill, Double Pipe Creek. The price for carding and rolling wool will be 10 cents per pound - Joshua Delaplane, James Walker/Andrew Stewart, Fred Co, 1 mile from Emmittsburg, offers reward for missing mare/Sale of farm and tavern on road from Fred. Town to Noland's Ferry; land will be shewn by John Hooper or Andrew Havner living on the premises or subscriber living two miles from Fred. Town - Levi Hughes

125. FHB May 28 1808/John Gerhard, living in Liberty-Town, offers reward for David Evans, apprentice to boot and shoemaking, about 5 ft 3-4 inch, 18-19 yrs of age, fair complexion, light hair; had on a white fur hat, brown coating doublet, one do. cotton cassimere mixed blue and white with several

waistcoats and other cloathing/Several parcels of land for sale by John Hughes, Fred. Town

126. FHB Jun 4 1808/Death announced here during last week of William Campbell, jun., eldest son of Capt. William Campbell of this neighborhood, who expired at sea on the 29th of April, aged about 28 yrs. The vessel in which Mr. Campbell went as passenger, sailed from Balt on 12 Apr and it appears left the capes on the 17th, on board Spanish Schooner St. Salvadore, 12 days from Havannah, captured by French privateer; experienced a severe gale; broached, upset and filled, probably because of lack of experience of Frenchman at the helm. She sank, but 5 persons, including Mr. Campbell were able to get on part of the deck that floated. They were picked up after 4 days but Campbell died on board the brig that picked them up. (additional details in the article)/Benjamin Galloway, Ht, candidate for elector of Pres of U.S./Margaret Reid admr of Hugh Reid/Benjamin Permillion, manager of Thomas Noland's manor farm, Potomac, has taken up a stray mare

127. FHB Jun 11 1808/Joel Marsh has his machinery for carding and rolling wool in complete operation at Jacob Ramsberg's mill in Fred. Town/Henry Williams certifies that Joseph Elders has taken up a stray gelding/Harrison Fitzhugh, living nr Centreville, Fairfax co, Va, offers reward for negro man Charles about 33, 5 ft 8 inch

128. FHB Jun 18 1808/John Baer of Henry has just received from Balt a number of groceries for sale/Jacob Steiner, Jun. exec of Jacob Steiner, Sen. to sell prop in Market St/George Peter, George-town, otters reward for mulatto man Isaac who ran away from his farm in Mtg Co, about 35, 5 ft 10-11 inch /William Gibbs has in complete operation at Thomas Hobbs mill on Linganore, 4 miles from Liberty and Newmarket machinery for picking and carding wool

129. FHB Jun 25 1808/John M'Kaleb has taken up a stray horse/Joseph Arthur has removed from Bush Creek Forge and deposited all his stock of iron with Addams and Wager in Fred. Town/Peter Shriner, miller, living on Linganore, offers reward for negro man Bill or Will, aged 45, 5 ft 7 inch/Andrew Tucker gives notice that his wife Elizabeth having left his bed and board, he forbids harbouring her and he will pay no debts of her contracting; cautions persons from taking assignment of a note given by Caleb House to him which she has taken with her

130. FHB Jul 2 1808/John Crapster has taken up a stray gelding/Samuel Ridgely of Charles, living on the Balt and Frederick turnpike road 19 miles from city of Balt, offers a reward for negro man Peter, 23, 5 ft 3-4 inch

131. FHB Jul 9 1808/Subscribers, appted by last session of the Gen Assembly, Trustees for the town of Bath, Berkely Co, Va, are entirely satisfied that these Springs may be resorted to as formerly without a risque to the health of visitors: Elisha Boyd, John Baker, Henry St. G. Tucker, David Hunter, Rawleigh Colston, Philip C. Pendleton/Frederick Linthicum and Ezekiah Linthicum of Zachariah Linthicum, exec of Zachariah Linthicum, Mtg Co, to sell pers prop of decd/Thomson Mason, The Retreat, nr Leesburg, Loudon Co, Va, offers reward for person named Theoderick Lyles, who rode away on Mason's horse; the man is an Englishman by birth, until a few months

past has been a sailor, nearly 6 ft, has good education, dark eyes, fair complexion, large whiskers, about 25-30

132. FHB Jul 16 1808/No additional item

133. FHB Jul 23 1808/George Miller has in operation a nail manufactory/John Sprigg, living 2 miles below mouth of Monocacy, offers reward for negro woman Hannah, took with her a child about 3 months old; was prop of Richard Laurence, decd, and since that of John S. Hall of Frederick/William Pole has taken up a stray mare/New Carding Machine in operation at David Kemp's Mill 3 1/3 miles south of Fred. Town - Thomas Gibbs

134. FHB Jul 30 1808/Daniel Trundle and Alfred Belt, exec, in pursuance of last will of Ann Trail, Mtg Co, to sell 7 negroes of decd, horses, cattle &c/James Daws, Georgetown, offers reward for apprentice to Boot and Shoe-making bus., named John Wayman, about 19 1/2 yrs old, dark complexion and hair, 5 ft 6-7 inch, strait and well made

135. FHB Aug 6 1808/George Baer candidate for Gen Assembly/Morris candidate for sheriff/J. Hunt, Coopersmith, as an assortment of kettles & stills/Thomas A. Davis, sheriff of Charles Co, offers reward for negro man who calls himself Davy, who broke jail; says he is prop of Raphael Boarman, jun, about 30, 5 ft 6-7 inch, stout; has a brother at Mrs. Digges, nr Bladens-burg/James Bickett, living nr Emmittsburg, offers reward for Christian Kauffman, apprentice to tayloring bus., 18-19, 5 ft 4-5 inch

136. FHB Aug 13 1808/Farm for sale in Balt Co, on the western run, 2 miles from the York Turnpike Road, about 16 miles from city of Balt, 275 a.; apply to John Dillon who I have empowered to contract - Moses Dillon/Tobias Belt, Merryland Tract, Fred Co, offers reward for missing gelding/John Benson, Mtg Co, nr mouth of Monococy, offers reward for negro man John, about 40, 6 ft/Wheat wanted at Bruce's Mills, on Big Pipe Creek

137. FHB Aug 20 1808/Doct. Samuel Johnson, res at John Biggs, adj Graceham, tenders his medicinal services/Henry & George Shultz, Fred. Town, have commenced the coach-making bus., in shop formerly occ by Mr. Dofler, from several yrs experience in and close attention to that bus. at York-town, Pa/Farm for sale 6 miles below Fred. Town, 270 a. - William Harding, living on the premises, bounded one side fully 1 1/4 mile/John Hanson Thomas candi-date for legislature of the state, recommending by Devalt Willard, Jacob Grove, Arthur Botelar, John Shaffer, Henry Bowles, George Hause, sen., Jacob Colman, David Arnold, Henry Asherman, Elias Willard, John Willard, George Blessing, Abraham Blessing, Eli Thrasher

138. FHB Aug 27 1808/Upton Bruce of Alleghany Co, candidate for 4th Congressional dist in opposition to Col. R. Nelson/Francis Brown Sappington candidate for Gen Assembly/Died 9 inst in 53rd yr of her age, Mrs. Elizabeth O'Neill, consort of Bernard O'Neill of Mtg Co, interred 11 inst

139. FHB Sep 3 1808/Taney-Town Races, purse of $50 - John Crapster, Joseph Taney, Jun

140. FHB Sep 10 1808/Meeting of 1st Frederick Troop of Cavalry, equipt agreeable to law, for purpose of marching to the Trap to join Col. Swearingen's regiment - Henry Kemp, Capt/Lawrence Brengle candidate for sheriff/Davis Richardson, guardian to S. & J. Pancoast, to rent farm on river Monococy, about 6 miles below Fred. Town, prop of Samuel and Joseph Pancoast, representatives of Stacey Pancoast decd

141. FHB Sep 17 1808/Philip Barton Key candidate for Congress for district composed of Mtg and part of Frederick Co, east of Monocacy

142. FHB Sep 24 1808/Blacksmith wanted at Buckey's Town - George Buckey/A. Graham at the sign of the Cask and Sugar Loaves, Patrick St, intends removing to Balt and will dispose of his remaining stock of store goods at reduced prices/John Young, on Gen. Nelson's farm nr Trammel's town has taken up a stray gelding/John Hull jun. has taken up a stray gelding

143. FHB Oct 1 1808/Died Mon last, Christian Brandt of this town/Died same day, Baalis Coomes of this co

144. FHB Oct 8 1808/Henry Grammer, 3 miles from Westminster on the Petersburg Road, offers reward for mulatto wench Jin, about 24, 5 ft/William Dydenhover has erected a fulling mill 3 miles from Fred. Town, on Tuscarora creek, nr the Emmittsburg road

145. FHB Oct 15 1808/Married Sat last by Rev Daniel Wagner, Charles Henry to Miss Polly Shriner, dau of Peter Shriner, all of Little Pipe Creek, Fred Co/James Wilson admr of Leven Wilson, Mtg Co, to sell 5 negroes of decd, and other items/Col. John Lynn of Allegany candidate for elector of Pres/Roger Brooke Taney candidate for elector of Pres/Ann Livers admr of William Livers Jacob Cookes has taken noted tavern stand, formerly occ by G. J. Schley as a tavern

146. FHB Oct 22 1808/Daniel Arthur candidate for Gen Assembly/Meshach Tucker, living in Clarksburg, offers reward for Jacob Brown, bound to Cordwaining bus.

147. FHB Oct 29 1808/Rachel Metcalfe and Thomas Boyer, admr of Thomas Metcalf, request claims be exhibited/C. W. Hanson, offers reward for horse missing from Hampton, nr Baltimore/Sale of mare and colt at plantation of William Crum, 2 miles from Fred. Town - William Crum, Senr

148. FHB Nov 5 1808/Three cents per pound for clean lines and cotton rags - David Martin/Sarah Evans, exec, to sell tract agreeable to last will of James Evans, 2 miles from Liberty town, 10 a./John Nicholls and George Leaply, admrs of John Nicholls, sen, to sell horses, cattle, sheep and hogs, &c. of decd/David Reifsnider has taken up a stray gelding/William Johnson of Thos. has taken up a stray steer

149. FHB Nov 12 1808/Janaro Farre, Buckeys-town, intending to remove to Mtg Court House, requests settlement of accounts/Aaron Hainsworth has taken up a stray gelding/Sarah Coomes adm of Baalis Coomes

150. FHB Nov 19 1808/Married Tues eve last, by Rev Daniel Wagner, John Baer of Fred. Town to Miss Catharine Hoffman, dau of John Hoffman, Esq. of Fred Co/Sale at the Plantation of Benjamin Hall, mouth of Bennett's creek, of horses, cattle, hogs, waggon and geers, two yoke of oxen and cart, &c. - John H. Simmons, Otho Sprigg/Urshula White admr of John White of Mtg Co

151. FHB Nov 26 1808/On Thurd last the 16th Regiment of militia, commanded by Col. Stoner, met nr this town for purpose of drafting the proportion of men which it is to furnish towards the quota of 100,000 militia, called for, from the state of Maryland, to be in a state of readiness. 180 privates volunteered

152. FHB Dec 3 1808/Death of Richard Potts, Esq., born in PG Co, has just finished the study of law and settled in Fred. Town, when the struggle for independence commenced; he was soon distinguished by a generous and ardent attachment to the cause of this country, apptd clerk to the committee of observation as a young man; served in the expedition to reinforce Washington in winter of 77, as aid to Thomas Johnson. Shortly after return he was apptd clerk of Fred Co, resigned a year or two afterwards and commenced law practice; elected delegate from Fred Co in 1780 and soon chosen by the Gen Assembly as member of the revolutionary congress, member of state convention, appted Judge of high court of appeals in 1800; died in 54th yr of his age (very long obit)/Died Thurs last at the seat of her brother, Major Henry Darnall, Mrs. Anne Dixon, in 77th yr of her age/John Hughes denies that he has made over his prop to his father, Levi Hughes, with a design to defraud his creditors/Sale of tract called Solomon's Flower, on Bennett's creek, adj lands of Capt P. Griffith and William Morsels, 350 a.; apply to subscriber, I. W. Worthington, at Ely Dorsey's, jun. No. 171, Market st, Balt

153. FHB Dec 10 1808/Ig. Davis and George Buckey, exec, give notice ath notes are due for those indebted for purchasing at public sale of Philip Sankstack, decd/Red Morocco Pocket book lost, containing among other items, receipt signed by Col. John Thomas for $470, one signed by George Creger, jun. for $100, two notes of hand of Otho Hughes, one of William Wards, one of Joseph Garrots, judgment agnst George Brown superseded by Lawrence Brengle courses and plets of Partnership and Jedburgh Forrests, receipt signed by Patrick Hall, for Mrs. Wolfenden, a note of hand of Maj. Ben. Stallings - John Hughes/Joshua Stevenson, applying to legislature for benefit of an act of insolvency/Chancery sale of plantation of William Hammond, decd, adj Annapolis, 90 a. - Basil Brown, trustee

154. FHB Dec 17 1808/Elias Crutchley at his store in Patrick nr the square will receive and give fair price for clean combed hogs bristles/Two stry stone hse to be let in Patrick st, formerly prop of Matthias Buckey, decd, lately occ by widow M'Graw as a tavern - Valentine Buckey, Guard./Thomas Chew Shipley, nr New Market, has taken up a stray gelding, certified by Silas Bailey/Married Tues eve 6 inst, William Emmitt, Esq. of Emmittsburg, to Miss Susan Shellman, dau of John Shellman of this town/Married at Woodsbury on Thurs 8 inst by Rev L. Browning, John Wireman, merchant, to Miss Elizabeth Campbell, all of this co/Died 6 inst in this town, Jacob Sinn, in 69th yr of his age/Trunk found on Balt and Fred. Town turnpike road - Philip

& Henry M'Elfresh/23 negroes for sale, prop of James Peter, decd at hse of Anthony Tracy on Senaka - David Peter, Admr, George-town

155. FHB Dec 24 1808/Dennis Sollers forwarns not to give his wife Priscilla Sollers credit on his credit, because of the gross misconduct of said Priscilla and her departure from his hse

156. FHB Dec 31 1808/Died Tues last in 62nd yr of his age, Henry Winemiller of this town/Doctor Jacob Baer, has commence the practice of medicine, in Fred. Town/Eleanor Offut, living near Mtg Court House, offers reward for yellow fellow George, about 22, 6 ft 5 inch

157. FHB Jan 7 1809/G. M. Conradt, Fred. Town, seeks 2 lads as apprentices to the weaving bus./William Lowe has declined bus. which will be continued by his sons John Lowe and William Lowe, jun.

158. FHB Jan 14 1809/Henry and Noah Worman offers land for sale, near the Sulphur Springs about 1/2 mile from Henry Landis' mill on Sam's creek, 221 a.; and a farm of 158 a., about 1/2 mile from above/Tavern for sale called the Stone House formerly occ by Nathan Randall decd as a tavern, at present by Frederick Collenberger, on main road from Liberty-Town to city of Balt, within 18 miles of latter; there is a school hse on said lot - Jonas Crum-packer/Richard B. Chenoweth has invented a new improvement on the plough which is made at his shop east of Market Street Bridge, near Christ's church, Balt/Payment requested by all who put mares to the horse North Star -James Anderson, at Mrs. Kimbolls/Fire Tues night in middle of Messrs. Ellicott's upper mill on Fred. Town road, about 10 miles from Balt

159. FHB Jan 21 1809/John Fry forwarns from taking assignment on note given by John Fry to John Sprigg and assigned by Sprigg to Nathan Neighbours/Half of hse for rent in Buckeys Town, lately occ by Jannaro Farre, taylor - George Buckey/George Baer offers reward for missing steer/James Clare wishes to sell his farm in Berkely Co, Va, whereon Benjamin Pendleton now lives, lying on the head of Falling Waters

160. FHB Jan 28 1809/Upton Beall of Mtg Co has not received papers sent from Mrs. Kimball's tavern; the gentleman to whom was delivered these letters please inform the printer what has done with them/Brick hse for rent, now occ by William Addams - John Doll/William Morland, near Emmitts-burg, exec of Francis Kane/Died 15 inst at his seat in Mtg Co, John Hender-son in the 40th yr of his age, father, master, husband (long obit)

161. FHB Feb 4 1809/Mill & lands for sale by virtue of a deed of trust from Henry Ambrose to Ludwick Kemp, decd, pt of Good Neighbour, 470 a., Charming Beauty, 25 a., Centre Bit, 12 a., 6-7 miles from Emmittsburgh; shewn by Peter Shover, living near the lands - Henry Kemp and Christian Kemp/Jacob Duckett in Piscataway, PG Co, offers reward for negroes, Pompey, 50, 5 ft 10-11 inch and Basil, 22-23, 5 ft 8-9 inch; Basil's father lives in Alexan-dria; his brother and sister live in Balt; it is conjectured that a black man named Jack Neale, who, it is said murdered his master on the Ohio river, has contrived to get them away/Died Thurs 25 ult, in 49th yr of her age,

Mrs. Margaret Barrick, wife of Col. Henry Barrick, nr Woodsborough, leaving 6 children and husband

162. FHB Feb 11 1809/Spring Rye & Barley Seed for sale - M. Brown, Montevino (formerly Amelung''s Old Glass Works)/Richard Johnson has taken up a stray mare, certified by Peter Burkhart/Schoolmaster wanted - George Buckey, or Ignatius Davis, Buckey's Town

163. FHB Feb 18 1809/Died Sun las, Mrs. Eunice Shelmerdine, consort of Stephen Shelmerdine of this co/Died Thurs morn last after a long and severe illness, in 36th yr of his age, Lieut. Alexander Contee Harrison of the U.S. Navy, leaving a young family and an aged mother/Because of political implications John Hanson Thomas will not speak at German Presbyterian Church in celebration of Washington's birthday (statements made in discussion of this issue by J. Baer, John Hanson Thomas, Jacob Steiner, Jun., and Nicholas Holtz)

164. FHB Feb 25 1809/To sell 100 a. of land 1 mile from Fred. Town, with merchant overshot mill, two pair of French Burrs - John Reynalds/Sale by order of Fred Co court, of prop of Michael Boyer, lot # 80 of the town - Otho Lawrence, Trustee/Benjamin Sedwick has taken up a cow which came to Johnson Furnace

165. FHB Mar 4 1809/Sale of pers est of Peter Stimmel, dec, nr Woodsborough - Barbara Stimmel and Jacob Cramer, admr/Sale of land nr Frederick, 1/2 of lot of 209 a. at present occ by Major Henry Barrick, a few miles from Fred. Town, 100 a. leased to Christian Barrick, present tenant, lot occ by Adam Smith and other lots; apply to Capt William Campbell nr Fred. Town or subscriber in city of Wash, John P. Van Ness/Farm for sale pursuant to last will of Jacob Sinn, 211 a., nr Fishing Creek, 5 miles from Graceham - Jacob Rouzong, Philip Hauptman, exec/George Trisler offers reward for information concerning author of gross, malicious and scandalous libel, communicted to subscribers of Mr. Cookes Coffee Hse, directed to care of editor of Herald

166. FHB Mar 11 1809/Persons having claims agnst William Lyles, decd, are requested to present them - Samuel Howard

167. FHB Mar 18 1809/Died Sat last aged 17, Miss Ann Potts, dau of late Richard Potts, esq. decd, from a lingering and cruel illness

168. FHB Mar 25 1809/Thorough bred horse, Speculator, will stand the season at Noland's Ferry and will be let to mares at $25 each - W. Noland/Sale of slaves at Bellview Farm of the Richard Potts, decd - William Potts, exec/ Tavern for rent at present occ by William Kerr, 3 miles from Balt - John Mitchel, No. 20, Cheapside, Balt/John Reynalds has determined not to dispose of the mill and farm nr Frederick as recently advertised

169. FHB Apr 1 1809/Died Wed eve last after an indisposition of a few weeks, Stephen Shelmerdine of this co; 6 weeks ago Mrs. Shelmerdine died; during the interval one of their little ones has also been removed from this vale of tears/Chancery sale of prop formerly owned by William Hammond decd, lot of 974 a., tract, Norwood's Fancy Resurveyed on Round Bay adj plantation

of Col. Manadier, tract Bachelors's Neglect of 15 1/2 a. on Elk Ridge adj land of Ely Dorsey of Fred Co; plots can be examined at tavern of Amos Gambril adj Hammond's Retreat Resurveyed; also to be exposed to sale at tavern of William Glover in Annapolis, the reversionary interest of William Hammond in lots in said city – Basil Brown, Trustee/Sale of farm called Supply to Parrons and West Time and pt of Middle Plantation, 75 a. about 3 miles from New-Market; apply to Mr. Miller living at said farm/Sale by order Orphan's court of Fred Co at the late dwlg of Philbut Grenwell, decd, a young negro man, horses, cattle, hogs and sheep, &c. – Raphael Jarboe, admr

170. FHB Apr 8 1809/A barn of Richard Cromwell was struck by lightning Wed night; during the fire vast quantities of wild ducks, attracted we suppose by the light, flocked to the place, many of them flew directly into the flames, others against trees, buildings, &c. and were killed and crippled in great numbers/Available to teach reading, writing, &c. – John Richmond at Benjamin Hughes, at Whipperwill run, 2 miles from Clarksburg

171. FHB Apr 15 1809/George Kolb has removed to hse of John Schley between stores of Jacob Shriver and Daniel Deveney, where he intends to keep private entertainment for man and horse

172. FHB Apr 22 1809/Three cents a pound for linnen & coton rages – Michael Ott/Abijah Fenn offers reward for negro man Moses, who ran away from manor of C. Carroll of Carrollton, 15 miles from Balt on Frederick town road, about 6 ft, 25 yrs of age/Sale at the farm of Stephen Shelmerdine, decd, of his pers est – William Campbell, Henry Koontz, jun., Nicholas Randall, Sebastian Graaff, exec

173. FHB Apr 29 1809/Married Tues eve last, by Rev Wagner, Michael M'Lanaghan, of Franklin Co, Pa, to Miss Susan M'Cleary, dau of Henry M'Cleary of this town/Sale of lot on which Mr. Hempey now lives – Joseph Smith for William Conn/Joshua Stevenson answers accusations of dishonesty

174. FHB May 6 1809/Dissolution of partnership of John Bayly & George Graff/Died Tues 2 inst after a severe and painful illness, William Purdy of this co, aged 74; he embarked early on our Revolution

175. FHB May 13 1809/Books will be opened to further subscriptions to complete the Turnpike road to Boonsborough; managers: Henry Stemple, sen; Joseph Swearengen; Lewis Creager; George Scott; Capt. Conn; Wiliam Good; Elie Williams; Samuel Ringgold; Col. Vanlear; John Buchanan; John Thompson Mason and Charles Carroll/Sale in Liberty-town of tavern stand, presently rented to Edward Hanna; also tavern stand 15 miles from Fred. Town nr William Hobbs, presently rented to Peter Orndorf – Jacob Kiler

176. FHB May 20 1809/Sale of horses, cattle, sheep, &c. at tavern of subscriber on Lancaster road – William Cookerly/Sale of 1109 a. with grist mill, on Passage Creek, 6 miles from Stoverstown, Va; for particulars enquire of Jacob or John Weaver, nr Winchester, or David Weaver on premises, being exec of est of Jacob Weaver/Jonathan Powell, living in Liberty-town, offers reward for apprentice boy Samuel Show, bound to the Shoemaking bus., about 5 ft 3 inch, about 18

Frederick-Town Herald

177. FHB May 27 1809/Detachment of Maryland militia, ordered under the act of Congress, discharged. The Commanding officers of companies, of the 16th regiment, will therefore discharge the volunteers who offered from their respective companies on the 24th Nov last for that service. The Cononel congratulates the detachment from the 16th regiment, on the happy change in our foreign relations, which has made their services unnecessary - Stephen Stoner, Lieut. Col. 16th Reg. Md. Militia/Peregrine Warfield wishing to removed from Fred Co, will dispose of his prop in New Market, 4 lots adj/George Keiler, Liberty, requests settlement of accounts

178. FHB Jun 3 1809/Married Thurs eve 25 ult by Rev Shaiffer, William Cockey of Balt Co, to Miss Catharine Graff, of Lancaster/Died Thurs last, Capt Adam Freshour, for many yrs an excellent peace officer/Sentance of death on Mon last pronounced by hon. Judge Buchanan, on Thomas Burk, who was found guilty at March court last, for committing a rape on a child between the age of 10 and 11 yrs (Hagerstown Gaz.)

179. FHB Jun 10 1809/A portion of this issue is missing

180. FHB Jun 17 1809/Col. Baker Johnson has taken up a stray gelding, certified Fredk. Heisely/Persons who purchased prop at sale of Gabriel Thomas, decd are request to discharge their notes - John Thomas and Henry Thomas, of Gabriel Thomas, admrs

181. FHB Jun 24 1809/William Baer of Henry offers for sale at his store on Market st, 2 doors below the bank, 30 barrels of herrings and a few barrels of shad

182. FHB Jul 1 1809/Levy Court orders that no allowance will be made to Justices of the peace for holding inquisitions on dead persons, unless held by permission of the Coroner - William Ritchie, Clk/Married Tues 27 ult by Rev James L. Higgins, Basil Crapster to Miss Harriet Dorsey, dau of Vachel Dorsey, both of this co

183. FHB Jul 8 1809/Thomas Gibson, having purchased the tavern for many yrs kept by late William Cookerly, is determined to be constantly supplied with the best of liquors, beds, hay, oats, &c/Daniel Smith, living nr Goshen Mills, Mtg Co, offers reward for negro man Ralph, about 30, 9-10 inch, stout /Died Fri morn 30 ult in 63d yr of his age, Edward Salmon, Mathematical teacher in the academy of this place, 40 yrs an instructor of youth/Sale by order of Orphan's court at hse of Adam Frushour, decd of pers prop of decd - Jacob Frushour & Christian Brengle, exec

184. FHB Jul 15 1809/Plantation for sale, 200 a., 1 mile of Potomack - Trammel Delashmet/Sale at his hse in Trap Town, of 2 stry hse, with cellar, kitchen, bake-oven, and other - Zach. Simmons/Basil Waters, living nr Clarksburg (in which there is a post office), Mtg Co, offers reward for negro man Sam, about 30, 5 ft 6-7 inch, has lost the sight of his left eye/William Conden to petition for benefit of insolvency act/Mr. Donlevy, Frederick Academy, to resign - P. Thomas, Chairman

185. FHB Jul 22 1809/Samuel R. Hobbs, requests meeting with his creditors at hse of John Dillin, Fred. Town/William Noland, Spring-Dale, offers farm for sale on which he now res, 470 a., 2 1/2 miles from Noland's ferry, 11 miles from Leesburg, Va

186. FHB Jul 29 1809/Joseph Miller, nr New-Market, has taken up a stray gelding

187. FHB Aug 5 1809/Daniel Arthur, offers reward for Aaron Lee, apprentice to the carpenter's bus., about 18, very stout, sandy hair, freckled, went off from a harvest field nr Fred. Town/Chancery case - Edward M'Carty vs John Reller's heirs, &c.; that James Reed, Trustee, to sell land to satisfy sum due Edward M'Carty; widow of John Reller having right of dower; ordered by court of Hampshire Co Court, Va/Edward Thomas, Jun. has taken up a stray gelding/Sale of 1680 a. in pursuance of will of Richard Potts - Eleanor Potts and William Potts, exec

188. FHB Aug 12 1809/Drugs, Medicines, Paints &c. - John S. Miller/John Nicholls and George Leapley, admr of John Nichols, notify persons that notes for sale of his prop are due/Isabella Munro, nr Emmittsburg, has taken up a stray gelding/Abraham Blessing candidate for Gen Assembly

189. FHB Aug 19 1809/Meeting of 16 Regt of Militia - H. R. Warfield, Adjutant/A quantity of clothes found by one of my negroes in a haystack - Thomas Noland, Bloomfields/George Attoo, living nr Fout's mill, 3 miles from Fred. Town, offers reward for stolen horse/Zach. Danner, living in Liberty-town, offers reward for apprentice to the harness and saddling bus. named Francis Simpson Hammond, 18-19, 5ft 8-9 inch

190. FHB Aug 26 1809/Teacher seeking position - John Richmond, at George Nicholls', Buckey's-town/Fuller wanted - Edward Magruder, nr Clarksburg, Mtg Co/Nathan T. Veatch, living about 2 miles from mouth of Monocacy, offers reward for stolen horse/Archibald Chisholm, West River, AA Co, offers land for sale in Allegany Co, tract called Shawney War, taken up in 1774; apply to Chisholm or to Thomas Shaw, at Fred. Town Bank/John Orme, Mtg Co, offers tract for sale he now occ, 250 a./Sale of hse and 1/4 lot at upper end of Market st, Fred. Town, prop of Adam Freshour decd; also 49 a. of Millers Chance - Jacob Freshour, Christian Brengle, exc/To rent farm in Loudoun Co adm farms of Samuel Clapham and William Noland, Esqrs. - Susanna Chilton/ Sale of plantations, one in Fred Co, nr Gettzinger's tavern, 176 a.; the other 3 miles of the former, 133 a.; apply to Jacob Rote, Middletown or subscribers in Hager's-town, Abraham King and Jacob King/John Clabaugh, living nr Little Pipe creek, on the Lancaster road, offers reward for stolen mare

191. FHB Sep 2 1809/Christian Freat has applied to Court of Common Pleas of Adams Co, for benefit of insolvent law of Pa

192. FHB Sep 9 1809/Chancery sale of tract of Thomas Price, decd, 113 a., nr Col. Baker Johnson's mill - George Price, Trustee/Sale on farm of Edward Salmon, decd, of negroes, horses, cows, hogs, sheep, &c. - Elizabeth Salmon, exec/Died Sat last at Boonsborough in Wash Co, George Scott, formerly res of this town/Christopher Keefer, nr Fred. Town, offers reward for stolen mare

193. FHB Sep 16 1809/Just received 21 boxes of lemons; to be sold very low - George Trisler/Citizens of Toms's creek and Catoctin hundreds to petition for road from Emmittsburg to George Oates' tavern/Thomas J. Hammond, Fred Co, to petition for relief under insolvency act/George Carter, Oatlands, nr Leesburgh, offers reward for mulatto Billy, sometimes calls himself William Jordan Augustus, light color, straight hair; also negro Isaac who calls himself Isaac Clerk, 5 ft 6 inch, about 40

194. FHB Sep 23 1809/John Winemiller, Mtg Co, offers reward for negro man Isaac Dorsey, about 35, 5 ft 6-7 inch; has a wife at Hagers-town/Sale of farm in Loudon Co, Va, 3 miles form Leesburg, 2 miles from Waterford, 300 a.; apply to John Williams, Waterford, to to subscriber, Joseph Janney, Alexandria/Fairfax Washington, Avon Hill, Jefferson Co, Va, wishes to sell 500 a. in Jefferson Co, called Fleetwood/Robert Johnson has taken up a stray mare/James Lackland, with a number of inhabitants of Mtg Co, to petition Gen Assembly for public road from lower end of William Darne's land thence to union mills and to intersect public road leading from John Orme's plantation to Mtg Court House/Tavern stand, in Liberty-town, for sale, formerly prop of Jacob Keiler, at present rented to Edward Hanna - George Keiler

195. FHB Sep 30 1809/Joseph Howard offers at public sale at his farm 1 1/2 mile from Howard's mill, horses, cows, sheep andhogs/Sale of negroes, horses, &c., 154 a. on Linganore creek; John Brengle nr Fred. Town or Otho Lawrence in the town will she the land - Joseph W. Lawrence/Patented condensing tub, to expedite the distilling of grain; one has been made by Job Hunt; a draught of this still can be seen in the hands of agent - Henry Witmer, patentee, George Miller, agent, Fred. Town/Chancery sale of land in Wash Co, on which Norman Bruce formerly lived and whereon William Bayley lived a few yrs since and conveyed by Mackall to Philip B. Key - James S. Morsell, Trustee

196. FHB Oct 7 1809/Married by Rev Ball Thurs 5 inst, John Hanson Thomas of Md to Miss Mary I. Colston dau of Rawleigh Colston, of Berkley Co, Va/Hauser & Thomas have just opened a new store, nearly opp Dr. Thomas's/George Creager, sen, candidate for sheriff/Sale on the Great Kanhawa, 580 a., pt of Gen. Washington's 10,000 a. tract - George C. Washington/Sale in pursuance of last will of Samuel Turner, of farm in Mtg Co, 300 a., negroes and other - Thomas Turner and Samuel Turner, exec/Sale of farm pursuant to last will of Jacob Sinn, 211 a., nr Fishing Creek, on road to Graceham - Jacob Rouzong and Philip Hauptman, exec

197. FHB Oct 14 1809/Sale of pers est of Capt. Thomas Chilton, decd, of Loudoun Co, negroes, horses, cattle &c. - Susanna Chilton, admr/Sale at subscriber's farm nr Trammelsburg, cattle, horses and hogs - Edward Thomas/ Sale of farm of late William Otto, on south side of big pipe creek, 5 miles from Taney-town, 120 a.; apply to Henry or Jacob Otto, living on premises - Commissiners: Joseph Taney, Jacob Cover, Conrad Stultz, William Jones, Thomas Todd/Andrew Williams and Daniel Smith exec of Ludwick Herbaugh/Horse race to be run nr Taney-town - John Crapster and Joseph Taney, Jun/ Union Bank stock (Georgetown, D.C.) will be sold - Robert Beverly, Thomas Beall of George, George Magruder/George Willson, living nr Mtg Court House, offers reward for stolen horse

198. FHB Oct 21 1809/Thomas I. Hammond applying for relief from debts/Lots for rent - Richard Ratcliffe, Fairfax Court House, Va/Vachel Hammond, Liberty, gives notice to persons indebted to make payment/Benjamin Carmin to sell farm of 80 a. on Linganore within 1 mile of Lawrence's mill/Married Thurs eve last by Rev George Bower, Doctor William B. Tyler of Balt to Miss Harriott Murdoch of this place/Died Sun last at an advanced age, Mrs. Jane Haff, consort of Maj. Abraham Haff of this co/Died Tues last, Jacob Levy of this town

199. FHB Oct 27 1809/(Date should 28th)/Receiving proposals for the erection of new court house in Leesburg; commissioners: William B. Harrison, Samuel Murry, Thomas Fouch, John Littlejohn, Charles Binns, C. F. Mercer/ Thomas Newens offers reward for apprentice to chairmaking bus. Orrell Murphy, about 12, 4 ft 2-3 inch/Committed to gaol of Fred Co, a negro man who calls himself Henaw, about 5 ft 9-10 inch, well made, about 30; says he belongs to John Ray of Bath Co, Va/A petition to open a road from Samuel Reynold's tavern by George Monse''s mill to intersect road lading from Taneytown to Westminster at or nr house of widow Smith/William Price admr of William Price, jun

200. FHB Nov 4 1809/Merchant Mill and saw mill for rent - Jacob Stoner, living on Sam's creek/Henry Baer, exec, to sell pers est of Jacob Levy/Sale of farm and mills pursuant to decree by court of Hamphsire Co in case of M'Carty vs Keller's heirs, at house of Thomas Dunn, in Frankfort James Reed, Trustee/Jacob Keiler cautions persons from taking assignment on note given to Ephraim Gaither of Mtg Co as Gaither has not complied with his contract/ Sale at late res of Stephen Shelmerdine, decd, of horses, hogs & milch cows - William Campbell, Henry Koontz, jun., Nicholas Randall, Sebastian Graff/ Samuel Pannabaker, living below Fred. Town on Balt turnpike road, has taken up a stray horse, certified by Peter Burkhart/Married Tues eve last by Rev Frederick Rahauser, Joseph Ogle to Miss Elizabeth Valentine, both of Fred Co

201. FHB Nov 11 1809/Married 5 inst at Shepherds-town, Va, by Rev Raebenach, Rev Lewis Mayer, formerly of Fred. Town to Miss Catharine Line, dau of John Line of the former place/Sale of hse and lot in Taney Town, lately occ by Thomas Gibson - William Cookerly/Sale of negroes, horses, &c. on Carroll's Manor - Lewis Hill/Sale of plantation, Conoi Island, nr Trammellsburg, 3 miles from Noland's Ferry and other - Trammell Delsahmutt/ Lancaster Times - died in this borough Fri last 3 inst, Philip Leonhard, aged 95, 2 months, 12 days; came to res here in 1734 when there were but 7 or 8 houses on the scite of the now populous town of Lancaster

202. FHB Nov 18 1809/Died Mon 15 inst at Georgetown, Maj. Henry Darnall of this co, at an advanced age, after a short illness in which he suffered extreme pain/Died Sat morn last in the 59th yr of her age, Mrs. Buckie/Died Mon morn in 72 yr of her age, Mrs. Catharine Kole/Loudon land for sale on which Judge Joseph Jones res - James Monroe, exec/Mason work on Monocacy bridge completed/P. Thomas, in want of money to pay his debts, warns those indebted to him to pay their debts

203. FHB Nov 25 1809/Frederick Stem to apply for benefit of insolvency act/John Scott exec of George Dickson/Farm for sale, 300 a. belonging to

heirs of General O. H. Williams, on west side of Catoctin mountain; apply to William Smith of Balt, Elie Williams nr Williamsport or P. Thomas in Frederick/Chancery sale at farm now occ by William M'Gary of real est of James Cooper, 200 a., 1 mile from Emmittsburg and other land - William Witherow, Trustee/Married Tues eve last by Rev Jonathan Rauhauser, Rev Frederick Rauhauser of Emmittsburg, to Miss Elizabeth Wagner, dau of Rev Daniel Wagner of this place/Died Sat last at an advanced age in this town, Gotleib Miller/Died Tues, Nicholas Hauer

204. FHB Dec 2 1809/Died Sat morn last in vicinity of this town, of a consumption, Gabriel Thomas in 26th yr of his age/Bernard O'Doherty, taylor, has just received from Phila, patterns of latest admired fashions

205. FHB Dec 9 1809/Died at his seat in this co on Sun last, Col. James Johnson in 74th yr of his age; active during revolutionary war/Died same day in this town at an advanced age, Adam Keller/Sale of 7 negroes at Mr. Cookes's tavern in Fred. Town - John Simmons, auctioneer/Sale of negroes, horses, cattle, &c. by virtue of deed of trust from Capt John S. Laurence - Allen Talbott, Peter Shriner, Trustees/Christian Freat, jun. has applied for benefit of insolvent laws in the court of Adams Co, Pa

206. FHB Dec 16 1809/Married Thurs eve last in this town by Rev Shaffer, Silas Engles to Miss Mary Hauer/Ferdinando Fairfax, Shannon Hill, Jefferson Co, Va, gives assurances re title to land he has for sale/Merchant mill with 200 a. for sale on Tuscarora, 1 mile of Leesburg, Va - Barnett Hough, Leesburg/Land for sale, 613 a. beginning 4 miles from town, adj lands of Marshall and John L. Harding - Thomas Johnson, nr town/Lottery for finishing Meth Meeting House in Libery Town; managers: Ephraim Howard, Abraham Crapster, Robert Cumming, Philip Hines, Curtis Williams, James L. Higgins, Abraham Jones, Sabritt Sollers, Dennis D. Howard, Frederick Unkefer/Sale at plantation of late Robert Peter in the Sugar lands, 1 mile. of Seneca Mills, of 50 slaves - Thomas Peter

207. FHB Dec 23 1809/Died on Carrol's Manor, 16 inst, Charles Smith, in 22d yr of his age. Captain John Smith died about 5 yrs ago leaving widow and 6 children of the decd was the eldest son/Alfred Belt adm of Henry A. C. Beld, to sell at dwlg plantation of Daniel Trundle 4 likely negroes, by order of Orphans's Court/Committed to gaol of Fred Co as a runaway, nego man who calls himself John Scott, appears to be 21-22, 5 ft 7 inch; had a piece of writing purporting to be a pass with the following names annexed, John Goff, Richard Evans, Jeremiah Cooksey; he says he belongs to James Harvey, nr to Clem Bayden's mill, 15 miles from Upper Marlborough in PG Co

208. FHB Dec 30 1809/Samuel Soaper exec of John Soaper, Montg Co/John Fluck has taken up a stray mare, certified by Abrham Lemaster/Jesse Petty, manager for Capt. William Campbell of Fred Co, brought before me a stray colt - Frederick Heisely, Justice of the Peace

209. FHB Jan 6 1810/Creditors of Samuel R. Hobbs are request to meet at Andrew Etzler's tavern in Liberty-town - John Glisan, Trustee/Henry Clary, living on Linganore, Fred Co, offers reward for apprentice boy Anthony Kline, 18-19, about 5 ft 5-6 inch/Peter Hawman has opened a house of enter-

tainment, at the sign of John Wilkes, Patrick St, Fred. Town, in the hse of Mr. Shellman lately occ by Henry Baer, nr the stone well and opp Dr. Baltzell's and the widow Birely's; he also carries on the tayloring bus./David Eador, Fred Co, offers reward for apprentice to blacksmith's bus., Solomon Eador, 19-20, stout made, stoop shoulder'd and grim countenance

210. FHB Jan 13 1810/Jacob Kessler, Fred. Town, seeks 2-3 journeymen taylors/Ezra Mantz, Sheriff, will sell est of Samuel Cromer, 44 a. of Mountain land adj lands of Yost Wyant, Fred Co, decd, by virtue of writ of fieri facias issued out of Wash Co court, at the suit of Christopher Burkhart/John B. Colvin, insolvent debtor, confined in prison of Wash Co/ Conrad Shaifer, Fountain Inn, Market St, Fred. Town, advises that Andrew England left in his possession a gelding, found in the possession of a negro man who said he came from Shenandoah nr Woodstock/Jonathan Powell, living in Liberty town, offers reward for Daniel M'Carty, apprentice to shoemaking bus., about 10 yrs of age/Newly apptd: Justices of the Levy Court: Joseph Swearingen, Alexander Warfield of Charles, Andrew Shriver, Christian Kemp, John Hoffman, John Clemson, Benjamin Biggs; Justices of the Peace: William Luckett, Francis B. Sappington, Joseph Swearingen, Henry Williams, John Schley, Patrick M'Gill, Ignatius Davis, Andrew Shriver, Henry Kuhn, John Hoffman, John Huston, Benjamin Biggs, John Wampler, Lewis Browning, Middleton Smith, John Creager, James S. Hook, Thomas Jones, Joseph Miller, Michael Myers, Edward Boteler, Sen., Henry Stembel, James Rice, Thomas Bond, Frederick Unkefer, John Jones of John, Thomas Wells, John H. Smith, James Mark, Frederick Heisely, Peter Burkhart, Henry Kemp, Jesse Wright, Silas Bayley, John Myers, Abraham Lemaster, Stephen Basford, Samuel Dawson, James Neale, Joseph Little, John Husselbaugh, John M'Kaleb

211. FHB Jan 20 1810/Meeting of Commissioners of the Tax for Fred Co - Richard W. Butler, Clerk/John H. Simmons, exec of Benjamin Hall/Jacob Steiner, Jun. exec of last will of Jacob Steiner, Sen., to sell prop of decd now occ by Henry Steiner in Market St/William Candler, Sheriff to sell dwlg plantation of John Reed, Mtt Co, tract called Johnson's discovery, 150 a., and 7 negroes, late the prop of John Reed and Archibald A. Reed, taken at the suit of Ignatius Davis/Sale of 10 horss, road waggon, 10 ploughs, harrows &c., 7 milch cows, 8 feather beds, 100 head of hogs, &c. John Hughes/Taxes for 1808 and 1809 to be paid during February Court - G. Baltzell, Collector/Sale of land of several thousand acres at Sharpsburg, Wash Co, named Semple's manor, by decree of Chancery Court in case of James Lawson agnst state of Md; the land belonged to John Semple who mortaged it to James Lawson and died without heirs; it escheated to state of Md - Elie Williams, William T. T. Mason, trustees

212. FHB Jan 27 1810/Died Tues night last, after a very tedious and severe indisposition, Mrs. M'Cully, relict of late Robert M'Cully of this place/ Sale of real est of John E. Young, nr waters of Pipe Creek and Beaver Dam, 187 a.; appl to Adam Young, living on the premises - Joshua Delaplane, Trustee/Farm for sale within 1/2 mile of Emmittsburgh, 200 a.; apply to Henry Williams nr Emmittsburg; Major John M'Kaleb, Taney Town; or subscriber, Patrick Davidson, living in Fred. Town/Jonathan Miller exec of Daniel Let/Apptd in Allegany Co: Justices of the Peace: John Reed, Jesse Tomlinson,

Frederick-Town Herald

William Shaw, Andrew Bruce, Benjamin Tomlinson, Aza Beall, John Rice, Thomas Pratt, George Rizer, Thomas Cresap, William Coddington, Thomas Parkenson, John Devillbiss, Hanson Briscoe, Thomas Greenwell, Nicholas Gower, Thomas F. Brooke, Ebenezer Davis, William H. Burnes, James Morrison, John M'Neil, Joshua Willson, Robert Armstrong, Lenox Martin; Levy Court: Benjamin Tomlinson, Thomas Pratt, Aza Beall, Upton Bruce, John Rice, Thomas Parkenson, Thomas Greenwell; Orphan's Court: Thomas Cresap, Hanson Briscoe, Upton Bruce

213. FHB Feb 3 1810/Thomas M'Giffin, atty for James Weldon, Washington, Pa, gives notice to heirs and legal representatives of Edward Weldon, late of Canton township, Washington Co, Pa, decd, that writ of partition has been ordered by Orphans's court on petition of James Weldon/the Loudon Lands, lying on Little River and the new turnpike road leading to Alexandria, being still unsold, will be disposed of by private sale; apply to Israel Lacey of Goshen, Col. Armistead T. Mason nr Leesburg, Major Charles Fenton Mercer of Leesburg or subscriber nr Milton in Albermarle Co, Va - James Monroe/Sale in New-town (Trap) of two stry log dwlg hse and lot in tenure of Jacob Martin jun - Zach. Simmons, Fred. Town/Stephen Stoner candidate for sheriff

214. FHB Feb 10 1810/John S. Miller and Frederick Heisely, exec of Godlob Miller, to sell a number of stocking looms of decd/Morris Jones candidate for sheriff/Sale by order of Orphans court of Montg Co on farm of Jeremiah Fowler, decd, lying on Broadrun, 4 miles from Conrod's ferry, of negroes, horses, cattle, &c. - Henry Fowler, exec/P. Edwards will open school in George Snatchel's stone hse, market st/Nicholas Worthington, intending to leave this place very shortly offers for sale his present stock, dry goods and groceries

215. FHB Feb 17 1810/Joshua Stevenson comments on his case against Myers/ Hugh Garvin will offers two hses and lots in creagers-town for sale/John Mitchell, Baltimore, No. 20, Cheapside, will rent the Tavern House, 3 miles from town (Balt) on Frederick-town turnpike road, formerly occ by William Kerr

216. FHB Feb 24 1810/George Baer, admr D.B.N. of Robert M'Cully, to sell pers prop of decd, including 4 new stills/James Johnson exec, Springfield, Fred Co, requests persons indebted to est of late Col. James Johnson to make immediate payment/Joseph Smith to sell lots in South st formerly in the possession of Wm. Clements/Otho H. W. Luckett to petition for benefit of insolvency act/Mills for sale on branch of Linganore called Bens Breanch, 65 a. - William Gipson, Gideon Gipson, Samuel Gipson, Joel Elliott, Hannah Elliott

217. FHB Mar 3 1810/Married Sun eve last in this town by Rev Daniel Wagner, John C. Thompson of George-town, to Miss Margaret Winemiller of this place/ All notes offered for renewal must be left at the Bank (Frederick Town Branch Bank) on Tuesdays preceding the discount day in each week - Thomas Shaw, Cashier/Ann Willis exec and James M'Cannon, Francis Hollingsworth, exec, to sell tract on Little Pipe Creek, formerly occ by James Poulson/John Glisan, Trustee of Samuel R. Hobbs, to sell lot in Liberty-town; also Hobbs' interest in tavern stand now in the possession of Andrew Etzler/Elegant

Summer Seat belonging to Conrad Doll adj Fred. Town, for sale or rent/Died Wed eve at the Retreat, Miss Mary Potts, dau of William Potts, in 19th yr of her age/Died in this town Fri 23 Feb, Mrs. Margaret M'Graw, aged 36 yrs, and on Sun following she was interred in Roman Cath Burial ground

218. FHB Mar 10 1810/Fire! About 1 o'clock Tues morn last a building in the skirts of this town, owned and occ by John Gomber as a brewery, was discovered to be on fire. It and small stable nearby were consumed/Mill of William Potts on Tuscarora Creek, 3 1/2 miles from Fred. Town, to be let/ John Baer of Henry intends removing from this place on 1 Apr next and wishes to settle accounts/Absconded from George Town, D.C., mulatto wench Lotty, 32, robust, formerly prop of Dr. Edward Gantt, has lived for some time past with Mrs. H. Hayward, and is well known in George-town/Appt commissioners to receive subscriptions for Westminster and Hagers Town Turnpike Road: James Johnson, Joshua Delaplane, Jacob Weller/To sell at his res in Wash Co, Salubria, 30 negroes, and other - Tench Ringgold/Sale at farm where he lives, 2 miles from Buckey's town, horses, cattle and hogs - Christian Hill/ William Barker and A. Hagan have commenced the tayloring bus. in Fred. Town, at corner of market and Patrick

219. FHB Mar 17 1810/Peter Ordner, living in Fred. Town, offers reward for apprentice boy, bound to the hand screw bus. James Augustus Norris, about 5 ft, 17-18/Sale of farm lying between sugar loaf mountain and Monococy, nr Colenburg's glass works, 145 a.; to be shewn by Robert Fish, present tenant - Nathaniel Hines

220. FHB Mar 24 1810/George Creager, Jun. having removed from town, will attend every Sat for a few months at the hse of John Gill for settlement of accounts/Amelia Wolfenden has removed to hse in Market st, lately occ by Mr. Worthington adj the Market hse, where she carries on the Millinery bus./Sale of horses, cattle and hogs, and 4 negroes - Elias Harding of Walter/Sale of farm pursuant to last will of John Paterson, sen., 1 mile of Creager's town, 200 a. - Ann Paterson, John Paterson, Michael Zimmerman, exec/John Glisan has taken up a stray mare/George French admr of George Scott and Michael Hauser admr of Robert T. Cary, make a joint sale of negro slaves

221. FHB Mar 31 1810/Stephen Joy cautions agnst taking assignment on note given to Adam Maine, jun/S. Baily, Hager's town, has taken that hse on public square in Hager's-town, lately occ by Mrs. Heister, where he has opened a House of Entertainment/Sale of tract of John Ried of Montg Co, of tract, Lost Breeches, 100 a. - Ignatius Davis/Schoolmaster wanted - John Johnson, nr Trammels-town

222. FHB Apr 7 1810/Married Thurs last by Rev Higgins, Vachel Worthington Randall to Miss Mary Dorsey, dau of Basil Dorsey, all of this co/Died at Hager's-town on 25 ult, William Clagett, Assoc Judge of the 5th judicial dist of this state, consisting of the counties of Fred Co, Wash and Allegany/Jacob Appler to sell at Mr. Hanew's tavern, Liberty-town, a 2-stry log hse and 3 lots, and 7 1/2 a. of timer land adj Mr. Albaugh's/John Main of George has taken up a stray gelding/W. C. Selden to sell farm of 337 a. in Loudon Co, Va; apply to Presly Saunders, jun., living on the premises

Frederick-Town Herald

223. FHB Apr 14 1810/Died Tues even last, Mrs. Charlotte Steckell, wife of
Solomon Steckell. Less than one hour previous she was apparently in perfect
health, but being alarmed by the cries of one of her children, which had
been playing in the yard, she ran out hastily and after assisting in with
the child was seized with a fever which proved fatal, although medical aid
was immediately called in. She left a husband and 6 little ones/Died Wed
last in 65th yr of his age, George Nicholl, of this co, after an illness of
nearly two yrs/Jacob Miller, at the sign of the Spread Eagle, Fred. Town,
has opened a House of Entertainment at the stand formerly occ by Benjamin
Stallings; he has provided himself with a billiard table; boarders by the
week, month or year; privte parties can at any time be accommodated. He has
provided himself with a careful and attentive ostler and stabling for horses
by the week, month or year; constantly keeping an assortment of the best
liquors/Jacob Keller, living next to Doct. Baltzell and Mrs. Byerley, Patrick St, has available ropes and twine/John Baer, having moved to Emmittsburg, requests settlement of accounts; pay to Henry Baer/Fleecy-dale Mills,
where carding and fulling will be done (formerly Amelung's old glass works)
on Bennett's creek - Matthew Brown, Montevino/Alexander Scott, Georgetown,
offers reward for mulatto man Charles, formerly an ostler at Lindsays'
tavern in Washington, about 25, tall, slender and ill formered/The horse,
Naraganset, stands at Cerisvill Farm - John Morrison, manager

224. Apr 21 1810/Married Thurs 12 inst by Rev Ryland, Doct. George Colegate
to Miss Mary M'Cannon dau of James M'Cannon, all of this co/Died 11 inst,
after an indisoposition of 3 days, Mrs. James, consort of Major Daniel James
of this co/Wool Carding Machine - Subscribers are ready to receive wool to
card at the machine formerly owned by Owings and M'Kinstry, at Thomas
Hobbs's mill on Linganore - Crapser & Jones, Joseph M'Kinstry, Avignon
Mills/Benjamin Penn, offers reward for negro lad who ran away from subscriber nr Fred. Town, about 20, who calls himself Moses Brisco; has a father and
mother living in city of Balt nr Chase's wharf; his father who is free, is
of the name of Brisco and follows something of the shipping bus.; Moses is 5
ft 8-9 inch/ Benjamin Penn will sell in Creager's Town, 4 lots; apply to
Cornelius Ridge, living in Creager's Town/ Committed to gaol of Fred Co,
mulatto woman Poll, about 27, 4 ft 10 inch, stout; says she belongs to Miss
Baque of city of Balt/Hezekiah Summers, Fred Co, to apply for relief of
debts/Land for sale in Berkely Co, Va, 1 1/2 miles from Martinsburgh, 226 a.
- Philip C. Pendleton, Martinsburgh/Sale of land on which he res on post
road from Fred. Town to Harpers Ferry, 311 a.; also farm nearby, 234 a. -
John Thomas, Merryland Tract/Pump making & pipe boring, at his hse at east
end of Patrick St - Absalom Caff

225. Apr 28 1810/Sale of tract in Loudon Co, Va, with merchant and saw
mill, 300 a. - Samuel Adams/Chancery sale of tract, Papaw Bottom on river
Monococy, now in possession of Jeremiah Browning, 163 a. in Fred Co   - R.
B. Taney, Trustee/Wood land for sale, 900 a., adj plantations of widow of
Peter Bussard, Benjamin Hatherly, Peter Leatherman, John Wiseman, on top of
Kittoctin mountain. The waggon road from George Oats' tavern, on the marked
Harman's Gap road, passes through it, down to John Devilbiss's sawmill at
the foot of the Kittoctin mountain and so on through Turk-Eye and Monococy
manor settlements. Mr. Laurence Brengle whill shew the land - William Hobbs
of Samuel/Married Sun last by Rev Shaffer, Thomas Stevens, to Miss Elizabeth

Graybell/Died 19 inst, Mrs. Mary M'Elderry, in 83rd yr of her age; she re-
tained all her faculties to the last/Died Thurs eve last after a lingering
illness, Mrs. Mary Beall, wife of William M. Beall of this town/Sale of prev
est of late George Nichol - Margaret Nichol, Henry Koontz, Jun., exec

226. FHB May 5 1810/Married Sun last by Rev James L. Higgins, Henry Bargman
to Miss Margaret Champer, all of this co/Sale of mill seat, late prop of
Elisha Janney, in town of Occoquan, 16 miles south of Alexandria - Richard
M. Scott, Trusteee for creditors of E. Janney/Sale of farm in Loudon Co, Va,
2 miles from Waterford, 300 a., in neighborhood where there are many of the
Society of Friends, within 2 miles of their meeting hse; apply to John
Williams, Waterford, or to subscriber, Joseph Janney, in Alexandria/ Committed to gaol of Fred Co, negro man, who calls himself Simond Adams, about 26,
5 ft 10 inch; says he is free born and served his time with Joseph Carter of
Charles Co, about 10 miles from Nottingham/Jacob Kesler, tayloring bus., has
removed to Patrick St, opp store of William and John Baer

227. FHB May 12 1810/Otho Lawrence asks for return of borrowed books/John
Bayly has just received from Phila at his store in Patrick st, 3 doors from
George Baer's corner, opp J. S. Hall's Boarding hse, an assortment of super-
fine and second quality broad cloths, and many other items (named)/Sale of
hse and lot in New Market - Israel French, Jun./Nicholas Turbutt, nr Fred.
Town, has taken up a stray gelding, certified by Peter Burkhart/Francis
Feelemeyer, living in New Market, offers reward for missing mare/Married
Tues eve last by Rev Daniel Wagner, John Buckey, to Miss Susan Hauser, dau
of Michael Hauser, all of this town/Married same eve by Rev P. Davidson,
William M. Beall, Jun., to Miss Fanny M'Cleary, dau of Henry M'Cleary, all
of this town/John Dertzbach has opened a house of entertainment in Market St
at the sign of the Eagle and Review in the hse lately occ and kept by Adam
Keller, decd

228. FHB May 19 1810/Two-stry log hse, 30x24 ft for sale in Cumberland and
other houses, tract of 90 a., 1 mile from Cumberland; apply to B. S. Pigman,
Fred. Town or subscriber, George Rizer in Cumberland/Lewis P. W. Balch,
Georgetown, has 10,000 a. of land in Kenhawa, Va, for sale, owned by Ezekiel
King of Wash City/Tanyard for sale, 5 miles north of Fred. Town - Richard L.
Head

229. FHB May 26 1810/John S. Lawrence, Fred Co, wishing to emigrate to
Tennessee this fall, to sell farm, 500 a., 5 miles of Liberty-town/Miller
wanted - William Johnson of Thos. nr Newtown/Married by Rev Lewis Mayer,
Tues evening last, Doct. Jacob Baer, of Fred. Town, to Miss Charlotte
Chinoweth, dau of Samuel Chinoweth of Berkley Co, Va/A new carding machine
is now erecting at John Cook's mills, on Bennett's creek, 5 1/2 miles from
New Market

230. FHB Jun 2 1810/Pine plank - Leonard Shafer, Williamsport/Henry Burkitt
wishes to let hse nr Merryland Tract/Committed to gaol of Fred Co, as a
deserter by name of William Peters, about 5 ft 10 1/2 inch, slender made,
pitted with small pox, pretty talkative, taylor by trade; says he res at
Great Choptank bridge, eastern shore Md; stated he enlisted at Charleston,
Va/Subscribers have purchased from Rev Patrick Davidson several lots laid

off of said Davidson's Farm, nr Emmittsburg; since then we have found on the records in Fred Co, a mortgage on said farm for 900 pounds, unto William M'Meeken now of state of Ohio; until release of mortgage is obtained, hands of Doct. Robert L. Annan, we forewarn persons from taking assignment on bonds used in payment - Lewis Weaver, Patrick Bradly, Joseph Hughes, James Hughes, Henry Hughes, Jacob Cress, Joseph Beahey, John Troxel/Escaped from Balt Co roads, nr Francis Snowden's: John Collins, native of Ireland, about 5 ft 7 inch, middling chunky, well made, light hair, marked on right arm with a mermaid and an anchor and cable on his right or left arm; Samuel Smith, white man, 25, 6 ft, fresh complexion, dark hair and eyes, front teeth decayed, thick lips; Thomas Harvey, white man, 25, about 5 ft 11 inch, slender, fair complexion, light hair, by occupation a saddler; William Carroll, white man, 40, about 5 ft 10 inch, sallow complexion, light brown hair; John Casey, white man, 35, about 5 ft 8 inch, stout, native of Ireland; Abraham Bannerkir alias George, a black man, about 27, 5 ft 8-9 inch, high forehead, hollow faced, very black; Charles Chapman, black man, about 5 ft 8 inch, well set, pleasant countenance; Samuel Green, a black man, supposedly went to Annapolis; Jacob Hazel, very black, full faced, about 5 ft 7-8 inch - made their escape by seizing the centinels and taking their arms from them - Richard Choate, supervisor/Frederick Linthicum, living in Hyatt's Town, offers for sale a hse in New-Market, lately occ by Miss Poultney and Miss Plummer/Grist Mill, Saw Mill, plantation of 150 a., formerly Morton's on Little Monocosy - Joshua Johnson/Died Sun 20th ult at the plantation of George Calver, PG Co, negro Jack in 120th yr of his age/Pine boards - Stephen Stoner in Frederick/William Scott has removed from Hanover, Pa, to Newtown and opened a House of Entertainment at the sign of the Black Horse/Solomon Davis has taken up a stray gelding, certified by G. W. Harwood

231. FHB Jun 9 1810/Hauer & Rohr have just received at their store in Patrick St, Sign of the Cask & Sugar Loaves, madeira, sherry, lisbon, port ... raisins, pepper, &c./John B. Beall, intending to remove from Cumberland, offers for sale brick merchant mill, nr centre of town; apply to John Michael Beatty, nr Fred. Town, Eli Beatty, Hagers-town/Mill seat for sale, nr turnpike bridge on waters of Linganore, 3 miles from Fred. Town - Charles Hammond, nr the premises/Joseph M. Cromwell adm of William Marshall, to sell negroes and other pers est of decd, 1 1/2 miles from Noland's ferry/P. Davidson states that incumbrance stated in earlier notice in the herald was known to many of the purchasers; at an early period he informed William Emmit who made the sales; informed those present: Patrick Bradly, Lewis Motter who refused to sign and Henry Need who also refused to sign/Baer & Hickson have just received from Balt at their store in Emmittsburg, a fresh assortment of dry goods & groceries

232. FHB Jun 16 1810/Thomas S. Lee, Fred Co, Needwood Farm, offers reward for slaves, Jim, mulatto, about 21, 5 ft 6-8 inch; and Charles, 5 ft 11 inch, 45-50/Vincent Moss, living on Goose creek, Fauquier Co, Va, offers reward for negro Dick, stout, 5 ft 9-10 inch, 27; a white boy 15-16 absconded with him/Pump making & pipe boring - Lewis Smith has commenced bus. in Emmittsburgh/Reward for negroes who ran away from Samuel Weaver and George M'Clanahan, living nr Faquier Court House, Va: Nicholas, 30, 5 ft 9-10; Bill Seaton, 20, 5 ft 7-8 inch, Robin, 40, 5 ft 8-9 inch, Jenny, belonging to Samuel Steel, 35-40, Hannah, prop of John Weaver, about 14/John Harnest

offers reward for horse stolen out of a waggon at Richardson's tavern, Fred. Town

233. FHB Jun 23 1810/Camp Meeting to be held at Francis Hoffman's farm, between Frederick and New-town/Sale of 5180 a. of timbered Mountain land, pt of real est of late George Murdoch, decd, 3/4 miles from Creager's-town, at Cornelius Ridge, Creager's-town; apply to George William Murdoch or Lawrence Brengle/During the gust of Tues last, the waggon shed of John Brengle, nr this place, was struck by lightning/Christopher Barickman will sell 154 a., formerly prop of Joseph W. Lawrence/Lancelot Wade, nr Hancock, Wash Co, offers reward for negro Dick, who ran away when Mr. Wade lived in Fred Co; he sometimes calls himself Dick Hawkins, 36, 5 ft 9-10 inch

234. FHB Jun 30 1810/Died Thurs morning last at an advanced age, William Crum, of this town/Luke Cannon, living in Prince William Co, nr Dumries, Va, offers reward for black man Jeffery, 29-30, 5 ft 2-3 inch, shoemaker by trade

235. FHB Jul 7 1810/Married 28th of last month in Phila, by Rev Dr. Helmuth, Rev David F. Schaffer of Fred. Town, to Miss Eliza Krebs dau of George Krebs of Phila/Farm to be rented, 500 a., Berkley Co, Va - John Hanson Thomas/James White, intending to remove to City of Wash the approaching winter, will sell farm on which he now lives, nr the mouth of Monococy, in upper part of Montg Co; also to sell lots in City of Wash/The Post Office will in future be open on Sundays for delivery 1 hour in the forenoon, 10-11 and 1 hour before sundown

236. FHB Jul 14 1810/Henry Poole, Sen., living on Linganore, offers reward for negro Davy, 5 ft 5 inch, 29, born nr Annapolis/Sale of 2 negro women at res of George Scott, decd, in Boonsborough - George French/Sale of tract 20 1/2 a. called Resurvey or Miller's Chance, 8 miles from Fred. Town - Jacob Freshour, Christian Brengle/Died Tues last, Capt. Thomas Sprigg, of this co, an old revolutionary solider/Died same day, Mrs. Pyfer, consort of Philip Pyfer of this town/Pump making and pipe boring in and around Emmitsburg - John Caff. "Through malice there is one Lewis Smith (who) advertises to follow the same business... having never served any time to it... about 4 weeks ago he took an old pump out of his brother's well to learn by it. ... There is a Jacob Rise married to a cousin of Smith's I understand means also to take up the trade. He went to my son in Frederick-Town for certain augurs, and told him that I sent him..."

237. FHB Jul 21 1810/Ambrose Moriantz or John Douglas, nr the Center Market, Wash City, offer reward for missing horses

238. FHB Jul 28 1810/If Mary, widow of William Perry (who some yrs ago kept a blacksmiths shop in Hagers-town) is yet living, she may hear of something to her advantage by applying to John Russell, living in New-market/Benjamin Stalling, having removed to Balt, notifies all those indebted, he will attend at August court next, for purpose of adjusting same/Ropes and twine - Jacob Keller, Fred. Town/Lot for sale on north branch of Bennett's creek, nr Yate Plummer's mill, 4 a. with frame hse; apply to Samuel Plummer, living nr the lot or Thomas Wood in Newmarket/Chancery sale of farm in Tom's creek

hundred, late the prop of Daniel M'Cormick, decd, 190 a., 2 miles from Graceham - Joseph Hughes, Trustee, Emmitsburgh/Died Wed eve last at hse of her son-in-law, Doct. William Tyler, in this town, Mrs. Lucy Addison, widow of late Col. John Addison of PG Co, after lingering illness, leaving relations, mother, and sister

239. FHB Aug 9 1810/Married Mon 23 ult by Rev David F. Schaeffer, Doctor Edward Henry Anderson to Miss Catherine Priscilla Morris, of this place/John Gerhard, living in Liberty-town, offers reward for apprentice to shoe making bus., named Thomas Leopard, about 15, 4 ft 7-8 inch

240. FHB Aug 11 1810/Sheriff's sale of right of Allen Simpson, Sarah Simpson, William Benson and Ninian Benson to tract, Goodport, 788 1/4 a., taken at suit of Henry Howard of John - William Candler, sheriff of Montg Co/Sheriff's sale, Montg Co, at Nathan Browning's tavern in Clarksburgh of right of Mesheck Browning to lot in Clarksburgh, tract called the Resurvey on Maple branch, 150 a., taken at suits of Humphrey Pierce and John C. Richards; also right of Jesse Browning to above prop; also hse in Clarksburgh, late prop of Archibald Browning, taken at suit of Lewis Browning, use of Henry Poole/Sale of pers est of Capt. Thomas Sprigg, decd, negroes, furniture, cattle &c. - Otho Sprigg, admr/A full bred Merino ram to be let to ewes - John Threlkeld, nr Georgetown/Fulling and dying at his mill, at mouth of Hunting Creek, bout 2 miles from Cregers-town; cloths will received at store of Francis Mantz, Fred. Town - Ignatius Lilly/Fulling, dyeing and dressing of cloths, a new erected fulling mill at his farm on fishing creek, nr Catoctin furnace, 8 miles from Fred. Town - John Cronise; cloths will be received by Hauer and son, Seth Clark, Fred. Town; John Baltzell, Woodsbury; and Jacob Beckenbaugh, Creagers-town/Jacob A. Powell, taylor, nr Burkett's & Harley's store, having a pressing demand for money, request persons indebted to him to make immediate payment/Morris Jones candidate for sheriff/Doct. William Potts having completed his medical education at the Univ of Pa, has just commenced the practice of physic, Market St, next door to Major Miller's and opp Mr. Beall's/Barn of James Downey, jun. living on the Antietem, nr the old Rock forge was struck with lightning Tues eve last, grain in the straw consumed and 3 horses killed

241. FHB Aug 18 1810/House and 4 a. for sale in Clarksburg, Montg Co, next door to Scholl's tavern; also 133 a. 2 1/2 miles east of Clarksburg/Elias Harding of Walter, intending to remove from state of Md, will sell 10 head horned cattle, milch cows, desk, &c./House and lot for sale on which is erected a frame hse occ by Joseph Hughes as a tavern and store, subject to annuity of 32 dollars, payable to Rev. Mr. Dubois who will sell the same; apply to Joseph Hughes on the premises, or to Grundys and Crossdale, Balt/John Hoffman, Muehlheim, living 4 miles from Fred. Town on Harper's Ferry road, offers reward for stolen mare

242. FHB Aug 25 1810/David Trundle, exec, in pursuance of last will of Ruth Trundle, Montg Co, to sell at dwlg of sd decd, 1 mile from mouth of Monococy, 11 negroes and other/Journeymen cooper wanted at Crapster and Jones's mill on Linganore, 3 1/2 miles from Liberty - John M'Daniel

243. FHB Sep 1 1810/Conrad Shaffer, Fountain Inn, Fred. Town, to sell a negro man/Sale on late farm of John Michael, 1 mill from Late's mill of horses, cattle, sheep &c. - Christian Hill/John Mayer, York Pa, has applied for relief of debt/Committed to gaol of Fred Co, negro man who calls himself Jerry Bryan, appears to be 44-45, 5 ft 4 inch; says he is free and drove a dray for Robert Clark in High-street, George-town

244. FHB Sep 8 1810/Frederick Augustus Schley, atty at law, has opened his office in upper end of Market st, 3 doors below Mr. Dertzbach's tavern/ George M. Conradt offers for sale at his cotton and woollen cloth manufactory and dye shop, chambrays, cotton stripe, &c./Public sale of Dry Goods & Groceries - Philip Hines, Liberty town/ White House Tavern for rent, lately occ by Samuel Sylvester, also known as Fountain Inn - Thomas Shipley/Lands for sale, 350-360 a., 7-8 miles from Fred. Town, one part of them occ by Col. Henry Barrick and another by Christian Barrick, another by Adam Smith; apply to Capt William Campbell or W. T. T. Mason at Frederick or in Wash city to John P. Van Ness/Dennis Pool, on Linganore, Fred Co, offers reward for negro man Reuben, calls himself Reuben Smith, 5 ft 8-9 inch/Bernard O'Neill, Mtg Co, offers reward for missing mare

245. FHB Sep 15 1810/John Hughes intending to return to Balt this fall, will sell farm where he res, 1 mile from Fred. Town/Merino sheep for sale; may be viewed at Seth Clark's tavern - Edward B. Gibbs, Samuel B. Clark/ Officers and non-commissioned officers of 16th Regt to meet - Stephen Steiner, Lieut. Colonel/John Hilleary has taken up a stray steer/Plantation with merchant mill, saw mill, fulling mill and blacksmith's shop for sale; apply to Thomas Francis, nr Paris, Loudon Co, Va/Sale by virtue of deed of trust from William Lee, at Beltzhoover's tavern, Hagers-town, lot in Hagers-town adj prop of John Ragen and other lots - George Grundy, Trustee

246. FHB Sep 22 1810/John Crum, exec of William Crum, to sell negroes/ Sheriff's sale at Mr. Dill's tavern of negro man named Ned, negro woman Rachel and 3 children, Nelly, Milly and Alfred, woman Claey and her 3 children, woman named Amey, tract Rock Hall, in Fred Co, 90 a., late the prop of Trammell Delashmutt, decd, at the suits of Francis Mantz, Sampson Delashmutt use of Francis Mantz, John Whiteneck use of same, Samuel Phillips, John Bruner and Jacob Grove

247. FHB Sep 29 1810/Sheriff's sale at Nathan Browning's Tavern in Clarks-burgh right of Mesheck Browning to lot in Clarksburgh, pt of tract called Resurvey on Maple Branch, 150 a., taken at suits of Humphrey Pierce and John Custis Richards

248. FHB Oct 6 1810/Married at Balt Tues last by Rev Beasley, Baker Johnson, jun. of Fred Co to Miss Hannah Sophia Grundy, dau of George Grundy, Esq. of the former place/Fred. Town Races - Jacob Cookes, Jacob Miller, managers/Henry S. Turner, Wheatland, nr Charles Town, Jefferson Co, Va, offers reward for 2 slaves, Rachel and Emiline/Fall Goods - Hauser and Thomas (items listed), Fred. Town

249. FHB Oct 13 1810/Store now opening in Market St - George Trisler/Basil Brown, on Severn river AA Co, offers reward for Ezekiel, about 6 ft/ Commit-

ted to gaol as a runaway, negro lad who calls himself Joe, 17-18, 5 ft 2 1/2 inch; says he belongs to Henry Peak, who owns a mill on crooked branch in Stafford Co, Va/Barton Philpott and Thomas Hawkins, admr of Joseph Gwinn, to sell 21 negroes, furniture, cattle, &c./House for sale in Emmittsburg - Samuel Noble, Emmittsburgh/William Dydenhover has commenced fulling & dyeing bus. for this season on Tuskarora creek

250. FHB Oct 20 1810/Chancery sale of farm, 270 a., prop of Charles Magruder of Montg Co, decd, adj Edward Magruder's plantation, 2 miles from Clarksburg - Samuel Claggett, Trustee/Sale of dwlg of Thomas Gibson, decd, horses, hogs &c. - Ann Gibson, exec/Elisha Beall, living on Bush Creek, nr Fred. Town, offer reward for yellow girl, about 17, chunky, ears are bored for rings/Hse to let next door to Samuel Duvall; enquire of subscriber, Conrad Doll or Solomon Steckle now living in the hse/Died Sat last at her res nr this place, Mrs. Rebecca Thomas, relict of Notley Thomas, in 82nd year of her age/Died at Balt Thurs morn last, after a long and lingering illness, David Smith in the 35th yr of his age

251. FHB Oct 27 1810/No additional items

252. FHB Nov 3 1810/Sale of tavern stand at the fork of the roads, the foot of the Allegany, 5 miles above Fort Cumberland (buildings described) - Evan Gwynn, on the premises/Chancery sale of real est of Richard Lawrence, decd, 313 1/3 a. in AA Co, 3 1/4 miles from Ellicott's mills; apply to Joseph Ratclift, who is tenant on it - Otho Lawrence, Trustee/Sale of 525 a. of land, pt of real est of George Murdoch, decd, formerly prop of Daniel Dorsey, 1 mile of Liberty Town; David Duttero, now res on the premises will shew the prop - George William Murdoch/Samuel Thomas admr of Rebecca Thomas, will sell 8 negroes, pt of est of decd/Married Sun eve last by Rev Mallavay, Terence M'Gowan of Balt to Miss Peggy Baltzell of this place/Died Sat morn last, at the house of General Nelson, in this Town, of a pulmonary disease and in the flower of life, Mrs. Kitty Harrison, widow of the late Alexander Contee Harrison of the U.S. Navy and on the following day her remains were removed to Conowaga, in York Co, Pa, and there deposited in the tombs of her ancestors/Nathan Maynard to sell 2 negro girls, furniture

253. FHB Nov 10 1810/Married Thurs evening 1st inst by Rev Jones, Lewis Augustus Beatty, to Miss Sarah Gist, both of this co/Married Tues last by Rev Grubb, John Baer of Henry of this place, to Miss Catharine Shriver, of Adams Co, Pa/Died in this town Mon last, Robert Potts, youngest son of William Potts, senr, of Fred Co, attacked just five weeks before his death by a highly inflammatory fever; at the age of 21 (long obit)/Committed to jail of Fred Co, mulatto man who calls himself Amos Hoe, supposed to be about 21, 5 ft 6-7 inch; says he belongs to James Mitchell, Innkeeper, in Stafford Co, Va/Committed to jail of Fred Co, negro boy who calls himself John Gassaway, supposed to be 17 yrs of age, 5 ft 2 inch; says he belonged to John Myers of Kent Island who sold him not long since to a man who was going to Natchez, and from who he absconded on the Allegany mountain/Sheriff's sale at the hse of John Dill, right of John Hummell to lot on Market St, between houses of Richard Potts, decd, and George Schnartzell/Horses for sale; also 50 head of hogs, sheep, cider, furniture and other - Dennis Sollers/New store by the Market House in Fred. Town, with general

assortment of goods - Lanes & Rutherford/Thomas Maynard exec of Brice Maynard, to sell crop of grain, furniture, and other

254. FHB Nov 17 1810/Wet and Dry goods - George Trisler/Meeting of first Frederick Troop of Cavalry - Henry Kemp, Captain/Persons are cautioned from receiving assignment of notes passed by Henry Willis, decd, to John Giger of Fred Co - Ann Willis, James M'Cannon, Francis Hollingsworth, exec/Married Sun eve last by Rev Daniel Shaffer, Mr. C.G. Miller to Miss Anna M. Conradt, all of this town

255. FHB Nov 24 1810/New Confectionary and Oyster House - G. G. Mueller, in Market st, next door to Mr. Cooke's Tavern/Statement by Francis B. Sappington, Justice of the Peace, that George Keiler in dealing with his brother Jacob Keiler, has not been benefited any farther than his just claim required (statement made to repudiate statment made by creditors of Jacob Keiler/William Hilliary has taken up a stray gelding/Richard Beall, within 3 miles of mouth of Monococy, has negroes for sale/John Fitzhugh, living on Cedar run, Prince William Co, Va, offers reward for negro man Reuben, black-smith by trade, about 30 yrs of age, 5 ft 9-10 inch

256. FHB Dec 1 1810/Died in this town on 22 ult, at an advance age, George Schnertzell/Died on 24th, Jacob Wise/Died on 25th in 80th yr of his age, Major Jacob Miller/Died on 26th, E. R. Stone, Esq./Sale of negroes and other pers prop of Charles Ridgely of William, Balt Co, decd - Samuel N. Ridgely, exec/Sale of prop of John Adams, Charles M'Kinny and Elie Williams, consist-ing of 7 draft horses, negro boy - John Adams, at his res, 2 miles from Boonsborough/Committed to jail of Fred Co, black or dark mulatto who calls himself Samuel Davis, about 35; says he is free and lived with a Col. Butler and Col. O'Hara in or nr Chambersburg, Pa; is in possession of certificate of freedom signed by Robert Allison and another certificate of his marriage to one Molly Lucas, signed by D. Denny

257. FHB Dec 8 1810/Married Thurs 5 ult by Rev Craver, John Stilly, to Miss C. Staley, dau of John Staley/Married Tues 27th by Rev Bower, William R. King to Miss Eleanor Thomas, dau of Edward Thomas/Married same eve by Rev Malavay, Thomas Powell to Mrs. Grinnell/Married Sun last by Rev David F. Shaffer, John Mahany, to Miss Susan Lantz/Married Thurs eve last by Rev A. Grubb, Henry H. Hickson, to Miss Mary Crapster, dau of John Crapster/Married same eve by Rev Shaffer, Captain John Michael Beatty, to Miss Charlotte Hughes, dau of Levi Hughes/Married same eve by Rev Craver, George Whip to Miss Susan Cast, dau of John Cast - All of this co/Committed to jail of Fred Co, negro man who calls himself Isaac, about 5 ft 6-7 inch, about 27; says he belongs to Andrew Offutt of Montg Co/John Owings, admr of Kitty Harrison

258. FHB Dec 15 1810/Just received assortment of Dry Goods from Phila - John Bayly/Female Academy, to be opened by Mr. and Mrs. Welch, Fred. Town/ Tavern stand to be let almost opp Mrs. Kimboll's, formerly occ by Benjamin Stallings - Jacob Miller

259. FHB Dec 22 1810/Died Sat evening last, Mrs. Nancy Pigman, in 75th yr of her age, after tedious and painful illness/Mill and farm for sale, adj seat lately improved as a cloth manufactory, at Amelong's old glass works -

- Matthew Brown, nr the premises/John Bayly admr of E. R. H. Stone/Committed to jail of Fred Co as a runaway, mulatto man who calls himself Harry, 5 ft 5 inch, appears to be about 21-22; says he belongs to William Valandigham, in Fairfax Co, Va/Journeymen tanners wanted - Isaac & John Mantz

260. FHB Dec 29 1810/Married 18 inst by Rev Chandler, Ely Dorsey jun. of the city of Balt, to Miss Sarah Johnson, dau of Major Roger Johnson of this co/Died at York, Pa, on 17 inst, in 61st yr of his age, Rev Daniel Wagner, formerly pastor of the German Reformed Church in this place, from whence he lately removed to Pa, compelled by ill health to relinquish his ministerial labours

The Maryland Herald and Hager's Town Weekly Advertiser, printed by Thomas Grieves.

261. Jan 3 1806/Married Tues evening last, by Rev Bower, Richard Ragan, merchant, to Miss Elizabeth Ragan, dau of John Ragan, all of this town/Wash Co Court Chancery case - Walter Boyd, complainant, agnst Mary Boyd, Conrad Frankenberger & Eleanor his wife, Peter Swartz, and Charity his wife and William Boyd, heirs of William Boyd, decd, defendants - to obtain decree for sale of real est of William Boyd, decd, for payment of his debts. The bill states that Mary Boyd, Peter Swartz and Charity his wife, res out of the state/M. Bayly has a number of Negroes, prop of John T. Mason, Esq., to put out upon hire; enquire at the farm of said Mason, under the North Mountain /Philip Mains, Justice of the Peace, certifies that William Murry has taken up a stray mare/Tavern to be rented with 3 a., and black-smith's shop and tools, within 1/4 of mile of the Cave, about 2 miles from Col. Hughes's Forge - William Allinder, living on the premises/Rezin Davis requests persons who were purchasers at his sale, to pay their obligations /John Wilson, near Sharpsburg, offers reward for missing horse

262. EAM Jan 10 1806/Married Thurs 2d inst by Rev Rahauser, Jacob Foutz, to Miss Elizabeth Storm, both of Wash Co/Died suddenly Tues morning last in the 58th year of her age, Mrs. Peitrey, wife of Jacob Peitrey of this co/Doctor Young has taken into partnership Dr. T. Walmsley, late of Phila/Samuel Miller adm of John Miller/Committed to custody of N. Rochester, Sheriff of Wash Co, negro man who calls himself John Williams; says he absconded from his master near Alexandria, Va, who was taking him and several other negroes to the southward, but whose name he does not know; he says he was purchased of John Dorsey, of St. Mary's Co; he appears to be about 25, 5 ft 8 inch

263. EAM Jan 17 1806/Sale at house owned by David Harry, opp R. Schnebly's in Hagers Town, furniture - Godfrey Glossbrenner/Sale of house in Old Town, also 300 a. - Caleb Corn, Old Town, Allegany Co/John Hyland has taken up at his plantation a stray shoat/Robert Hoey, living on the late Peter Baker's old place, near Scott's Mill, has negro girl for sale

264. EAM Jan 24 1806/Married Tues last by Rev Rahauser, Leonard Shafer, merchant of Hancock-town, to Miss Mary Shroeder, dau of Henry Shroeder, of Funcks-town/Sale of farm on which John Hunt now lives, 130 a. - M. Vanlear /Peter Malott, near Major Langley's Tavern, has taken up a stray bull/Hats

for sale - Castors and Rorams; also a quantity of wool hats - John Anderson /Rags wanted, delivered at the Paper-Mill - George Miller/Journeyman coopers wanted - Henry Grubb/Bolting cloths for sale - Alexander Neill, next door to Mittelkauf's Tavern, Hagers Town

265. EAM 31 1806/Died Fri 24 inst at her res in this co, Mrs. Rachel Cromwell, relict of the late Richard Cromwell, Esq., leaving family of children /Michael Tice adm, to sell at dwelling house of Henry Tice, decd, 4 miles from Hagers Town, pers est of decd/Christian Artz, adm, to sell at dwelling house of Henry Artz, decd, at Booth's Mill, pers est of decd/Sale of farm, 322 a., pt of tract called Swan Ponds, in Berkeley Co, Va - Richard Clagget, living in Shepherd's Town/Thomas S. Lee, offers reward for negro Tolly, who left his farm near George-Town, aged 24-25, blacksmith; deliver to Mr. Lee at Needwood, Fred Co, or Hagers Town jail/Sale of plantation whereon George Kershner, decd, lately lived, 4 miles from Hagers Town, 1/2 mile from Major Martin Kershner's, 100 a. - Martin Kershner, jun/Notice by George C. Smoot, Register of Wills/Tavern in Hagers Town for rent, known as Red Lion - Henry Shane

266. EAM Feb 7 1806/John Buchanan, appointed trustee for benefit of creditors of Samuel Bayly, insolvent debtor, will sell real est of said Bayly, consisting of a reversion in fee, after the death of his father William Bayly, in one undivided eighth part of tract, called Part of Clift Spring, containing 300 a./Daniel Fetter, acting admin of John Hesselius, request settlement of accounts with him at Old Town/Meeting of Commissioners of Tax Resin Davis, Clk/Sale of house in Old Town - Gotleib Conn, Old Town, Allegany Co

267. EAM Feb 14 1806/Sale of tract in Montgomery township, Franklin Co,, 144 a. - John Collins, living on the premises/Daniel Bowman exec of John Bowman, to sell tract called Poor Land, 1 miles from Williamsport/Rebecca Stoops, exec, request payment on notes given at sale of pers est of Nicholas Stoops, decd, to Thomas Compton at Samuel Ringgolds', Esq./Committed to gaol of Wash Co, negro Sally, about 20; says she was purchased from John Smith of Stafford Co, Va/Ann Moore, adm of John, late of Wharton Township, decd, to sell real est of John Moore, 400 a., on road from Cumberland to Geneva/Henry Kealhofer, Hagers Town, offers reward for apprentice lad to the saddler's bus., named John Taylor, about 18 yrs of age, fair complexioned; had on black coat, snuff coloured roundabout, two swandown waistcoats, pair of Bennet's cord pantaloons/George Hammel, to sell at the plantation where he now lives, 1 1/2 miles from Hagers Town, horses, colts, milch cows and other

268. EAM Feb 21 1806/Daniel Nead, living near the Big Spring, 12 miles from Hagers Town, offers reward for Negro woman Dinah, about 5 ft 3 inch, 23-24 /Sale of prop of the est of late Abraham Van Bibber, called Paradise, 300 a. - Andrew Van Bibber, Washington Van Bibber/Store-room for rent on corner of the public square in Hagers Town, formerly occ by Benjamin Clagett; apply to Philip or George Binkley, on the premises/Michael Hager to sell at his house, 3 miles from Hagers Town, plantation whereon he res, 90 a.; also horses, cows, sheep and hogs/Ambrose Geoghegan, to sell at his place of res, on Little Conococheague, furniture, plantation utensils, smith's bellows, anvil and vice, and remainder of his stock, and other; also one set of Laws

of Md./John Hammel to sell at his dwelling, on David Long's place, Franklin Co, Pa, near David Schnebly's (formerly Dr. Schnebly's Tavern), cows, hogs, sheep, grain in the ground and other/Elisha Hyland forewarns persons from taking assignment on note give to Benjamin Connerly

269. EAM Feb 28 1806/Married Tues evening last, by Rev Rahauser, Joseph M'Ilhenny, merchant, of this town, to Miss Elizabeth Newcomer, of Wash Co/Died Fri 21st inst. at Hopewell Iron-works, near Bedford, Pa, after a few days illness, Daniel L. Reynolds, late of this place, in the 21st year of his age/Died in this town, Capt. Nathan Poor, Aet. 65. On Sabbath morning last, he went in usual health to attend divine service at the Rev Dana's meeting house, where he had not been many minutes, before he wsa discovered to be indisposed, in a fit, died within 15 minutes/Rezin Davis candidate for sheriff/Chancery sale of real est of Zachariah Magruder, of Allegany Co, part of tract adj Cumberland, called George's Adventure/Conveyancing - George C. Smoot/Robert Mackey to sell plantation, 118 a., on West Conoco-cheague, at the Mouth of the Welsh Run, Montgomery Township, Franklin Co, Pa/Plantation for sale, 300 a., prop of Benedict Cautzman, decd, 150 a. - Apply to Cornelius Thompson, or to Henry Cautzman, Berkeley Co/House for rent which he now occ - Stephen M'Closkey, Hagers Town/Jacob Knode has taken up 5 stray sheep, at his plantation near Funks-town/Josiah Price, 7 miles from Hagers Town, has taken up a stray steer/Jacob Harry has removed his store nearly opp to where he formerly lived, lately occ by John Hefleich, next door to John Harry, formerly J. Geiger & J. Harry's Store, where he has taken his son into partnership - Dry Goods, Hard-Ware & Groceries/Matthias Smith and John Middlecauf to sell at their dwelling house (formerly res of Martin Bachtel, decd), near David Schnebly's, milch cows, furniture and other/Kinsey Hughes, to sell at his plantation, 3 miles from Hagers Town, negro lad, about 18, and other/Tan Yard, of John Geiger, decd, containing 36 vats, in Hagers Town to let - John Harry/David Denwiddie, 5 miles from Hagers Town, has taken up a stray Ram/John Sibert, Hagers Town, cautions persons agnst trusting his wife Nancy, as she refuses to res with him, and he is determined to pay no debts of her contracting

270. EAM Mar 7 1806/Married yesterday by Rev Bower, Col. Josiah Price, of this co, to Miss Sarah Scott, of Franklin Co, Pa/Adam Ott certifies that Christian Miller, living on Dr. William Downey's plantation, near the Widow Renche's Mill, has taken up a stray colt

271. EAM May 9 1806/Died suddenly Sat last in city of Balt (whither he had gone to attend the Synod with Rev Rahauser), Martin Kreps, Joiner, an old inhabitant of this town, husband and parent/F. Kemmelmeyer, Limner, contin-ues to carry his bus., two doors from John Hershey's in the Main St /Old copper & brass wanted for cash - Wm. Heyser, Hagers Town/Tan Bark for sale - Susanna Geiger, and John Harry, adm of John Geiger, Hagers Town /Dissolution of partnership of Peter Miller, Matthais Miller, and John Julius, to be carried on by Peter & Matthias Miller, who will have on hand an assortment of hats, wholesale or retail/Wash Co Levy Court May term, to convene - O.H. Williams, Clk./Henry Homes, to sell two story log dwelling 13 miles from Hagers Town/Tract for sale, 200 a., on Back Creek, Berkely Co, Va - Thomas Keenan, Winchester, Va/Joshua Fletcher, Fauquier Co, Va, near Rectortown, offers reward for negro man Tom & Phillis his wife/John Ringer, adm of

The Maryland Herald and Hagers-town Weekly Advertiser

Michael Snyder/Samuel Young notifies creditors of Jacob Nichol's est that a small dividend will made/Joseph Cheney has taken up stray sheep/John Blackford, Swearingen's Ferry, having withdrawn himself from the Ferry and Tavern opp Shepherd's Town, which bus. he has attended to for the last 6 yrs, request those indebted to pay Presley Marmaduke, who has present management of the Ferry and Tavern/John Heddinger to sell brick dwelling house adj jail in this town, includes spring house on the premises/Miss Elizabeth Majors informs the ladies of Greencastle, Hagers Town, Mercersburg and Chambersburg and their vicinities, that she has just opened a sewing school in Greencastle/Samuel B. Davis, has commenced an English Free School in Meth Meeting House in Hagers Town

272. EAM May 9 1806/Orphans' Court of Wash Co has ordered the prop in the hands of Elizabeth Brumley (late Elizabeth Heckrotte) and John Heckrotte, adm of Henry Heckrotte, decd, to be delivered over to Daniel Weisel and David Sellers, Williamsport, who were securites for the performance of said administration/Peter Smith offers his services as an auctioneer/George Scott, certifies that George Glading, near Boonsborough had taken up a stray gelding/G. M. Conradt has begun the dying bus. in the house formerly occ by Daniel Nead/John Greiner, brass founder, continues his bus. at his shop, nearly opp Rev Rahauser's/Francis Gardner, has removed to house opp Adam Ott's, Esq. next door to Mr. Cook's Tavern/Isaac S. White, John Ragan, Jun. and Adam Ott candidates for sheriff/John Barr, Spred Eagle Mill, Wash Co, has hops for sale/Frederick Miller, Druggist and Apothecary, Hagers Town, seeks apprentice/Christian Fechtig, Hagers Town, offers reward for apprentice boy to the shoemaking bus., named Joseph Logan, about 14; he took a blue striped cotton roundabout, blue cloth pantaloons, an old fur hat and coarse shoes/Thomas Shuman has removed his tinner's shop to house where he now keeps tavern, nearly opp Dr. Woltz's/U. Lawrence, near Hagers Town, offers reward for negro man Tom, about 30; formerly belonged to Jeremiah Cheney, senr. of this co/Barton Carricoe, living on Little Conococheague, within 2 miles of Big Spring, offers reward for negro woman Priss, formerly prop of John Geiger, late of Hagers Town, decd/Benjamin Galloway to rent dwelling house he now occupies in Hagers Town/Thomas Kennedy, Williamsport, will receive and forward flour during the boating season, at a certin fixed price or at the current rates - Washington Ware House

273. EAM Jun 6 1806/Henry Sheets to sell at his dwelling house at the Mill of John T. Mason, milch cows, hogs, case of drawers, feathers and feather beds, dressing and other tables, chairs, grindstone, new hogsheads and whiskey barrels, set of cooper tools, two chests and other/Gabriel Nourse, Sharpsburg, offers reward for stolen watch/Sale at late dwelling house of Peter Malott, decd, 1 miles below res of Samuel Ringgold, Esq., pers est of decd, including life lease of 1-6 a., pt of Conococheague manor - Peter Malott, Michael Malott, Daniel Malott, exec/Gibbs & Westover, have just erected a carding machine in George Miller's Mill (formerly the Boring Mill) on Antietam, 1 1/2 miles of Hagers Town, for carding wool/John Langley, Justice of the Peace, certifies that William Starling has taken up a stray mare/William S. Compton, certifies that Joseph Cox has taken up a stray horse/William M'Coy, Williamsport, requests payment of debts/Sale of 160 a. adj Williamsport, prop of Gabriel Friend, decd - Thomas Helm, Robert T. Friend, exec/John Scott, Franklin Co, Washington Township, has taken up a

46

stray horse/Henry Lewis has stills for sale/Wm. Carroll, T. Miller & A. Leopard, tailors, have commenced bus. at shop lately occ by John Gruber, Printer, opp David Harry's, and near the German Luth Church/John Reynolds, watch & clock maker, has removed to shop next door to Messrs. Coffroth and Kreps's store/Peter Sutter has commenced the nailing bus. at shop lately occ by Col. N. Rochester, nearly opp Timothy Monahan's in the Back St, Hagers Town/Henry Dillman adm of Peter Schlimmer

274. EAM Jun 13 1806/Christian Artz adm of Nicholas Beard, to sell at late res of decd, pers est of decd/Joseph Sprigg has taken up a stray - S. Ringgold, Justice of the Peace/John Hershey, junr, Hagers Town, offers reward for Negro man William Paul, about 36/Jacob Mumma, 1 mile from Sharpsburg, offers reward for Negro man named George Amos, about 26/John Shimer, living about a mile from Barnet's Fording, on Big Conococheague, to sell Negro woman/Journeymen millwrights wanted - Conrad Piper

275. EAM Jun 20 1806/Allegany Equity court sale of real est of John Otewalt, decd, by Roger Perry, trustee, a lot in Cumberland/Christian Gerhart and Jacob Lamber, exec, request payment of notes given at sale of Elias Gerhart, decd

276. EAM Jun 27 1806/Sale of land, 900 a., merchant mill and distillery in sight of the Potomak river, Berkeley Co, Va - George Newkirk

277. EAM Jul 4 1806/Whereas Charles O'Neal, who is in my employ, left my house for Balt on 17 Jun, under an impression that he had lost a pocket book between the subscriber's and Fred Town I wish to make known that all contents have been found amongst my papers at home - John Booth

278. EAM Jul 11 1806/Thomas Ringgold to apply for relief from debts /Matthias Shaffner to sell house where he now lives on the Main st, with Tan-Yard/Purchasers at the sale of pers est of Dr. Henry Schnebly, decd, are given notice that notes are due - John Schnebly, Jacob Schnebly and David Schnebly, exec/Christian Nighswanger, living near David Schnebly's, has taken up a stray mare

279. EAM Jul 18 1806/Died Mon morning 14th inst, after a lingering indisposition, Jacob Harry, merchant, of this town, in the 50th year of his age

280. EAM Jul 25 1806/Died 16 inst in 31st year of her age, at her father's in the city of Balt, Mrs. Janet Clagett, consort of Benjamin Clagett, of Hagers Town, after a long and painful illness, wife and mother of 3 little daus/John Rahp, breeches maker, to sell stone house on Main st, Hagers Town /To sell stalls in the Market house for one year to highest bidder - A.M. Waugh, Clk/Henry Stembel, living in Middletown, offers reward for horse, formerly prop of Bennet Peak/Samuel Smith, living 1 miles of Mercersburg, Franklin Co, Pa, offers reward for missing horse

281. EAM Aug 1 1806/Examination of Messrs. John and P. C. Young's pupils who acquitted themselves well - Benjamin Galloway, John O'Neill, Thomas Grieves/Sale agreeable to will of Jacob Harry, decd, of furniture, horse, cows, Negroes, and other - Mary E. Harry, George J. Harry, exec/Wash Co

Court - Casper Moudy vs John Moudy, Henry Moudy, George Moudy, Martin Moudy, Adam Moudy, Peter Moudy, Michael Moudy, Jacob Moudy & Mary wife of Jacob Ash regarding election to take the est/Sale of stone house in Hagers Town, formerly known by Eichbaugh's Pottery - Christian Fechtig/Co-partnership of Jacob Harry and son is dissolved

282. EAM Aug 8 1806/General Committee Meeting (political) - John Langley, John Shafer, John Adams, John Ashbury, Samuel Lynch, William S. Compton, R. Doughlass, Martin Kershner, David Schnebly, Henry Shafer, Thomas Sprigg, Emanuel Franz, Peter Brewer, John Berry, Martin Myer, Daniel Kershner, William Yates, John Honn, James Saunder, John Ocks, David Rowland, Jeremiah Stillwell - Thomas Kennedy, sec'ry./Sale at his res beetween Rohrer's and Funk's Mill on Antietam, 2 miles from Hagers Town, horses, milch cows, beehives, wagons, iron mill for grinding apples, furniture and other - Matthias Kessler/Sale of plantation on Main road from Hagers Town to Mercersburg, 117 a., alos 656 a. in Sandy Creek Glades, Monongahela Co - Michael Tice, exec, 4 miles from Greencastle, Pa/Matthias Kessler, acting exec, to sell prop of Jacob Rohrer, decd; also pt of est of decd adj lands of William Shycaw and Peter Umrickhouse/James Smith, Hagers Town, to apply for relief from debts

283. EAM Aug 15 1806/Jacob Friend forewarns persons from coming on his premises/Magdalena Kreps adm of Martin Kreps, to sell pers est of decd /Esther Neal, surviving adm of Aquilla Neal/Hughes & Fitzhugh, offer reward for negro Jack, or Jack Forest, who eloped from their nail factory

284. EAM Aug 22 1806/Married last evening by Rev Bower, Jonas M'Pherson, merchant, of Balt, to Miss Margaret James, of Sharpsburg, in Wash Co/Joseph Kennedy, insolvent debtor/Philip Household has taken up a stray horse/Bull and milch cows to be sold at William Delahunt's on the Long Meadows/Thomas Glissan, living near Moorfield, Hardy Co, Va, offers reward for negro man, Joe, raised in Anne Arundel Co, Md/George Marsteller, Junr, offer for sale 75 a. 3 miles from Hagers Town

285. EAM Aug 29 1806/George Nigh, exec, to sell at late dwelling house of Henry Bowser, decd, 3 miles from Hagers Town, pers prop of decd, including 2 weaver's looms with gears/Petition for laying out and opening a public road from state line at Peter Baker's/N. Rochester offers reward for negro man Isaac, about 22, who ran away from Sprigg and Rochester's Nail Factory /Committed to jail of Wash Co, negro man who calls himself William Smith /Chancery sale of tract occ as a tavern by John Shelhorn, decd, necessary for the payment of debt, in the case of Robert Sturgeon, use of Jacob Zarley, agnst John Shelhorn's minors and heirs at law in Chancery Court of Allegany Co - Beene S. Pigman, Trustee; also in the case of Jacob Fauty agnst John Shelhorn's minors/Reward for James Jackson, about 30, 5 ft 10 inch and John Collins, 18-19 upwards of 6 ft and John Board, 176-18 about 5 ft 6-7 inch, all broke jail, committed for stealing

286. EAM Sep 5 1806/William Delahunt has taken up at his plantation on Long Meadow, 4 miles from Hagers Town, a stray cow/John Guswa and David Gushwa, exec, give notice to persons who made purchases at the sale of the effects of John Gushwa, that notes are due/John V. Kelly continues to carry on Fulling and Dying bus. at the Fulling Mill of Martin Baechtel, near Hagers

Town; Robert Douglass will receive woollen yarn for thick cloth or linsey, which he will weave at the usual rates at the above mentioned mill/Thomas Edwards, exec, requests payment of notes given at sale of est of John Edwards, decd/Samuel M'Lind, Williamsport, to sell stills, tubs, kegs, &c.

287. EAM Sep 12 1806/Benjamin Malott, senr., to sell at his dwelling house, near the res of Samuel Ringgold, horses, cows, steers, hogs, hemp and other /Sale of plantation, adj land where Jacob Kershner now lives, 100 a., and other parcels of land - Martin Kershner/Sheriff's sale at house of Barton Carricoe, on Little Conococheague Creek, of tract called Resurvey on the Mountain of Wales, adj lands of Nathaniel Nisbett, Henry Prather, John T. Mason and others, prop of Denton Jacques, at the suits of John Singleton and Nicholas Carroll/John Slagle, on Col. Walling's place, 6 miles from Hagers Town, has taken up stray shoat/Tho. Crampton certifies that George Eichelberger has taken up a stray horse/Sale at dwelling of David Denwiddie, decd, 1 miles from General Sprigg's, Negroes, horses, cattle, sheep and hogs, wagon and gears, sleighs, ploughs, harrows, and other farming utensils and furniture - Isabella Denwiddie and N. Rochester, adm

288. EAM Sep 19 1806/A mare was left in the stable of Benjamin Leight, Hagers Town, by a name named Lee/Sheriff's sale at house of Barton Carricoe, on Little Conococheague, 120 a., prop of John Juin, by virture of two writs of Fieri Facias, at the suit of Samuel Miller, adm of John Miller, decd/M. Bayly to petition for relief from debts/Williamsport Races - Jacob Brosius, junr., and George Moudy will pay purses/Adam Ott, surviving exec, to sell house now occ by John Conrad, next door to Henry Lewis on the Main St, agreeable to will of William Conrad, decd/William Moore to sell house in Cumberland, at the corner of Paca and Smallwood sts/Amos Dilworth cautions that his wife Margaret has left him without any just cause or provocation

289. EAM Sep 26 1806/Thomas Meredith to sell at his res on Ringgold's Manor, 1 1/2 miles from Williamsport, pers prop of late John Jones, decd, 5 head of horses and a variety of wearing apparel/Night school - John & P.C. Young/John Adair, Adams Co, Pa, offers reward for stolen horse/Jacob Rohrer to sell house he now occ, next door to Mr. Leight's Tavern

290. EAM Oct 3 1806/Married Thurs 25th ult by Rev Schmucker, Philip Binkley, Merchant, of this place, to Miss Jane Locke, dau of George Locke, of Wash Co/Married Tues evening last by Rev Schmucker, George W. Ent, of Fred town, to Miss Margaret Woltz, dau of Dr. Peter Woltz, of this town/Died Wed last, after a short illness, Mrs. Barbara Mittelcauff, wife of David Mittelkauff, of this town/Sale of a tract of 275 a. on West side of west Conococheague creek, in Peters township, Franklin Co - Elizabeth Wilson and Robert Wilson, adm/James Garrett, weaver, has removed to shop lately occ by Mr. Cook, a few rods below brick house now occ by Mr. Galloway, formerly by Mrs. Ringgold on Main St/John Peter Herr to sell house in Hagers Town wher he now lives in the Main st/R. Pindell offers reward for colts which strayed from Mr. Ashberry's pastures on Ringgold's Manor/John Armstrong to have a carding machine erected in the mill lately purchased of the Messrs. Scotts, by Gen. Sprigg/Application of Jacob Brumbaugh for the sale of real est of Jacob Brumbaugh, decd. Rule that Jacob Brumbaugh, John Brumbaugh, Mary intermarried with Samuel Ulry, David, Henry, Daniel and George, heirs of Jacob

Brumbaugh, decd, to show cause at the court at Bedford why est should not be sold/Joseph Phenicie to sell at Warfordburgh, Bethel township, Bedford Co, Pa, taynard, house and other

291. EAM Oct 10 1806/Esther Neal and William Neal, adm, gives notice that notes are due from sale of pers est of Aquilla Neal/Stray steer has come to John Johnston's planation - William Anderson

292. EAM Oct 17 1806/Died last evening in this town, after a short illness, Timothy Monahan, in the 43d year of his age, leaving a widow and 6 children /James Anderson, overseer for Upton Laurence, near Hagers Town, has taken up a stray horse/Sale of tract in Fred Co, on Cotoctin creek, prop of William Cheney, late of Fred Co, decd - Robert Cheney/William Cromwell, adm, gives notices that notes are due from sale of pers est of Richard Cromwell/Conrad Crumbauch to sell brick house he now occupies in Hagers Town; on premises are a brewery and potter's shop, a never failing pump of excellent water, stable and a garden/Lewis Blaire will sell prop in Elizabeth-Town, near the Roman Cath Chapel

293. EAM Oct 24 1806/Sale at late dwelling house of Stephen Slifer, decd, on Ludwick Young's plantation, 2 miles from Hagers Town, pers prop of decd /Committed to jail, Charles Bowman, alias Charles Butler, about 35, dark mulatto

294. EAM Oct 31 1806/Jacob Bowlas, to sell house in Williamsport/Mrs. Diffenderffer, milliner, next door but one to Robert Douglass, Esq., and near the German Luth Church, has just received an elegant assortment of millinery goods from Phila/Meeting of Prot Episc Church at Col. Rezin Davis - Elie Beatty, Register/Sale at the house of Timothy Monahan, decd, Hagers Town, real and pers est of decd - Frances Monahan and N. Rochester, exec /Sale at dwelling house of William Neal, decd, 2 miles from Williamsport, pers prop of decd - Elizabeth Neal and St. Leger Neal, adm

295. EAM Nov 7 1806/Died Mon morning last by a fall from a horse, George Sharkey, Joiner and cabinet-maker, in this town, in the 31st year of his age, leaving a widow and 2 small children/Died at Carlisle, a few days since, on his way to the Genesee Country, Samuel Bowles, inhabitant of this co; remains deposited in the family burying ground/Robert Benson, No. 92 Baltimore St, Balt, seeks 6-8 journeymen tailors/Sale at late dwelling house of Martin Rohrer, decd, on Antietam, 2 miles from Hagers Town, pers est of decd - Daniel Rench, Christian Newcomer, exec/Sale at late dwelling house of Richard Sprigg, decd, near Upper Marlboro, PG Co, slaves/Tho. Fisher, living in East-Pennsboro' township, Cumberland Co, Pa, offers reward for Negro man Harry Collins, alias William Powell, aged 40; also seduced to go with him a Negro woman named Letty, aged 23/Wm. Runner, near the mouth of Back Creek, Berkeley Co, Va, offers reward for missing mare

296. EAM Nov 14 1806/David Hammett, has taken up a stray hog at his farm, 3 miles from Hagers Town

297. EAM Nov 21 1806/Married Tues evening last, by Rev Bower, Francis Dorsey, to Miss Sally Forbes, all of this co/Cabinet making to be carried at

the shop lately occ by George Sharkey, decd/William Gabby, adm of William
Allen/Information wanted on some evil disposed person or persons who have
frequently thrown down the fences of the farms and lots of Mrs. Rosanna
Heister/Sale of plantation, 142 a., agreeable to will of Henry Bowser, decd
- George Nigh, exec/Sale at house of Daniel Harbine, at the Big Spring, near
the premises, undivided moiety of 2000 a. now in the possession of Denton
Jacques; Mr. D. Jacques, living at the Furnace will shew the land - Lancelot
Jacques, Trustee/David Harry, admin with the will annexed, gives notice to
persons indebed to est of Abraham Bower

298. EAM Nov 28 1806/William Webb adm of John Webb, to sell pers prop of
decd, including joiner's tools, 8-day clock and other/Mary Bowles and
Albertus Miller, adm, to sell at the late dwelling house of Samuel Bowles,
decd, 1 1/2 miles from Fiery's mill, pes est of decd/Sale at res of John
Stoner, decd, neare Mr. Barry's Mill, of pers prop of decd - Christian Good,
and Jacob Barr, adm/Samuel Finlay adm, to sell two story log dwelling house,
in Hagers Town, near the German Luth Church, late the prop of Samuel Finlay,
decd/Joseph Latshaw to sell tract, 50 a., 1 miles from John Barr's Mill and
4 miles from Antietam Forge/Alexander Kennedy adm, to sell at the dwelling
house of Jane Short, decd, in Boonsborough, pers est of decd/Wash Co Court -
Samuel Ridenour vs Jacob Ridenour, Conrad Ridenour, John Markley and Susanna
his wife, Catharine Ridenour, Sarah Ridenour, Milley Ridenour & Mary Ridenour - under the act to direct descents/Peter Righter, Sharpsburg, has taken
up a stray bull/James Belch, living on the lands lately owned by Richard
Cromwell, decd, 7 miles from Hagers Town, has taken up a stray sow

299. EAM Dec 5 1806/John Heddinger, Hagers Town, has commenced the bus. of
auctioneer at the house of David Mittelkauff, in Hagers Town/Sale areeable
to direct descents, of real est of Baltzer Moudy, decd, several tracts -
James M'Clain, Jacob T. Towson, George Locke, Commissioners/Person indebted
to William Begole, on vendue notes are hereby informed to make payment
/Persons are forewarned from taking assignments on notes given to Alexander
Boteler, of Pleasant Valley, Wash, given by Peter Miller, Sen., Alexander
Grim, and Dennis Byrne/Jacob Barr has taken up a stray heifer which came to
his farm near John Barr's Mill/Philip Mains, near Parkhead Forge, has taken
up a stray steer

300. EAM Dec 12 1806/On Sun evening last, Jacob Dagy and his wife, two very
old people, who lived in an obscure place, at the foot of the South Mountain, 1 1/2 miles from Road leading to Fred Town, were found in their bed
with their scull fractured in a most shocking manner; the former was still
alive, incapable of giving any information and survived til next morning,
the latter already dead/Married last evening by Rev Rahauser, Levi Price,
Merchant, of Martinsburg, to Miss Fanny Baird, of this town/Reward for
deserted, Henry Besser, a German, aged 23, 5 ft 8 inch, fair complexion,
brown eyes, fair hair, bald headed, occasioned by sickness, speaks bad
English, a weaver; went away with a drab coloured great coat, dark coloured
velvet pantaloons - John Miller, Lieut., 2nd U.S. Regt. Inf'ry/Margaret
Gabby and William Gabby, exec of John Gabby/Sale of house now occ by John
Haun, prop of said Haun, at the suit of Jacob T. Towson/Michael Tice exec of
Henry Tice

301. EAM Dec 19 1806/Married Tues evening last by Rev Bower, Milton
Sackett, to Mrs. Sterett, of Williamsport/Died Wed evening last, after a
short illness, Philip Hornidge, candle maker, an industrious citizen of this
place/Geo: M'Irvine has commenced the cabinet making bus. in the shop lately
occ by Conrad Crumbauch/Sale of plantation, 200 a., 1 mile from Hughes's
Furnace, late the prop of Daniel Renoll, decd, sold in pursuance of an order
of Wash Co Court. Mrs. Renoll, widow of said Daniel Renoll has life est in
about 70 a. Lodowick Hewitt who lives near the land will shew the same -
William Webb, George Nigh, Peter Seibert, Walter Boyd, commissioners/William
Jones offers reward for sheep which strayed from his living in Paty Valley,
near Mount Pleasant furnace, Pa/Three tracts for sale - John M. Beatty,
Charles A. Beatty, George-town/Jacob Barr, 3 miles from Hagers Town, offers
reward for Negro man Peter about 35/Frederick Brown, Hagers Town, offers
reward for indented servant James Jackson, about 30, about 5 ft 10 inch,
mason by trade/Sale at dwelling house of George Sharkey, decd, in Hagers
Town, pers est of decd - Alice Sharkey and Michael M'Kiernan, adm/Profiles
taken by calling at the house of David Middlekauff, Inn-keeper. Price for
cutting 25 cents - painting, one dollar

302. EAM Dec 26 1806/Died in this town Sat morning last, in 32d year of his
age, Samuel Sleigh/Died in Wash Co, Frederick Foutz, old and esteemed inhabitant, at an advanced age/Jacob Kessinger gives notice to purchaser at the
sale of Andrew Kessinger's prop to make payment on notes/William Allinder
exec of Anna Allinder/Young man capable of teaching an English School is
wanted - John Hanna, Ch. M'Calley, Henry Landers/Edmund Tarlton, 2 miles
from Lantz's Mill, has taken up stray sheep/Deserted Joseph Morell, French
man, aged 25, 5 ft 7 1/2 inch, dark complexion, black eyes, black hair cropt
short, by occupation a butcher - John Miller, Lieut, 2nd U.S. Regt, Inf'ry
/Theobald Kendel, 3 miles from Hagers Town, has taken up a stray mare

303. EAM Jan 2 1807/Married on Sun evening last by Rev Rahauser, Mr. David
Mittelkauff, of this town, to Miss Hannah Sailer, dau of Peter Sailer, of
this co/Married last evening, by Rev Bower, Col. Daniel Hughes, to Mrs. Ann
Elliott/Died Mon evening last after a lingering illness, Mrs. Hogmire, in
the 73d year of her age. On Wed her remains were interred in the German
Lutheran Burial ground in this town/Sale of two story stone house in
Williamsport, late the prop of Henry Heckrotte, decd - Daniel Weisel,
Williamsport

304. EAM Jan 9 1807/Died last week, after a painful illness, in the
meridian of life, Mrs. Sarah Price, consort of Col. Josiah Price, of this
co/Last Sat Mr. Michael Tice was unfortunately drowned, in attempting to
cross the dam at Mr. Hoffer's Mill, with a wagon and four horses, near the
Broad-fording on Conococheague. All the horses were also lost. On Sunday
his body was found near the fatal spot, brought home the same day, and
decently interred on Monday. He has left a widow and an infant son/Sale of
real est of Richard Cromwell, Esq. of Wash Co, decd, tract on Conococheague
Creek, about 7 miles from Hagers Town, upwards of 1300 a.: (1) late res of
the said Richard Cromwell, 450 a.; (2) at present in the occupation of
Oliver Cromwell, divided from the former by Conococheague Creek, 340-350 a.;
(3) adj the first mentioned tract, at present occ by Richard Cromwell - Com-

missioners: Walter Boyd, Martin Kershner, Henry Ankony, Josiah Price/David Hammett candidate for sheriff

305. EAM Jan 16 1807/Robert Brent, Brentfield, a few miles below Port Tobacco, on Wicomico river, Charles Co, offers reward for negro James, hired some few years ago as a labourer, at Col. Hughes's Furnace; has been seen at Mr. Wm. S. Compton's on Ringgold's Manor/Sale of plantation of William Bay-ly, on Potomac river, Wash Co, adj George Snyder's, and lately occ by Samuel Bayly - M. Bayly/Conveyancing services offered - Archibald M. Waugh, Hagers Town/Jacob Rench, about 2 miles from Hagers Town, has taken up stray sheep /Sale of brick house occ by Henry Kaelhofer, adj Christian Fechtig, on Main St in Hagers Town - Conrad Crumbauch/House for rent wherein I now dwell, next door to Samuel Hughes - Jonathan Hager/Negro woman for sale - S. Ring-gold, Fountain Rock/Sale of mill and 85 a. in Virginia, adj Buckles-town - Daniel Imbody, Berkeley Co/Candle making - Catharine Hornidge dips candles on same terms as her late husband, Philip Hornidge, at one shilling per hun-dred

306. EAM Jan 23 1807/Sale at dwelling house of John Rahp, in Hagers Town, pers prop of Samuel Sleigh, decd, consisting of a fresh milch cow, quantity of hay, furniture - John Sleigh, adm/Dissolution of partnership of Coffroth & Kreps/Committed to jail, mulatto man, who calls himself George; also negro Fanny and child; George says he belongs to Benjamin Fayton of King George Co, Va; Fanny says she is the wife of George and belongs to Col. Taylor, of a co adj King George Co; her child is about 13 months

307. EAM Jan 30 1807/died Sat last at his res, near Col. Hughes's Forge, William Webb, Esq. for several years a magistrate of this co/R. Pindell adm of Jane Short/John I. Stull and O.H.W. Stull, desirous of entering into the mercantile bus., have concluded to sell their estate, adj Hagers Town, for-merly the res of Col. John Stull, decd, upwards of 400 a., embracing a considerable extent of the Antietam creek/John Bartlett, living at Gen. Sprigg's res, Was Co, offers reward for apprentice to the house carpenter and jointer's bus., named John Stiner, about 20, 5 ft 10-11 inch, fair complexion, dark brown hair, has large lump on the thumb of his left hand/Mary Tice, adm, to sell at late dwelling house of Michael Tice, decd, about 4 miles from Hagers Town, pers est of decd, horses, cows, young cattle, sheep, hogs, wagon, ploughs & harrows, wind-mill, horse gears, furniture and other /House for rent in the Square, now occ by Mr. Young - Henry Lewis, Hagers Town

308. EAM Feb 6 1807/To sell prop and stand occ many years by Melchor Beltzhoover as a tavern and at present by Jacob D. Dietrick as a store, adj prop of Alexander Clagett - Richard Pindell & Otho H. Williams/Sale of tract of 700 a. on which is erected a grist and saw mill, 700 a. - Richard Stephen, exec/Meeting of commissioners of the tax - Rezin Davis, Clk.

309. EAM Feb 13 1807/Present at an examination of Messrs. John and P.C. Young's scholars who acquitted themselves in a superior manner - Geo. Bower, Tho. Grieves/Jacob T. Towson, adm of Daniel Toncrey, to sell house of decd in Williamsport/Peter Miller to apply for relief from debt/U. Laurence to sell at his farm near Hagers Town, his stock and farming utensils and other;

also to rent in Hagers Town, store house lately occ by Peter Miller, house in possession of John Crumbauch, houses occ by Andrew Allison/Jacob D. Dietrick, intending to decline his present bus. will sell his stock of books /Frederick Miller, druggist and apothecary, has removed his shop to his dwelling house 2 doors below Dr. Samuel Young's, nearly opp Peter Hefleich's store/John Cook offers reward for mare stolen from his tavern in Hagers Town /Partnership between N. Rochester and Elie Beatty is dissolved/Tench Ringgold to rent his farm near John Shafer's Mill, 400a./Susanna Futz, Jacob Foutz, Jacob Alter - exec of Frederick Foutz, to sell pers est of decd, at res of decd about 4 miles from Hagers Town

310. EAM Feb 20 1807/Washington County Court case, Michael Thomas and Elizabeth his wife, Joseph Deener and Catharine his wife, and Christian Bealer and Susanna his wife vs. Peter John, John John, Abraham John & Elizabeth John, Catharine wife of Daniel Cretzer, Margaret Bell, Elizabeth Bell, Rachel Bell, Daniel Bell, John Bell, Elizabeth Hoffman, Susanna Hoffman, and Christian Hoffman. Commission appointed and recorded that Peter John, the eldest son, entitled to make his election, to take the est therein not appearing to make selection/Orphans Court to meet to take the probate of the testament and last will of Robert T. Cary, late of Wash Co, decd - Geo: C. Smoot, Register of Wills/John Hanna, about 1 1/2 miles from Hughes's Furnace, has taken up a stray barrow/John Harry, Hagers Town, to give highest price on hides and skins at his store in Hagers Town/John Carr offers reward for hogs missing from his farm, about 2 miles from Williamsport/William Webb adm of William Webb to sell at dwelling of decd, 1 mile from John Barr's Mill, all pers est of decd/John Ardinger adm of Christian Ardinger, to sell 2-story log house of decd/David Harry and Peter Hefleich, exec of John Protzman

311. EAM Feb 27 1807/Robert T. Friend, Thomas Helm, exec of Gabriel Friend /Jacob Shimer to sell at his dwelling house, 1/2 mile of David Schnebly's, horses, cows, sheep, hogs, wagon, horse gears, ploughs, harrows, windmill, grain, ten-plate stove, furniture/Christian Lantz, sen., exec of Jacob Ritter, sen., to sell tract of decd/David Hager to sell at his res on John Hager's Farm, 2 1/2 miles from Hagers Town, horses, colts, and other/John Shafer adm to sell at dwelling house of Christian Maughler, decd, pers prop of decd (located at John Shafer's mill)/Samuel M'Lind to sell lots in Williamsport

312. EAM Mar 6 1807/To sell plantation in Wash Co, 200 a., late prop of Daniel Renoll, decd, by order of Wash Co Court; Mrs. Renoll, widow of said Daniel Renoll has life est in about 70 a.; Lodowick Hewitt who lives near the land will shew the same - Commissioners: George Nigh, Peter Seibert, Walter Boyd, Samuel Hogmire/William Webb adm de bonis non of Adam Haun/John Miller exec of Matthias Ridenour, to sell log house on North East corner of Church and Conococheague sts, in Williamsport, now occ by Adam Householder, prop of said Ridenour/Sale of house in Hagers Town, whereon George Rinehart now lives, opp Gelwicks's Brewery - Jacob Stomm/Having rented my farm adj the plantation now in the possession of William Dillahunt, I intend to offer for sale my stock and other prop on said farm - O.H. Williams/John Bowles, exec, to sell prop of Andrew Morrisson, late of Montg township, Franklin Co, Pa, adj lands of Capt. George Crawford, Rev Robert Kennedy,

within 1/2 mile of Tent Meeting House/George Nigh gives notice to persons
who purchased prop at sale of Matthias Kessler, to make payment on obliga-
tions/John Klein to sell at his dwelling house in Hagers Town, next door to
Peter Hefleich, milch cow, stoves, bureau, cupboard, tables, chairs and
other/William Allender exec of Anna Allender/John Harry has taken his
brother George into partnership

313. EAM Mar 13 1807/Sales of John Haun's house in Wiliamsport and Jacob
Baltzel's house in Elizabeth-town are postponed/Henry Kaelhofer, saddler &
harness maker has removed his shop to house lately occ by Conrad Crumbauch,
a few doors above Mr. Beltzhoover's Tavern/John Sleigh, Hagers Town, offers
reward for stolen horse/Tench Ringgold having rented his farm, near John
Shafer's Mill, shall sell negroes, farming utensils and other/Deserted from
the barracks in Hagers Town, Abraham Edging, born in Franklin Co, Pa, aged
21, 5 ft 7 1/2 inch, fair complexion, blue eyes, round shouldered – John
Miller, Lieut., 2nd U.S. Regt., Inf'y, Hagers Town/Alexander Neill has just
received an additional supply of warrented bolting clothers

314. EAM Mar 20 1807/On Sat afternoon last, in consequence of some differ-
ence between the parties, a duel took place, near Shepherds-town, Va, between William L. Brent, Esq. and Mr. Otho H.W. Stull, both of this co. We
are sorry to say, that the former received a wound in his leg, a little
below the knee, the ball struck the larger bone, passing quite thro' the
leg. No dangerous consequences, however, from the effects of the wound, are
at present apprehended/Dr. Wm. Downey has removed from Mercersburg, and
opened his shop next door to Mr. Beltzhoover's Inn, Hagers Town/Frederick
Alter, Hagers Town, has for rent two rooms next door the Rev Schmucker
/Certifying to the colts sired by horse North Star of George Beltzhoover –
Jacob Graeff, Adam Reigart, jun., John Baer, Andrew Graff/M. Bayly, Mountain
of Wales, Wash Co, agent for John T. Mason, seeks overseer/John Hanna, 1 1/2
miles from Hughes's Furnace, offers reward for negro man Harry, about 22, 5
ft 6-7 inch/Milton H. Sackett offers for rent two story stone house wherein
he now lives in Williamsport/Christian Fechtig, Hagers Town, has just
received for sale, bar iron, from Hopewell Furnace, Bedford Co, Pa/John
Tharp certifies to pedigree of horse, Herod, owned by William Davis/John
Gerlough, 1/2 mile from Conococheague, to sell colts, cows, sheep, hogs,
wagon, ploughs, harrows, windmill, watch, smoothbore gun, cupboard, ten-
plate stove

315. EAM Mar 27 1807/To be sold at dwelling house of subscriber, 1/2 mile
from Kershner's Fording, on West Conococheague, colts, cows, and other –
Adam Gerlach/J. Schnebly, candidate for sheriff/Meeting of Prot. Episc. at
Hagers Town – Elie Beatty, Register/Jacob Rohrer, Hagers Town, intending to
move from this place in a short time, requests that those indebted to him,
settle their accounts/Sale of milch cows, cart, two 8-day clocks with cases,
one a mahogany, the other a wild cherry case, quantity of beef and bacon,
furniture and other – William Reynolds/The spinning wheel and chair making
bus. will be carried on at the ship now occ by Wm. Reynolds after 15 Apr
next by the subscriber who returns sincere thanks to friends and old
customers for the share of the custom he received when he formerly lived in
this town – John Watt/Elizabeth Orndorff to sell lots in City of Washington

/John P. Herr, Hagers Town, offers reward for apprentice to the tailor's bus., named William Conrye, about 15

316. EAM Apr 3 1807/Jacob Mumma, living near Sharpsburg, Wash Co, offers reward for negro man Perry, about 26, 5 ft 7 inch/P.C. Young has removed to the Back St. near the Public Spring and will recommence School on 6 inst, in the room formerly occ by Mr. Riddell; Mrs. Young intends at the same time to open a sewing school/Henry Carter, manager, offers reward for negro men who ran away from Northampton Furnace, near the City of Balt: Charles known as Skinner's Charles, about 35; Frean about 28, purchased of Edward Ireland about ten years since, raised in PG Co where his relations now live; Daniel who called himself Daniel Hall, about 45/Chancery case of John Harry agnst Jacob Harry, Elizabeth Harry, George Harry and Amelia Harry. The bill states that Martin Harry the complainant's father died seized of lots in Elizabeth-town, numbers 118 and 112 which he purchased of Henry Schnebly. Martin Harry died intestate. Jacob Harry res outside the state. Object of bill is to obtain decree for the division or sale of land/John Peter Herr, tailor and habit maker, has removed to house lately occ by Jacob Harry, decd, next door to George Beltzhoover/Blacksmiths wanted - Thomas Quantrill, Hagers Town/John Harry, Hagers Town, to let house now in the tenure of Christian Fechtig/Henry Strause and Wendel Gilbert to rent stand, for many years occ by Melchor Beltzhoover as a Tavern, at present by Jacob D. Dietrick as a store/The horse, Knight of Malta, will stand this season at my farm, about 4 miles from Hagers Town - Wm. Fitzhugh/Jacob D. Dietrick, Hagers Town, to sell furniture (described)

317. EAM Apr 10 1807/William Kreps appointed Post-master for Hagers Town, in the room of Jacob D. Dietrick/Died at Sharpsburg, Fri night last, Capt. John Ritchie, for many years manager at Antietam Iron Works in this co; left a widow and an only son/Died Sat last, Mrs. Elizabeth Carr wife of Major John Carr, of this co. She sustained a short but painful illness; she has left 9 children and a distrest husband/Married Thurs 2d inst, by Rev Schmucker, George Brumbaugh, to Miss L. Gelwicks, dau of Charles Gelwicks of this town/Married Sun evening last by Rev Schmucker, Jacob Binckley, to Miss Elizabeth Miller, both of this town/Married Wed last, by Rev Bower, Esau Bicknell aged 60 to Miss Susanna Rodgers, aged 16, both of Wash Co/Sale at dwelling house of subscriber, Daniel Bowman, 1 mile from Williamsport, on Conococheague, grain, colts, cows, plantation utensils, furniture

318. EAM Apr 17 1807/Married Thurs 9th inst, by Rev Schmucker, Dr. John Hofius, of Chambersburg, Pa, to Miss Peggy Harry, dau of David Harry of the town/Jacob Root and John Hammond, adm, to sell at late dwelling plantation of Henry Fasnacht, near Peter Newcomer's Mill, 3 miles from Boonsboro', pers est of said decd/George Grubb, cooper, has removed his shop to house where Mr. Ashcom formerly kept school within two doors of the corner house in the Back st, occ by Thomas M'Cardell, about Rev Rahauser's/Wildair will stand for mares this season at Jacob Sharer's mill near Funks-town and Charles Worland's stable in Hagers Town - James Breathed, owner/James Carroll, Balt, offers reward for negro man who ran away from his farm on Rhode River, AA Co, named Gilbert, 35-40!; he has a wife belonging to William Johnson, who is now moving out to Kentucky with his family; will endeavour to pass for free man named Peter Moore/George Brumbaugh has purchased tavern at the sign

of the Swan near the Court house in Hagers Town, lately occ by David Middlekauff where he has just commenced Tavern Keeping/Deserted from Hagers Town
Baracks, William Murphy, born in Pa, aged 23, 5 ft 11 inch, fair complexion,
blue eyes, fair hair - John Miller, Lieut, 2nd U.S. Regt, Inf'ry/John
Creager, saddler, carries on his bus. at the corner house, lately occ by
Francis Gardner, tailor, next door to Mr. Cook's Tavern, opp dwelling house
of Col. A. Ott/Journeymen weavers wanted - James Garrett, Hagers Town/The
person who borrowed a flax hackle from the subscriber last fall, will be so
obliging as to leave it at the English Printing Office - William Reynolds,
Hagers Town/Samuel Armor, tailor, has removed his shop to Back st, to house
formerly occ by Stephen M'Closkey, next door to the late dwelling of George
Sharkey, decd/Henry Strause at his shop opp Jacob Binkley's, Blue Dyer,
Hagers Town, has just received a large assortment of burr pieces

319. EAM Apr 24 1807/Died Fri 17th inst, in the 18th year of his age, at
the house of Col. Hughes, Samuel Hughes, junr. of Balt Co/George Nigh exec
of Henry Bowser/George Nigh exec of Conrad Knode/Book binding - Samuel B.
Davis who continues to teach school at the German Impartialists Meeting
House/Gera South, boot and shoemaker, has removed to the house lately occ by
Adam Miller, Joiner, directly opp dwelling of Samuel Ridenour, Tanner, in
the Main St/Peter Sailor, 1 1/2 miles from Hagers Town, offers reward for
negro man Richard, about 35, 5 ft 8-9 inch, has very large feet

320. EAM May 8 1807/Died Fri evening last in Greencastle, John Nigh,
Innkeeper/Jacob Walters, Balt Co, near Rannal's Town, near Hagers Town,
offers reward for negro Jack and his wife Jane; Jacks is swarthy color, 5 ft
3-4 inch, aged 25; Jane is about 30 who escaped from Walters near Hagers
Town; they may call themselves, Charles and Nancy Maxwell/William Clements
offers reward for negro man Frank, 5 ft 10 inch, aged 25, who ran away when
subscriber at M'Connel's-town, Pa, on his way to Kentucky. Deliver to
Greenberry Howard, Montg Co, Md. about 3 miles from Clarkesburg/Elie
Williams adm of Thomas Worley/Christian Good and Jacob Barr, adm of John
Stoner/Carroll, Miller and Leopard, tailors, have removed to shop lately occ
by John Creager, saddler, in the Main st//Rachel & Sarah Wilson have moved
to house formerly occ by Mr. Baltzell, saddler, in the Back st opp Capt
William Lewis's, where they continue to make Rouandabouts, Vests and pantaloons; also ladies dresses, and white sewing of every description/Picking,
breaking and carding machines are in readiness to receive wool for manufacturing into rolls for spinning at the mill - George Miller, Edward A. Gibbs,
Henry Hoffman/Dancing School in Hagers Town - James Robardet/Peter Smith,
auctioneer and vendue crier; apply to him at his dwelling nearly opp Henry
Strause, Burr maker, 2nd door below Jacob Binkley, Blue Dyer

321. EAM May 15 1807/Married Thurs 7 inst Thomas Quantrill to Miss Judith
Heyser, both of this town/Died in this town 14 inst after a lingering ill-
ness, Mrs. Elizabeth Smith, wife of James Smith, tailor, leaving husband and
4 small children/Chancery sale in case between Thomas Beall of Samuel com-
plainant and John J. Bugh defendant, to sell lot fronting on Mechanic st -
Roger Perry, trustee/John T. Shrader has opened a tavern in Funks-town
/William Reed, tailor, has removed his shop to house lately occ by George
Rinehart/Ann Jacques and Lancelot Jacques, adm of Joseph Hurst

322. EAM May 22 1807/George Beltzhoover has commenced running a Line of Mail stages from Fred Town via Middletown, Boonsborough, Hagers Town and Greencastle to Chambersburg, 3 times a week/Tho: Kennedy certifies that Benjamin Meeds, living with Samuel Lynch, has taken up a stray mare/George Watterston, Atty at Law, has opened an office in the room formerly occ by Col. N. Rochester

323. EAM Jun 5 1807/William L. Brent has removed his office to the house lately occ by Jonathan Hager opp Mr. Gruber's German Printing Office/Henry Strause has opened a House of Entertainment on the south west corner of the Court-house square, in Hagers Town/Committed to the jail of Washington Co, a negro boy, who calls himself James, about 15, 5 ft 3-4 inch, says he belonged to Dr. Thornton, Washington City and sold by him to Mr. Rodgers of Carolina - Isaac S. White, Sheriff/John I. Stull, adm, to sell pers prop of John Haun, Williams-Port, consisting of Hatters' tools and other/David Middlekauff requests settlement of debts/T. Bruff, dentist of Wash City to visit in a few days/A good road wagon for sale - Christian Fechtig, Hagers Town/Cash for hides and skins - John Harry, Hagers Town

324. EAM Jun 12 1807/Jacob Hewitt and Henry Hogmire, exec of Daniel Hogmire /Conrad Flora exec of George Ridenour/Francis Breathed adm of Edward Breathed/Adam Ott certifies that Christian Hawken has taken up a stray mare/Esther Ritchie adm of John Ritchie/Daniel Rench and Christian Newcomer exec of Martin Rohrer

325. EAM Jun 19 1807/Meeting of Polemic Society William Hammond to read the Dec. of Independence; George G. Ross and Samuel Sprigg to deliver orations on the 4th of July/New store - J. Kessinger & P. Artz - mercantile bus. in house lately occ by Mr. Conrod, joiner, opp two story red frame house formerly occ by Daniel Nead, tanner/Magdalena Kreps, adm of Martin Kreps, requests payments be made on sale of decd est/James Walker to erect a machine for breaking and carding wool into rolls at Peter Miller's mill (formerly Swingley's) on Conococheague, 1 1/2 miles from Williamsport /Charles Scott, living at Philip Spreacher's Mill, 2 miles from Williamsport, offers reward for missing mare

326. EAM Jun 26 1807/Sale of real est of John J. Bugh by Roger Perry, trustee/Wm. Gunnell, jun., 2 miles from Great Falls of Potomack river, Fairfax Co, Va, offers reward for mulatto man Tom Poston, about 33, 5 ft 10 inch

327. EAM Jul 3 1807/William Webb adm of John Webb

328. EAM Jul 10 1807/Celebration of the 4th of July - repaired to Frederick Rohrer's spring adj the town for repast prepared by George Smith/Portrait painter from Paris, has just arrived in this place, apply to him at his painting room in the house occ by Mrs. Heister, corner of the public square/Fuller wanter, in Morrison's Cover, Bedford Co - David Holsinger, res near Waynesburg, on Little Antietam Creek/Michael M'Kiernan and Alice Sharkey, adm of George Sharkey requests payment on sale of pers prop of decd

329. EAM Jul 17 1807/Sale of farm on which he now res (James Redman, Senaca, Montg Co), about 8 miles from Rockville, 422 a./Chancery sale of

land in Allegany Co, called Addition, 469 a., on road from Goff's Mill to
Morefield, Hardy Co, Va - James C. Goff, Trustee/John Langley requests
persons indebted to estate of Henry Artz to make immediate payment

330. EAM Jul 24 1807/Thomas Kennedy, Esq. of Williamsport, Notary Public
for the state of Md. to reside at Hagers Town/Chancery sale by John Buchanan, trustee for benefit of creditors of James Chapline/Sale of Negro man,
about 51 - John Ground, living on Potomak river, 3 miles from Sharpsburg
/Sale at plantation of George Harman, in Berkeley Co, Va, 1 mile above Peter
Light's Ferry, cows, sheep, hogs, furniture/Milton H. Sackett has opened a
tavern in Greencastle, formerly kept by John Nigh/Stolen from printing room
of Hagers Town Bank a number of notes - N. Rochester, Pres./Clerk's Magazine
available from John & George Harry - Jacob D. Dietrick/Negro man committed
to gaol of Wash Co, who calls himself David Jones, alias Israel Davis,
appears to be about 30; says he was formerly a cook on board the frigate
Chesapeake and latly lived in Alexandria and George town

331. EAM Jul 31 1807/Died Mon 20th inst at his res, about 14 miles from
Hagers Town, Nathaniel Nisbet, sen., old res of this co, in 82nd year of his
age/John Hanna, 1 1/2 miles of Hughes's Furnace, offers reward for negro man
Harry, about 22, 5 ft 6-7 inch

332. EAM Aug 7 1807/Officers commanding companies in the 8th Regt are
requested to make out rolls of their respective companies and attend with
them at Hagers Town - John Carr, Lt. Col. 8th Regt./John Armstrong informs
that machines are now in operation for carding wool at Gen. Sprigg's Mill
(formerly Scott's)/Jacob Mumma, 1 mile from Sharpsburg, offers reward for
negro wench Sarah, 25-30, speaks tolerable good German and English, formerly
prop of Jacob Schnebly/Jacob Zeller offers reward for missing steers/The
bus. carried on by Carroll, Miller & Leopard, tailors, has been dissolved -
Adam Leopard/Seth Lane, Hagers Town, offers reward for apprentice boy named
Henry Figly, about 17/Jacob Bowe, Jun., exec of Stephen Slifer, requests
settlement of accounts/Rochester & Beatty request settlement of accounts

333. EAM Aug 14 1807/Died Mon 10th inst in or about the 28 year of his age,
after a short but painful sickness, John O'Neill, who was for some years a
res in this vicinage/R. Pindell and O.H. Williams request persons who purchased prop at the vendues of Jacob D. Dietrick, in Hagers Town, to make
immediate payment, as Mr. Dietrick's bus. which has devolved on them, is of
a pressing nature/To let the house now in the occ by Mrs. Harry opp Dr.
Schnebly; apply to the subscriber at his store - George J. Harry/Distiller
and blacksmith wanted - James M. Cresap, Old town, Allegany Co/Reward
offered for negro Jerry, age 20, 5 ft 11 inch/R. Pindell, adm of Jane Short,
requests settlement of accounts/Thomas Hobbs, Fred Co, 3 miles of Liberty
Town, offers reward for negro man Bill, who calls himself William Scott, age
30-40, about 5 ft 8-9 inch; chews and smokes tobacco; sold last summer out
of Frederick-town jail to Adam Freshour, who sold him to Hobbs; he says he
was raised at Norfolk, Va, and that hs is free

334. EAM Aug 21 1807/Died yesterday in the 62 year of her age, Mrs.
Catharine Light, wife of John Light of this town/Died Mon 17th inst, after a
short illness, Mrs. Catharine Kuther, widow of the late Engelhard Kuther, in

the 89th year of her age; she was a native of Germany, upwards of 40 years and inhabitant of this town; remains interred on Wed in the Lutheran burying ground/Died 28 Jul 1807, at Balt, in the 62nd year of her age, Mrs. Susanna Scott Levy, wife of Levy Andrew Levy, formerly of this town (long obit.) /Elizabeth Neal and St. Leger Neal, adm of William Neal, request settlement of accounts/To sell at subscriber's res, 1/2 mile above Jacob Rohrer's mill on Antietam, horses, cows, etc. - John Hammel/Margaret Gabby and William Gabby exec, request pers indebted to est of John Gabby to make immediate payment/Adam Horine and Conrod Horiine adm of Jacob Dagey/Samuel Bayly available to draw all kinds of instruments of writing

335. EAM Aug 28 1807/Henry Lewis intending next spring, to absent himself for some time from Hagers Town, requests settlement of accounts/Sale of dwelling house in Funks-town - Christian Boerstler/William S. Compton certifies that Susanna Roby has taken up a stray cow/Sale of a number of blooded horses - S. Ringgold, Fountain Rock/Sale of house occ by Thomas Kennnedy, Williamsport - William S. Compton/James Belch forewarns persons from taking assignment on note given to Richard M'Daniel/John Langley certifies that Robert Cowen, living about a miles from Mr. Galloway's Mill, has taken up a stray mare

336. EAM Sep 4 1807/William Bayly, Williamsport, will sell plantation where he formerly lived and whereon James Amos now lives, 4 miles above Williamsport, 300 a., adj Howser's Mill, now Middlekauff's/Sale of 400 a. in Hampshire Co, Va, 20 miles west of Romney, adj land of Col Edward M'Carty; apply to Presley Marmaduke, Swearingen's Ferry, opp Shepherds-town or to the subscriber, Nicholas Seavers (Paddy Town), on the premises/Thomas Quantril, blacksmith, carries on the bus., has erected a machine for the purpose of shoeing unruly horses/Mary Bowles, adm of Samuel Bowles

337. EAM Sep 11 1807/Upton Lawrence, candidate for delegate in Gen. Assembly/John V. Kelly continues to carry on the fulling and dying bus. at the fulling mill of of Martin Baechtel near Hagers Town; cloth will be taken in a Mr. Brumbaugh's tavern to which place it will be carefully sent back when dressed/Robert Douglass will receive woollen yarn for thick cloth or linsey which he will weave at the usual rates/Application will be made to the Legislature of Md to complete the title of the Vestry of the German Evangelic Lutheran Congregation, in and about Elizabeth-town at St. John's Church in Wash Co, to 3 lots, heretofore conveyed to Lodowick Young, Martin Harry, Leonard Schryock and Conrod Hogmire, by Jonathan Hager, decd, in trust for the use of the Dutch Lutheran Congregartion belonging to Elizbeth-town/John Wagoner has taken up a stray horse/John Kennedy to apply for relief from debts/James Walker adm of George Walker/To let a tanyard in Williamsport lately occ by John Russell - 17 vats - John Sterrett, Wm. M'Cleland, Jacob T. Towson, exec/Thomas Quantrill, Samuel Martin, Philip Kellar, John Sleigh, Abraham King, John King, John Weis and Adam Boreoff, blacksmiths, have agreed to raise the prices upon their work/Nathl. Nisbitt and Peter Nisbitt, exec, to sell at the dwelling of Nathaniel Nisbitt, decd, 1 mile from Mr. Mason's mill (formerly Barnes's) the pers est of decd/Matthias Spangler, about 2 miles below Mr. Brinn's Ironworks on Potomac river, has taken up two stray oxen/John C. Williams has lost a pair of

leather saddle bags/Peter Umrickhouse, Hagers Town, seeks two journeymen blacksmiths

338. EAM Sep 18 1807/Sale pursuant to will of Edward Watkins, decd, of tract of 950 a. in Culpeper Co, Va, - William Pendleton, exec, Berkeley Co, Va/George Yost forewarns agnst taking assignment on bonds given to Abraham Karns/John Britner, a mile from Cave Tavern, offers reward for apprentice to the cooper's bus. named Nathan Henning, about 5 ft 5-6 inch, about 22 years old

339. EAM Sep 25 1807/Died on Mon last at M'Connels-town, on his return from Bedford Springs, Ignatius Taylor, Esq. one of the Judges of the Orphans Court for Wash Co/John Bowles, David Schnebly, William Gabby - Republican candiates as delegates in the next Gen. Assembly/Shepherd's Town races - E.O. Williams, H. Boteller, managers/Sale at subscriber's plantation, about 2 1/2 miles from David Schnebly's, of cows, hogs, coopers tools, farming utensils - Michael Hager

340. EAM Oct 2 1807/Married Sun last by Rev Schmucker, John Wolfkill of Williamsport, to Miss Betsey Reynolds of this town/Married same evening by Rev Schmucker, Jacob Kaelhofer, to Miss Amelia Ridenour, all of this town /Moses Tabbs, Republican, candidate for Gen. Assembly/Archibald M. Waugh, candidate for sheriff/Sheriff's sale of lot in Williamsport, prop of John Haun, to satisfy debt to Jacob T. Towson//P.C. Young adm of John O'Neill /John Gear has taken stable belonging to George Shall, Hagers Town, to establish a livery stable/Sale of tract in Fayette Co, Pa, 70 a., on Cheat river, millhouse 45x35 ft, 3 pair of mill stones - John M'Farland

341. EAM Oct 9 1807/Matthias Shaffner and Daniel Gehr candidates for sheriff/P.C. Young, adm, to sell pers prop of John O'Neil, consisting of silver watch, saddle horse, saddle, bridle and martingale, number of books, historical, geographical amd mathematical, wearing apparel and other/Henry Deehl, taylor, continutes to carry on his bus. in the house of Henry Middle-kauff, next door to Frederick Brentlinger, in Market St/Fire Company - Adam Ott, Richard Pindell, John Ragan, David Harry, George Woltz, Robert Douglass, Frederick Alter, George Shall, Samuel Young, George Shank, Nathaniel Rochester, Alexander Clagett, Charles Gelwicks, William Hess, Henry Cake, Peter Hefleich, Conrad Coffroth, Peter Miller (Hatter), Peter Woltz, William Clagett, Thomas Grieves, Peter Miller (merchant), Henry Middlekauff, and James Ferguston are directed to attend at the Courthouse square 17th inst. precisely at 3 o'clock in the afternoon for the purpose of working the Fire Engines; those who do not attend or furnish persons in their places, will be fined 25 cents agreeable to resolution of the said company - Wm. Heyser, Director General/Lewis Chastain, Frederick Co, Va, 12 miles from Winchester, near the Newtown Sulpher Springs, offers reward for yellow man slave named Moore who has obtained 3 forged passes signed John S. Woodcock/Sharpsburg Races - Philip Myers, manager

342. EAM Oct 23 1807/Died Sat 17th inst, Coleman Combs, old inhabitant of this co/Isaac Taylor, living in Mercersburg, Pa, offers reward for appren-tice to the shoemaking bus., John Crumbauch, about 5 ft 7-8 inch, 19; had on new blue cloth coat, cross-barred cotton coatee, pair of homemade cloth

overalls of a drab colour, high crowned roram hat/Peter Sailor, 1 1/2 miles of Hagers Town, offers reward for negro man named Richard, about 35

343. EAM Oct 30 1807/John Witmer, adm, to sell pers est of Jacob Ruch, at res of decd, formerly the res of Andrew Kessinger, 2 miles from Hughes's Furnace/Jonathan Hager offers reward for steer which strayed out of George Bond's pasture, near Newcomer's Mill, 5 miles from Hagers Town/Thomas Quantrill, Hagers Town, offers reward for negro man who calls himself Groner Packet; he formerly lived at Ellicott's Mills, about 34 years of age/Ordered that colonels of their respective regiments of the 2d Brigade to direct their adjutants to distribute to captains of companies the blank returns to be filled and returned with name of every white man within their districts, from the age of 18 to 45 years – Thomas Sprigg, Brig. Gen., 2d Brigade/Henry Ankony, near St. Paul's Church, on West Conococheague, about 10 miles from Hagers Town, has taken up stray hogs/George Nigh and Thomas Shuman to sell pers prop of Daniel Clapsaddle, decd, 1/2 miles from Hagers Town

344. EAM Nov 6 1807/Married Tues evening last, by Rev Rahauser, Joseph Graff of Northampton Co, Pa, to Miss Sally Kausler, dau of John Kauser of this town/John Combs, exec, to sell at late dwelling of Colman Combs, decd, 4 miles from Hagers Town, on Mr. Ringgold's Manor, pers prop of decd/J.M. Cresap, Old-town, Allegany Co, living on the premises, to sell 500 a.

345. EAM Nov 13 1807/Daniel Weisel, living in Williamsport, offers reward for negro man Isaac/William Kreps adm of Frederica Brown, Wash Co, decd /George C. Smoot will attend to any bus. of mine that may offer during my absence to the Legislature – Moses Tabbs, Hagers Town

346. EAM Nov 20 1807/Joseph C. Kellar and Archibald M. Waugh, candidates for sheriff/John T. Mason has a number of young negroes who will soon be free, wishes to sell for remainder of their time

347. EAM Nov 27 1807/On Fri morning, Nov 6th, the trial of Edward Donelly, for murdering his wife, Catharine, came before the Court of Oyer & Terminer in this place. Neighbours held her cries and screams as if in torment for more than an hour, till they gradually died away, since which time (last August) she has never been heard of. Blood was discovered in the bed and on the bedsteads; a very unusal quantity of fresh ashes were found in the fire place, all impregnated with something like lime; a great number of small bones were produced to court. Donnelly's son, a child of 7 years of age, could not be admitted as a witness on account of his extreme youth and ignorance. Jury returned with verdict of guilty after an hour of delibera- tion/Sale at late dwelling of George Ankony, decd, in sight of St. Paul's Church, on the West side of Conococheague Creek, pers prop of decd – Henry Fiery and Catharine Ankony, adm/Henry Barnet, living near Lantz's Mill, has taken up a stray bay and two colts/Andrew Charles, taylor, has taken a part of the house occ by Mrs. Kreps, widow of the late Martin Kreps, Back St, Hagers Town/Esther Ritchie, adm, Sharpsburg, to sell pers est of John Ritchie, decd/Henry Fiery, 1 1/2 miles from John T. Mason's Mill, has taken up stray cattle/Henry Yakle, near the Cave Tavern, about 4 miles from Mount Etne Furnace, offers reward for apprentice to the shoemaking bus., named

Elias M'Clure, about 19, 5 ft 3-4 inch/Jacob Zeller, offers reward for missing steer

348. EAM Dec 4 1807/Died Fri 27th ult, Miss Mary Light, dau of John Light, of this town, in the 22nd year of her age; for many years sustained the infirmities of a feeble constitution/John Langley, Wash Co, to sell at his tavern, about 7 miles from Hagers Town, horses, cows, hogs, hay, grain, set of blacksmith's tools, and other/Margaret Gabby gives notice to person who purchased prop at sale of est of John Gabby, decd, to make payment on their notes, to John Cochran, Esq. near Waynesburg/Jacob Ridenour, 4 miles from Hagers Town, has taken up a stray hog

349. EAM Dec 11 1807/Married Sun evening 6th inst, by Rev Rahauser, Henry Adams to Miss Mary Knode, both of this town/Married Tues 8th inst by Rev Schmucker, Peter Glosbrenner to Miss Christiana Shane, dau of Henry Shane of this town/William Hammett, living near Col. Hughes's Furnace, offers reward for two indented boys named John and James M'Kenney; John is about 14; James is about 12/Mrs. Eichelberner, opp the Lutheran Church, has just rec'd elegant assortment of hats and bonnets/Chancery case - Elie Williams vs. Anne Elliot, Nathaniel Rochester, Callender Irwin and Patience his wife, William, Robert, Wilson, Daniel, Harriot, John, Jesse, St Clair and Elie W. Elliot - object of the bill is to obtain sale of real estate of Robert Elliot, decd, for payment to his debts. Robert Elliot died intestate, leaving defendants or some of them, his heirs at law. Defendants Callender Irwin and wife, William, Robert, Wilson, Daniel, Harriot, John, Jesse, and St. Clair Elliot, all res out of the state/Milton H. Sackett, Greencastle, has negro woman for sale

350. EAM Dec 18 1807/Sale of Tan Yard in Warfordsburg, Bedford Co, Pa - Enquire of subscriber, John Mason, about 3 miles from Hancock-town, or Jeremiah Mason on Licking Creek, about a mile from Parkhead forge/Died in York Town, Pa, on 27th ult, Rev Jacob Goering, Pastor of the German Luth Church in that place/Mary Tice adm of Michael Tice, requests settlement of accounts/Robert Stewart gives notice that stray shoats came to the plantation of Hugh Stewart, Ringgold's Manor

351. EAM Dec 24 1807/Jacob Foutz exec of Frederick Foutz/Thomas Beall of Samuel, Allegany Co, to sell mills adj Cumberland, mill on Evets's creek and mills at mouth of Town Creek, 5 miles below Old-Town/Mary Snyder and George Snyder, exec, to sell prop of Caspar Snyder, decd, on road to Hancock town /William S. Compton to sell warehouse in Williamsport; also house formerly owned by Thomas Kennedy/Peter Glasbrenner has opened a tavern in Hagers Town, at the sign of the billiard table, formerly kept by Henry Shane

352. EAM Jan 1 1808/Married yesterday by Rev Bower, John Brenham, to Miss Mary Hanna, dau of John Hanna, of this co/John Dixon to sell farm lately occ and owned by Alexander Pitt Buchanan, Esq., in Jefferson Co, Va, 900 a., adj land of Rich Willis, Mr. Weaver, Mr. Dandridge and Mr. Baylor, 10 miles from Martinsburg/John Watt to sell tavern in Hancock-town, formerly occ by John Protzman, decd/Frederick Fishach and Elizabeth Kuhn, adm of Jacob Kuhn/Cash for hides and skins - Brocius & Towson, Williamsport/10 to 30 cords of

The Maryland Herald and Hagers-town Advertiser

hickory and oak wood wanted for the poor house - George Nigh, David Harry, Matthias Shaffner, trustees/James Buchanan offers reward for mare stolen out of the stable of Andrew Armstrong, in Wash City/Peter Humrickhouse, Hagers Town, has taken his son into partnership

353. EAM Jan 8 1808/Commissioners for Wash Co to open books for insurance company: N. Rochester, J. Schnebly, Wm. Heyser, F. Dorsey, Henry Lewis/Sale of real est of Richard Cromwell, decd, 1300 a. - Martin Kershner, Josiah Price, Walter Boyd, Henry Ankony, David Schnebly/Died in Williamsport Tues 5th inst, after a short illness, John Wolfkill/Died in Williamsport Wed 6th inst, Jacob Bowlas, blacksmith, leaving wife and 5 children/Died Tues Dec 22 1807, Mrs. Annaballa Johnston, consort of John Johnston, of Washington township, Franklin Co, Pa/House for sale now occ by Lawrence Shick, prop of heirs of George Young, decd/Daniel Miller, 1 1/2 miles below Broad Fording on Conococheague Creek, has taken up a stray bull/Adam Gerlaugh and John Gerlaugh have put their vendue notes in the hands of Martin Kershner for collection/Moses M'Namee has rented Miller and Julius's Mill, near the New Bridge, on Antietam

354. EAM Jan 15 1808/Jacob Root and John Hammond adm of Henry Fasnacht/Tho: Sprigg forewarns persons from hunting within his enclosures/Joseph Sprigg, exec, to sell at the res of Ignatius Taylor, decd, a portion of his pers est/Jacob Whiteman, Williamsport, adm of Jacob Whiteman, decd, to sell all pers prop of decd/Robert Smith, near Hess's Mill, about 2 miles from Sharpsburg, has taken up a stray sow/Rags wanted, at the old and new Paper-Mills, near Hagers Town - George Miller/Married Tues even last by Rev Rahauser, George Shryock, to Miss Betsey Lewis, dau of of Capt. William Lewis, of this town

355. EAM Jan 22 1808/Married at Staunton, Va, Thurs 14th inst. John Schnebly, of Wash Co, to Miss Catharine Witzel, of that place/Appointed as officers of the 8th Regt, of Maryland Militia: Anthony Howard; John Hivling; James Bowles; Christian Lantz, jun; Henry Barnet; William Yates; Christian Hager; Jacob Barnet, jun.; Anthony Snyder; Jacob Dunn; Nathaniel Nisbet; Jonathan Nisbet; John M'Clain; George Snyder; Jacob Smith; Henry Brumbaugh; Samuel Miller - John Carr, Lieut. Col./Fresh garden seeds - Theo: Holt/John Shafer adm of Christian Mauchler/Christian Langenecker forewarns persons from taking assignment on note given to Conrad Pecker, left in the hand of Conrad Yantz/Thomas Peter and others, exec of Robert Peter, to sell horses cattle, sheep and other, at Anthony Tracy's in Montg Co, within 2 miles of Bowie and Hersey's Mills, Seneca/Christian Fechtig offers reward for apprentice to shoemaking bus. named James Ashcom, about 17/House for rent which he occupies - Henry Lewis; also officers now occ by George Watterson and office above occ by George C. Smoot

356. EAM Jan 29 1808/Married Tues evening last by Rev Rahauser, John Swope, of Huntingdon, Pa, to Miss Mary Stemple, dau of Christian Stemple of this town/Died Mon last at his farm, about 3 miles from Hagers Town, David Hammett, after a short illness, aged 36 years, leaving widow and 5 young children/George Woltz, Hagers Town, has taken his sons into partnership in the Clock and Watch making bus., Emanuel Franz to sell plantation, 153 a., agreeably to will of George W. Stoud, decd/Sale of house wherein he now

64

lives on north side of German Reformed Church - Conrod Coffroth/Wash Co
court case - Ignatius O'Farrall & Frances his wife, Andrew Golding and
Catharine his wife vs. Peter Kiernan, Patrick Tiernan and Margaret his
wife, George Quinn and Susanna his wife, Lawrence Kiernan, Frances Monahan,
Michael Kiernan, Alice Sharkey, John Kiernan, Peter Kiernan, Francis Kiernan
and Barney Kiernan. The Commission under the act to direct descents has
determined that notice be given that above Ignatius OFarrall and Frances his
wife, Peter Kiernan, Patrick Tiernan and Margaret his wife, George Quinn and
Susanna his wife, John Kiernan and Barney Kiernan, some of the persons
entitled to make election to take the est therein mentioned, being absent
from the county when such election ought to be made/John Farren to apply for
relief from debts/House for rent where Adam Doyle now lives, and house occ
by subscriber near the Lutheran Church - Jonathan Hager

357. EAM Feb 5 1808/Married Tues evening last by Rev Gueding, John Hershey,
to Miss Barbara Hershey, of this co/Married yesterday by Rev Rahauser,
Michael Greybill, of Lancaster, Pa, to Miss Esther Lambert, of this co/Died
yesterday morning in this town, after a short illness, Robert Miller, weaver
/Margaret Gabby gives notice to those persons who purchased prop at the sale
of pers est of John Gabby/Henry Houck and Christina Ford adm of James Ford
/William Webb adm of John Webb/Performance by Mr. and Mrs. Mestayer/Chancery
sale in behalf of the creditors of Samuel Bayly/David Grim gives notice that
stray hogs have come to Alexander Grim's plantation, 5 miles from Harpers
-Ferry/Christian Fechtig, being much embarrassed in his circumstances, and
wishing to wind up his bus., requests all those who are indebted to him to
come forward and settle their accounts; the boot and shoe-making bus. will
still be carried on at his house in Hagers Town/Barton Carrico to sell at
his res in Wash Co, near the Big Spring, horses, cows, hogs, furniture,
farming utensils, grain in the ground, rye in stacks, quantity of bacon,
quantity of seasoned plank

358. EAM Feb 12 1808/Thomas Kennedy and John Kennedy, both of Wash Co,
insolvent debtors, discharged from imprisonment/Elizabeth Wolfkill adm, to
sell at late dwelling of John Wolfkill, decd, in Williamsport, pers prop of
decd/Wm. Heyser to sell 4 lots in Rohrer's Addition to Hagers Town/Henry
Adam exec, to sell at dwelling of John Adam 1/2 mile from John Schnebly's,
pers prop of decd/Rezin Davis, Hagers Town, to rent two rooms in the house
where he lives, known as Judge Buchanan's Office/Joseph Stewart has lost a
red morocco pocket book

359. EAM Feb 19 1808/Chancery case - Christopher Miller vs Joseph Frye, to
obtain decree for the conveyance of two tracts in Allegany Co/William Delahunt forewarns persons from hunting within his enclosures/Peter Seibert,
living on Beaver Creek, near Henry Newcomer's mill, offers reward for
missing filly

360. EAM Feb 26 1808/Joseph Butler to apply for relief from debts/Chancery
sale of real est of Gustavus Scott, decd/Died in this town Tues, 23d inst.
after a lingering illness, Dr. Peter Woltz, in the 63d year of his age
/Taking subscriptions for 800 shares in the Union Manufacturing Co. of Md:
N. Rochester, J. Schnebly, Wm. Heyser, H. Lewis, F.Dorsey, Commissioners/The
horse, Young Paul Jones, to cover mares this season at Hugh Cooper's stable

in Mercersburg and stable of Jacob Barnett, 6 miles from Hagers Town — John M'Kigney/Carlisle — Edward Donally was executed; a few days before his death he acknowledged the murdering of his wife

361. EAM Mar 4 1808/Sale at subscriber's res near John Shafer's Mills, horses, cattle, and other — John Adams/To be rented — brick house next door to Messrs. John & Joseph M'Ilhenny's store — Christian Lantz, senr./Married Tues evening last, by Rev Rahauser, Peter Humrickhouse, to Miss Sarah Shuman, dau of Thomas Shuman, of this town/Died Tues evening last, after a lingering illness, Mrs. Rebekah Reynolds, wife of William Reynolds, of this town/Died Sat evening last, at an advanced age, Sebastian Baker, for many years crier of Wash Co Court/John C. Williams, adm of Amos Davis/The horse Cotoctin will stand for mares at stable of Henry Strause, Hagers Town and John Stover's Tavern, formerly occ by Major John Langley

362. EAM Mar 11 1808/John Reynolds has again commenced the clock and watch making bus. at his dwelling/The horse President will stand the season — Benjamin Pettit/The Arabian Ranger will stand this season in Hagers Town and at Mr. Sherer's Mill — Francis Breathed/Sharpsburgh Independent Blues to meet in Sharpsburgh — Nathaniel W. Hays, Sec'ry/N. Rochester intending to discontinue his nail manufactory; will offer for sale the house in Rohrer's Addition to Elizabeth town in which J. Coke now res adj George Gresinger's

363. EAM Mar 18 1808/Ann Hammett adm, to sell at late dwelling of David Hammett, decd, 3 miles from Hagers Town, pers est of decd, 3 negro men, 1 woman and 2 children and other/Jacob Zeller adm of Christian Witmer/English and American Garden seeds — Frederick Miller, Druggist & Apothecary, Hagers Town/Mary Woltz exec of Peter Woltz/Joseph Little continues to carry on the plough and cradle making bus. at his dwelling nearly opp German Luth Church /The horse Fox Hunter will stand for mares this season at subscriber's farm on road leading from Greencastle to Williamsport, 2 1/2 miles from Jacob Zeller's, 1 1/2 mile from Michael Tice's Mill — Daniel Miller, Jun./The horse Wild Herod will stand this season at Stephen Barton's Tavern and other places (indicated) — Philemon Cromwell

364. EAM Mar 25 1808/Horse, Young President, wil stand this season — Daniel Rench/Young Clifden will stand — Michael Kessinger/Knight of Malta will stand — William Fitzhugh/James Ferguson to rent one of those new two story brick houses, in Hagers Town, on st leading from the Court house to Stull's old mill/Jacob Leider cautions persons from taking assignment on note given to Philip Sherban

365. EAM Apr 1 1808/Samuel B. Davis has removed his school to an apartment in the house of Wm. Patterson, next door to the Rev. Bower/Member of the Volunteer Troop of Horse to meet at house of Henry Strause — Otho H. Williams, Capt./To sell at house of Thomas Helm, Williamsport, warehouse formerly owned by Thomas Kennedy/George Watterston, Atty at Law, has removed his office to apartment in house of J. P. Herr, next door to George Beltz-hoover's tavern/Doctor Scott has taken his res in Col. Wm. Van Lear's new house in Williamsport/John M'Ilhenny and Joseph M'Ilhenny request those indebted to settle their accounts/Partnership of J. Kessinger and P. Artz is dissolved/The horses, Regulater & President, will stand for mares the ensu-

ing season. Good attendance will given by Benjamin Pettit. John M'Masters
and Co. previously owned Regulator and sold this stud horse to Enoch Armi-
tage of Montgomery Co for $1000. Statement by Elnathan Pettit has a colt by
Regulator (witnessed by Benjamin Field, Jacob Conrad). Joseph Harvey sold
a colt of Regulator for $400; his brother Robert raised two colts by said
horse.

366. EAM Apr 8 1808/George Shryock, pump maker, has removed from Samuel
Beelor's(?) near the German Reformed Church to the house next door to Henry
Barckman's and opp Abraham King's Blacksmith Shop in the Back st leading to
Chambersburg/Adam Leopard, tailor, has removed to shop in corner of the
public square between George Binkley's and Messrs. Perrin and Sweitzer's
store/Philip Binkley, Hagers Town, requests those indebted to him to call on
Dr. Jacob Schnebly/David Hammond, living in Greencastle, Franklin Co, Pa,
offers reward for two apprentices to the house joiner & cabinet making bus.
named John Sailor and Samuel Wise. John Sailor is about 18 year of age, 5
ft 9-10 inch, pitted with the small pox.   Samuel Wise is about 17, 4 ft 10
inch, full faced./Those in possession of public arms, furnished to Capt.
Joseph Chapline's and Capt. John Abel's Company of select militia are hereby
directed to deliver the same to Capt. John Blackford, at the house of Philip
Myers in Sharpsburg/Partnership of J. Kessinger and P. Artz is dissolved
/Geo: Scott adm of George Kennedy, to sell in Boonsborough, sundry dry goods
belonging to est of George Kennedy, decd/House of Entertainment - Benjamin
Bean has removed from his late stand near Parkhead Forge to the house lately
occ by Valentine Dyche, at the West end of Hancock-town, sign of the Green
Tree/Jacob Mumma, living in Wash Co, on Antietam creek, 1 mile from Sharps-
burg, seeks to hire a miller.

367. EAM Apr 15 1808/Jacob Ridenour, exec, to sell at late dwelling house
of Jacob Ridenour, decd, 4 miles from Hagers Town, pers prop of decd/Tench
Ringgold, candidate for elector of Pers. and Vice-Pres./Partnership of John
Beard and Christian Artz is dissolved/Peter Baker, 1 1/2 mile from Sharpsburg, offers reward for indented boy named James Box, about 4 years of age,
taken away by his mother/Peter Miller insolvent debtor

368. EAM Apr 22 1808/Schoolmaster wanted - apply to Andrew Snivley, Esq.,
Jacob Byers, John Gerhart and Alexander M'Cutchen, trustees in Antrim town-
ship, Franklin Co, Pa, near Greencastle/Thomas Crampton certifies that John
Philips has taken up a stray mare/William Easton has taken up a stray mare
/Henry Edllinger, living at Matthew Van Lear's mill, 1 mile of Williamsport,
offers reward for missing colt

369. EAM Apr 29 1808/Married Tues evening last by Rev Schmucker, William
Beatty, to Miss Elizabeth Miller, dau of Peter Miller of this town/John
Fiery, offers reward for negro boy Harry, about 19, 5 ft 3 inch, who ran
away from his mill, near John T. Masons' plantation/Samuel Lynch has taken
up a stray horse

370. EAM May 6 1808/Sale of farm, 300 a., 1 mile from Hagers Town, includ-
ing a meadow adj Daniel Stull's mill - John I. Stull, Otho H. W. Stull/The
President and directors of the Hagers Town Bank have declared a dividend   -
Elie Beatty, Cashier/Wm. Carroll, tailor and habit maker, has taken the shop

in which he last conducted the above bus., under the names of Carroll,
Miller and Leopard/George Bean will take in horses and cows to pasture ·by
the month, at Mr. Lawrence's farm, near Hagers Town

371. EAM May 13 1808/Captains commanding companies of the 1st Battalion in
the 10th Regt. are ordered to parade their companies at Sharpsburgh - John
Good, Major, 1st Battalion, 10th Regt./To sell - at late dwelling of Jacob
Ridenour, decd, 4 miles from Hagers Town, wagon and sleigh, kitchen dresser,
beds and bedsteads, chests and other - Jacob Ridenour, exec/New Store -
Christian Artz has just received from Phila and Balt and now opening at the
new two story brick house, two doors above Geo. Brumbaugh's Tavern, dry
goods, groceries & Queens Ware/George Nigh certifies that Francis Breathed,
living about 2 miles from Funks-town, has taken up a stray mare/To be let -
house and store now occ by Messrs. John & Joseph M'Ilhenny - Christian
Lantz, Senr., Hagers Town

372. EAM May 20 1808/The Captains commanding companies of the 2nd Battalion
in the 10th Regt, are ordered to parade their companies at John Stover's
(formerly Major J. Langley's) - Thomas Helm, Major 2nd Battalion, 10th
Regt/Sale of real est of Gustavus Scott, decd - Roger Perry, Trustee,
Cumberland/Journeymen gunsmiths wanted - Jacob Resor, Mercersburg, Pa/Sale
of plantation called Shadrach's Lot, alias the Cave Land - Thomas Charlton,
acting exec/Michael Snider living near John Booth's and John Shafer's mill,
9 miles from Hagers Town, offers reward for negro girl named Abby, about 13

373. EAM May 27 1808/Jacob Waltz, living 2 1/2 miles from Hughes's Forge,
Wash Co, offers reward for stolen horse/Excellent Pasturage, $1.00 per month
for horses and cattle - Tho: Kennedy,   formerly part of Chew's Farm
/Appointment of board of Agriculture of Wash Co: Tho: Sprigg, Frisby Tilgh-
man, Ch. Carroll, Wm. Fitzhugh, Elie Williams, Martin Kershner, Jacob
Zeller, Richard Pindell, Samuel Ringgold, Daniel Hughes, John Buchanan, John
T. Mason, John Clagett/David Harry and Peter Hefleich exec of John Protzman
/Sale of land by Mahlon Anderson lying with a miles of Charlestown, Jeffer-
son Co, Va/J. Holker, near Berryville, Va, offers reward for missing horse.
Deliver to Samuel Hughes of Hagers Town or to Thomas Flag at Charlestown or
to J. Holker.

374. EAM Jun 3 1808/On Monday last the 2d Battalion of the 24th Regt, com-
manded by Major John Reynolds, consisting of Capt. Thomas Fost's Volunteer
Rifle Company, and Capt. George Binkley's, Capt. Henry Lewis's, Capt. John
Harry's, and, and, and Capt. John Hefleich's Company of Light Infantry, met in
conformity to the orders of the Brigadier General, upon the parade ground,
in the vicinity of this town, where they were joined by Capt. O. H.
Williams's Troop of Horse. They were reviewed by Colonel John E. Howard, of
Baltimore, attended by Brigade Major Buchanan/Robert Douglas, Hagers Town,
offers reward for apprentice to the weaving bus., Daniel Shupe, about 18
years of age/Missing books from the library of William L. Brent, Hagers
Town, are listed/Peter Rench, 5 miles from Hagers Town, has taken up stray
mare/American Blues are requested to meet at Mr. Geo. Brumbaugh's tavern
/Notes passed at sale of pers est of John O'Neill are now due - P.C. Young,
adm/Machinery for picking, breaking & rolling wool are in readiness at
Philip Stern's, 7 miles from Hagers Town - Abraham Kagey

375. EAM Jun 17 1808/Married Tues 7th inst, at George-town, by Rev Sears,
John Harry, merchant of this town, to Miss Marianne Clagett, of that place
/Married Tues 14th inst, by Rev Rahauser, Christian Newcomer, of York Co,
Pa, to Miss Barbara Barr, of this co/Died yesterday morning in this town,
Mrs. Julianna Wounter, mother of George Shall, in the 86th year of her age
/Susanna Robey has taken up a stray horse/Dissolution of partnership of
Henry Middlekauff and William A. Beatty; firm to be carried on by Beatty
/Henry Middlekauff to carry on hat manufactory next door to George Binkley's
store/John Hunter certifies that Joseph Hunter, living near Parkhead Forge,
on Licking Creek, has taken up a stray horse/James M'Clain certifies that
Peter Brewer, living on Little Conococheague Creek, about 3 miles from the
Big Spring, has taken up a stray mare/James L. Hawkins, Hagers Town, offers
reward for mare stolen from stable of Alexander Clagett; return to Alex.
Clagett or to Major James S. Hook, near the mouth of Cotoctin Creek in Fred
Co

376.   EAM Jun 24 1808/Married Sun evening last by Rev Rahauser, Jacob
Kausler, to Miss Catharine Shall, both of this town/Died Wednesday 1st inst.
in Winchester, Va, Richard Bowen, editor and proprietor of the Winchester
Gazette; remains interred in the Episc Church burial ground, attended by his
Masonic breathren and friends/Fire Company to meet for the purpose of
working the Fire Engines: Leonard Kuhn, John Hershey, John Wise, Christian
Hawkins, George Binkley, Philip Kellar, William Kreps, John Miller, John
Reynolds, Christian Langernecker, Alexander Neill, John Cook, Peter Umrick-
house, Samuel Beelor, George Kreps, Henry Lewis, John P. Herr, Seth Lane,
John Conrad, Frederick Miller, Jonathan Hager, Devalt Eichelberner, Geo.
Crissinger, and Frederick Dorsey/Jacob Whiteman exec of Jacob Whiteman/John
Hilleary, on the Merryland tract, offers reward for negro man Will, 33 year
of age; calls himself William Pedit, chew tobacco

377. EAM Jul 1 1808/Philip Mains certifies that Richard Dowler has taken up
a stray gelding/John & Joseph M'Ilhenny, Hagers Town, intending to leave
this place in a short time, request settlement of accounts

378. EAM Jul 8 1808/Wm. B. Williams, near Williamsport, offers reward for
negro man Jack, about 30, 5 ft 6-8 inch; his father and mother are living
with John Muloy near the mouth of Seneca/Cash or Earthen ware given for rags
at the new Paper-Mills, near Hagers Town - George Miller

379. EAM Jul 15 1808/Died suddenly on Sunday evening last, at his res,
about 3 miles from Hagers Town, Jacob Sherer, an old and respectable
inhabitant of this co/Robert Cheney, 2 miles from Boonsborough, offers
reward for missing gelding/John Gruber, Hagers Town, offers reward for
apprentice to printing bus., named Robert Moore, about 5 ft 8 inch, 18 years
oag age, has light hair

380. EAM Jul 22 1808/Lexington, Kentucky – Died on 22nd day of this month,
after a severe illness, in the 77th year of his age, Col. Thomas Hart.   He
was for many years a citizen of this town, and one of the most active pro-
moters of its increase and prosperity/Catharine M'Lind and Alexr. Dougherty,
exec of Samuel M'Lind to sell pers prop of decd, at his dwelling in
Williamsport/To sell plantation 9 miles from Hagers Town, adj lands of Henry

Ankony and Samuel Miller, 270 a., prop of heirs and representatives of Michael Kiernan the younger, decd; Nicholas Smith, who lives on the plantation, will shew it to amy interested person/Committed to jail of Wash Co, negro man, who calls himself Alfred, says he belongs to James Bowling, near Middleburg, Loudon Co, Va; 5 ft high, about 27/John Ragan, senr. & John Kaelhofer, saddlers & harness makers, have commenced bus. next door to Mrs. Heister/Ebenezer Steel, living at Peter Middlekauff''s mill, at the mouth of Little Conococheague, offers reward for misssing horse

381. EAM Jul 29 1808/Married last evening by Rev Bower, James Shelby, of Lexington, Kentucky, to Miss Mary Pindell, dau of Dr. R. Pindell of this town/David Schnebly, appointed Lieut. Col. Commandant, 8th reg. Wash Co/Died last evening about 11 o'clock, Mrs. Elizabeth Sprigg, consort of General Thomas Sprigg, of Wash Co, after a short illness/George Woltz, Junr., brass founder, clock maker & silver smith, has commenced bus. at house nearly opp the jail; all orders left with his brother, Samuel, next door to Mr. A. Neill's store will be strictly attended to/Sale of house in Williamsport, formerly prop of John Haun, decd – George Haun/Conrad Coffroth, living in Greencastle, offers reward for missing horse/Adam Ott certifies that Christian Myer, living near John Barr's mill has taken up a stray mare /Wanted – a fuller – William Elliott, 8 miles from Mr. Ramsay's store, Westmoreland Co, Pa/Gabriel Nourse has lost an umbrella between Mr. Stover's Tavern and Sharpsburg

382. EAM Aug 5 1808/Died Thrus night last about 11 o'clock, Thomas James Grieves, son of the editor of this paper, aged 7 years and 5 months/American Blues to meet at the Captain's Quarters – Moses Tabbs, Sec'ry

383. EAM Aug 12 1808/Married Thurs evening 4th inst. by Rev Schmucker, John Worley, to Miss Eve Tice, dau of Michael Tice, of Franklin Co, Pa/Fulling & dying at the fulling mill of Martin Baechtel, near Hagers Town – John V. Kelly

384. EAM Aug 19 1808/Died Tues morning last, Mrs. Mary E. Harry, widow of the late Jacob Harry, of this town, in the 50th year of her age/Jacob Houser, 6 miles from Hagers Town, has taken up a stray horse/Susanna Russell and Jacob Lambert and Wm. Gabby, adm of John Russell, to sell pers prop of decd/Josiah Price, between Hagers Town and Mercersburg, offers reward for missing horse

385. EAM Aug 26 1808/Married Wednesday evening last, by Rev Rahauser, Michael Kapp, to Miss Mary Lorshbaugh, all of this town/Christian Baughman, Chambersburg, Pa, has applies for relief from debts/U. Lawrence, Hagers Town, to clear, this fall and winter, about 15 acres of woodland, 2 1/4 miles from Hagers Town, adj Major Carroll's land to be laid off in one acre lots/Jacob Hammon, Junr., living on Millcreek, Shenandoah Co, offers reward for horse stolen from his wagon about half a mile from Strasburg, Shenandoah Co/John Miller, weaver, continues his bus. at his old stand, near Mrs. Bower's Brick Yard/William Walker, has applied in Franklin Co, for relief from debts/James M'Lenahan, Senr., living in Antrim Township, Franklin Co, Pa, offers reward for missing mare/Henry Adam carries on the potting (pottery) bus. at the shop formerly occ by Henry Strause, burr maker, next door

to Samuel Ridenour, tanner, and opp Jacob Binkley, blue dyer/Mary Johnson and Tobias Belt, adm of Robert Johnson/Richard Allinder, near Col. Hughes's Forge, offers 6 cents and a good drink of grog reward for apprentice to the wagon making bus., named Hugh Meek, about 5 ft 9-10 inch, between 18 and 19, black hair, strong beard, large whiskers, dark complexion, kind of stoppage in his speech

386. EAM Sep 2 1808/Christian Stoffer, living in Franklin Co, Pa, about 5 miles from Mercersburg, offers reward for missing horse/Distiller wanted - James Prather living near Mr. Harbine's Tavern, at the Big Spring/Henry Adam exec of John Adam, gives notice that notes given at sale of pers est of decd, are now due/John Stover requests those indebted to him while he kept tavern in Hagers Town, to pay Robert Douglass/James Hughes, 3 miles from Hagers Town, has taken up stray heifers

387. EAM Sep 9 1808/Died Mon morning last after a lingering illness, Mrs. Susanna Geiger, relict of late John Geiger, of this town, in the 48th year of her age/John Combs exec of Coleman Combs, requests payment on notes due from sale of prop of decd/Roger Perry, of Allegany Co, adm of William Shircliff, late of Allegany Co, decd/Mary Helm and John Ashbury, adm of Thomas Helm, to sell at late dwelling of Thomas Helm, in Williamport, his pers est

388. EAM Sep 16 1808/Died Sun night last after a few days illness, John Clagett, inhabitant of this co; remains interred in Prot. Epis burying ground in the vicinity of this town/Persons who made purchases at sale of pers est of Michael Lowry are notified that their obligations have become due - Barbara Lowry and George Lowry, adm/Reward offered for deserters from the rendezvous in Hagers Town, on Monday night, 12th inst.: (1) Samuel Vincent, 5 ft 8 inch, 21 years old, fair complexion, blue eyes, dark hair, born in Maryland, and lately res in Greencastle, Pa, by profession a tailor, a little round shoulders; took with him a brown coat, two pair of green linen pantaloons, and two shirts ruffled at the bottom ; (2) Elias Gassaway born in Maryland near Frederick-town, 5 ft 8 inch, fair complexion, face has the appearance of his having been addicted to liquor, grey eyes, light brown hair and by profession a laborer; took with him a blue coat, a green linen frock fringed with yellow, two pair green linen pantaloons, and two shirts ruffled at the bosom - John Ragan, Junr, Capt. U.S. Rifle Corps/Hugh Caldwell/Robert Hughes certifies that Andrew Irwin, living at Major John Beard's, has taken up a stray horse/Henry Strause and John Heddinger apprehended near the Cave, on the Baltimore road, about 6 miles from Hagers Town, a person who calls himself Jacob Baker, who had with him a black gelding (supposed to be stolen); he says he came from Cumberland Co, Pa; and formerly lived in Berlin, Westmoreland Co; he is a blacksmith by trade, about 5 ft 8 inch, about 47 years of age, dark complexioned, dark brown hair, blue eyes, speaks English and German tolerably well/Committed to jail as a runaway, a negro who calls himself Tom, alias Michael Thomas, says he belongs to Robert Locher, living between Winchester and Romney, Fred Co, Va, about 5 ft 6-7 inch, 71-22 years of age/Susanna Russell to rent merchant mill on Antietam, about 2 miles above Hughes's Forge, late the prop of John Russell, decd

389. EAM Sep 23 1808/John Witmer adm of Jacob Ruch/Elizabeth Wolfkill adm of John Wolfkill/Richard M'Daniel in Hagers Town, offers reward for apprentice to the butcher's bus., named Jacob Miller, about 17 years of age, 5 ft 8-9 inch/Moses Nelson to sell plantation, late the prop of John Eberhart, decd, 200 a., lying between Green-Castle and Hagers Town, in Franklin Co, adj Brumbaugh, 1/2 miles from Md. line/William B. Williams, offers reward for horse missing from Miller's Mill, near Williamsport

390. EAM Sep 30 1808/Married at Mercersburg, Pa, Mon last, by Rev Dr. King, Dr. Peter W. Little, to Miss Mary Parker, of that town/Geo: J. Harry surviving execs of Jacob Harry to sell at late dwelling of Mary E. Harry, decd, pers prop of decd/Edmund M'Coy and Robert Cheney, adm, to sell at the late dwelling of John Fond, decd, 1 miles of Samuel Funk's Mill (formerly Christian Newcomer's) pers prop of decd/Jacob D. Dietrick to petition for relief from debts/John Hivling to sell at his dwelling house, on Henry Ankony's old place, 1/2 mile of Stone meeting house, about 2 1/2 miles from Fiery's mill, horses, cows, cattle, sheep and other/Samuel Funk, living at Newcomer's Mill, about 6 miles from Hagers Town, has taken up a stray colt /Barton Bean, living about a mile from Gen. T. Sprigg's place, has taken up a stray cow

391. EAM Oct 7 1808/Married Tues last by Rev Bower, Hon. John Buchanan, to Miss Sophia Williams, dau of Elie Williams, Esq., of this co/Michael Kessinger has rented Captain Daniel Stull's Mill

392. EAM Oct 14 1808/Deserted from the rendezvous in Hagers Town, Jacob Caufman, 5 ft 6 inch, 28, fair complexion, blue eyes, brown hair, born in Va, by profession a laborer - John Ragan, Junr. Capt. U.S. Rifle Corps /Michael Yerger to sell house in Market St, Hagers Town/Pair of black saddle bags left at tavern of John Cook, Hagers Town/Deserted from the rendezvous in Hagers Town, Jacob Rinehart, 5 ft 8 1/4 inch, 20, dark complexion, hazel eyes, brown hair, born in Pa, by profession a laborer; has a piece out of this side of his right eye, some marks on his arms made with India Ink - John Ragan, Junr. Capt. U.S. Rifle Corps.

393. EAM Oct 21 1808/Committed to jail as a runaway a negro man Philip, says he belongs to Margaret Rucket of Orange Co,Va, about 5 ft 5 inch, about 30/Committed to jail of Wash Co, negro man, who calls himself Jerry, says he belongs to Elijah Edwards of Orange Co, Va, 5 ft 7 inch, about 30/John Ragan, senr. & John Kaelhofer, saddlers & harness makers, have removed their shop to brick house nearly opp Mr. Beltzhoover's tavern

394. EAM Oct 28 1808/John M'Alester, Greenwood Mills, near Winchester, Va, offers reward for negro men, Dick, between 30 and 40 and Abram, about 21 born in N. Carolina/John Berry, within 1 mile of John T. Mason's mill, Wash Co, to sell horses, cows, cattle, sheep, and other

395. EAM Nov 4 1808/Frederick Zigler, living near Christian Lantz's mill, has taken up a stray mare/New Goods - George Binkley/George Nigh and Samuel Hogmire, exec, to sell at the lae res of Henry Snyder, decd, about 5 miles from Hagers Town, pers prop of decd/Samuel Ross to sell two houses on corner

of public square in Williamsport, or two story log house a short distance brom Mr. Brosius's Tavern

396. EAM Nov 11 1808/Hagers Town Bank - Dividend declared - Elie Beatty, Cash'r/John Harry and George Harry, exec, to sell pers est of Susanna Geiger, Hagers Town, decd/George Rutter, to petition for relief from debts/Joseph C. Kellar candidate for sheriff

397. EAM Nov 18 1808/Died Tues morning last at his res near this town, after a few days illness, James Hughes, leaving wife and 3 small children; buried in Port Episc burial ground/Chancery decree to record deed executed by Joseph Crawford to complainant Joseph Slagle on 10 Oct 1805/Jacob Fiegley forewarns persons from trusting his wife Polly Fiegley as he is determined not to pay any contracts she may make/Polly Fiegley cautions that she holds herself totally exonerated from all obligations to Jacob Fiegley and is determined not to pay any debts of his contracting

398. EAM Nov 25 1808/Negro named Frank Johnston, convicted at the last court, held in this place, of the crime of furnishing arsenic, to poison a negro girl, the prop of Thomas B. Hall, Esq., to be executed this day at 12 o'clock/Jacob Miller, senr., Hagers Town, offers reward for missing gelding /David Shonk has lost a red morocco pocket book between Blackford's Ferry and William Zigler's Store/Isaac Patrick has commenced the bus. of coverlet, counterpane, carpet and diaper weaving in Funkstown, near opp Jacob Knode's Tavern

399. EAM Dec 2 1808/Died Frid morning 25th inst, at his seat near Green-Castle, in Franklin Co, Major General Robert Johnston, aged 58 years/Died same day at Frederick Town, Richard Potts, Esq. and old and respectable inhabitant of that place/Land for sale adj lands of Henry Ankony and Samuel Miller, 270 a., about 9 miles from Hagers Town, prop of heirs and represent-atives of Michael Kiernan, the younger, decd - Jacob Zeller, Walter Boyd, Jacob Sibert/To sell at his dwelling on Ringgold's Manor, various prop including cider and cider royal - Hugh Stewart/Christian Fechtig to sell lots in vicinity of Harry's town, at George Smith's Tavern/Sale at late dwelling house of General Robert Johnston, decd, Antrim township, Pa, horses, &c. - Archibald Bard, John Findlay, Robt. Johnston of John, exec

400. EAM Dec 9 1808/Married Tues evening last by Rev Rahauser, Peter Cromer to Miss Elizabeth Keller, dau of Caspar Keller, all of this town/Henry Lewis is appointed Director of the Hagers Town Bank/Ringgold & Boerstler have opened a store near the courthouse in Hagers Town/Charlotte Muse and William Muse, adm of Sanford Muse/Tenth Regt. ordered to meet at Sharpsburgh - Lieut. Col. S. Ringgold, John L. Beall, Adj. 10th Regt., Md. Militia /Partnership of John Hogg and John Irwin, Williamsport, is dissolved

401. EAM Dec 16 1808/23 negros for sale with horses, cattle, sheep and other, prop of James Peter, at house of Anthony Tracy on Senaka - David Peter, adm, Georgetown/John West has rented the Grist and Merchant Mill, lately owned by John Russell, about 1 mile from Christian Lantz's Mill, and 6 from Hagers Town/Thomas Williams has taken up stray calves/Jacob Kershner

requests settlement of accounts/Caleb Tarleton, 1 1/2 mile from Hagers Town, has taken up a stray cow/Farm for rent, 350 a. - Tench Ringgold

402. EAM Dec 16 1808/24th Regt of Maryland Militia to parade opp Colonel's Quarters at 9 o'clock Sat 17th inst, provided with 6 rounds of blunt cartridges, for the purpose of ascertaining whether a sufficient number of Volunteers will tender their services to the government. It is expected, that at this crisis, a sufficient number of Volunteers will offer to prevent a draft. By order of Liuet. Col. Jacob Schnebly, U. Lawrence, 24th Regt /John West has rented the Grist and Merchant Mill lately owned by John Russell, 1 mile from Christian Lantz's Mill/Thomas Williams has taken up a stray calf/Jacob Kershner requests persons indebted to him to settle their accounts/Caleb Tarleton, 1 1/2 miles from Hagers Town, has taken up a stray cow

403. EAM Dec 23 1808/Married last evening at the house of George Bean, near Hagers Town, by Rev Bower, Hugh Bean, to Miss Alice Nowell; and at the same time, James Harper to Miss Sarah Bean, all of this co/A large number of militiamen volunteered Sat last - All the men of Capt. O.H. Williams' troop called American Blues, tendered their services/Philip Kershner, 4 miles from Hagers Town, offers reward for missing hogs/John Brewer, Junr., 2 miles from John T. Mason's Mill, has taken up a stray gelding/A bay horse was left at the tavern of Thomas Shuman, Hagers Town, by a person named Samuel Crawford with a wagon saddle and an old bridle/Frederick Miller, Druggist & Apothecary, Hagers Town, has just received and has for sale: bloom raisins, zand currants, almonds (soft shell), filberts, mace, cloves, cinnamon & nutmegs

404. EAM Dec 30 1808/On Monday 12th inbst, the 29th Regiment of Md Militia, under the command of Col. Barrick, met at Woodsbury, in compliance with general orders. Col. Barrick delivered a handsome address, recommending unity and harmony to his regiment, and beseeching them to discard those rancorous feelings of party spirit, which if persevered in, would make us an easy prey to our enemies/Married Tues evening last, by Rev Schmucker, George Stonebreaker, Merchant, to Miss Elizabeth Neff, dau of George Neff, of this town/Plantation for rent, lately occ by James Hughes, decd - Henry Lewis /Thomas B. Hall, having established his res in Hagers Town, will attend to the bus. of his profession in the Room occ by the Register of Wills/To sell the prop of Jane Short, decd, a corner lot and houses in Boonsborough - John Brandner, Frederick Woolf, Michael Beard, Jacob Summers, Wm. Good, Junr. - Boonsborough

405. EAM Jan 6 1809/Daniel Middlekauff has taken up a stray colt/James Clare to lease for 4-5 years his farm in Berkeley Co, whereon Benjamin Pendleton now lives on the head of Falling Waters on the road from Martinsburg to Williamsport/Anna Hammett adm of David Hammett, requests payment of notes given at sale of pers prop of decd to Alexander Neill, merchant/John Westeberger, 5 miles from Hagers Town, offers reward for stolen mare/John S. Williams, No. 246, Market St. Balt, purchases and receives on consignment, country produce of every description, viz. tobacco, flour, hemp, whisky, iron, &c./Wm. L. Brent offers reward for information on thief or thieves who broke open his office during his absence from home some few weeks ago

The Maryland Herald and Hagers-town Advertiser

406. EAM Jan 13 1809/Tench Ringold forewarns person from hunting on his farms/Charles Worland, Hagers Town, requests settlement of accounts

407. EAM Jan 20 1809/James Clare, Long Marsh, Fred Co, Va, to sell farm in Berkeley, Va/Blacksmith's shop and tools with house and garden to be rented, 2 miles from Hughes's Forge - William Allinder/George North, 1/2 mile from John Fiery's mill, has taken up a stray red bull/Elijah Cheney requests persons with claims agnst est of Joseph Cheney, decd, to present same/Martin Startzman, 1 mile from Hagers Town, offers reward for missing bay horse

408. EAM Jan 27 1809/Married Tues evening last by Rev Bower, George C. Smoot, Esq. Register of Wills, to Miss Matilda Stull dau of late Col. John Stull, of this co/William Gabby, exec, to sell prop of John Gabby, decd, 123 1/2 a., on Antietam/Blacksmith wanted; apply at Col. Samuel Ringgold's mill /Yellow frame house lately occ by Wm. L. Brent to be rented, next door to Samuel Hughes - Jonathan Hager/George Bean, living on Mr. U. Lawrence's Farm, has two stout negro men available for hire.

409. EAM Feb 3 1809/American Manufactory - George Miller and Edward A. Gibbs, Hagers Town, have commenced the spinning of cotton; have on hand cotton yarn of different sizes, suitable for common use/Ringgold & Boerstler have removed their store to Col. Ringgold's Mill/Frances Monahan offers her house & lot to be let/Meeting of the Commisssioners of the Tax - Rezin Davis, Clk/House to be rented, 6 miles from Hagers Town on road to Mercersburg - Josiah Price/Samuel Miller, living on West Conococheague, within half a mile of Kershner's Fording, has taken up a stray cow

410. EAM Feb 10 1809/Died in this town Sat morning last, after a short illness, John Rhape, in the 67th year of his age/Died yesterday morning, in this town, in an advanced age, Adam Doyle/Boonsborough Church Lottery - George Scott, John Brandner, Henry Nyman, John Ludy, Henry Locher, jun, George Troutman, managers/Persons indebted to est of John Russell, are requested to make payment to Thomas Edwards, Innkeeper, Williamsport - Susanna Russell, Jacob Lambert and William Gabby - adm/John Houck to sell at his dwelling about 2 miles from Miller's Mill (formerly Swingley's), negro boy, about 15 years old, horses, cows, sheep, hogs, farming utensils and household furniture to tedious to mention; also plantation adj land with Jacob Kershner and near Ritter's Old Fording

411. EAM Feb 17 1809/Lottery for finishing the steeple and discharging the arrears of the Lutheran congregation in Hagers Town - George Nigh, George Shank, Peter Miller, John Kaussler, Jacob Young, managers/Mary Snider and Geo. Snider, exec, to sell prop of Casper Snider, decd, tract 3 miles from Williamsport/Jacob Ridenour exec of Jacob Ridenour/Sale of Mills and lands by virtue of deed of trust from Henry Ambrose to Ludwick Kemp, decd; Peter Shover, living near the lands will shew them - Henry Kemp, Christian Kemp /Cash for old copper and brass - John Reynolds/Michael Hensell and Henry Couchman, exec of Laurence Hensell, Jefferson Co, to sell 10 a. near Opeckon Creek, Va/David Harry for George Bomgardner, to sell house now occ by Jacob Myer, near the Poor House/Persons having claims agnst est of James Hughes are requested to exhibit same to Samuel Hughes/Brick house to be rented as a

tavern, nearly opp George Brumbaugh's Tavern - Christian Lantz, Senr

412. EAM Feb 24 1809/Married Tues evening last by Rev Bower, Otho H. W. Stull, to Miss Letitia Hall, both of this co/Married Tues 14th inst by Rev Rahauser, Nathan Cromwell, to Miss Mary Zeller, dau of Capt. Jacob Zeller, all of this co/Chancery sale by Thomas Charlton, Trustee, of 262 a. of Henry Charlton, decd/Wm. & Peter Bowler have rented the Mill formerly occ by Gen. William Reed, 3 miles from Emmittsburg/Daniel Gehr candidate for sheriff /Sale of plantation 10 miles from Hagers Town, 208 a. - Isaac Bowser, at his mill (formerly Eversole's)/John Hiffner and John Baker, exec, at dwelling house of Albertus Hiffner, late of Washington township, Franklin Co, decd, horses, cows, sheep, hogs, grain in the ground, windmill, and other

413. EAM Mar 3 1809/John Fultz and Jacob Lowman adm of Samuel Summey, to sell at late dwelling of decd, about 1 mile from John Wolgamot's Mill and same distance from Stover's Tavern (formerly Langley's), pers prop of decd /Samuel Gardner, living on Cotoctin Creek, about 3 miles from Middle-town, offers reward for stolen horse/George Haun to sell at his dwelling, 3 miles from Hughes's Forge, horses, cows, hogs, farming utensils, 8-day clock and other furniture

414. EAM Mar 17 1809/Married Tues evening last by Rev Bower, Wm. Fitzhugh, Jun, to Miss Sophia Clagett, dau of late John Clagett, of this co/Married same evening by Rev Rahauser, Frederick Dietrick, to Miss Eve Gilbert dau of Christian Gilbert of this co/Land for sale, 227 a., in Berkeley Co, on Opeckon Creek, about 1 mile from the Potomac River - Apply to George Strode on the premises, or James Forman, Forman's Ferry/Jacob Reichard and Daniel Reichard, exec of Jacob Reichard

415. EAM Mar 24 1809/Died Fri evening, 17th inst, in this town, Col. Rezin Davis, in the 54th year of his age; remains interred with military honors, in the Prot Episc burial ground. Col Davis took an active part in the rev war, since which he has filled the office of Sheriff and acted as Coroner of this co for many years/Married Tues evening last, by Rev Schmucker, William Woltz, to Miss Mary Simkins, dau of Wm. Simkins of this co/Married last evening by Rev Schmucker, Adam Leopard, to Miss Mary Deterly, both of this town/William L. Brent has removed his office to the house belonging to George Beltzhoover, opp Hagers Town Bank/Stone house for rent in Boonsborough - George Scott, Boonsborough/Tract for sale, 105 a., 2 miles from Boonsborough - Peter Summers/House for rent, now occ by Miss Davis's on Main st in Williamsport; apply to John C. Williams near Williamsport or to subscriber, John I. Stull, in Hagers Town/Mill and lands for sale, 400 a., at the mouth of Town creek - Thomas Beall, of Samuel, Cumberland/Peter Baker offers reward for information on robbery of his weaving shop in Boonsborough /Sale of house now occ by subscriber Samuel Beeler, in Hagers Town, near German Reformed Church

416. EAM Mar 31 1809/Married Thurs 16th inst by Rev Craver, Lewis Bireley, papermaker, to Mrs. Catharine Zimmerman, all of Fred. Co/Sale at late dwelling of Rezin Davis, decd, of large brick house adj Mr. Ferguson's store, negro man, woman and two children and other - Eleanor Davis/Joseph

Hite to sell plantation whereon he now lives, 400 a., Jefferson Co, Va
/Samuel B. Davis has removed his school to house formerly occ by George
Sharkey, decd, Back St, near the Public Spring/The horse Paul Jones will
stand this season at the farm of subscriber, David Washabaugh, where Peter
Adam formerly lived, 1 1/2 miles from Col. David Schnebly's, 1 mile from
Capt. Jacob Zeller's/Joseph Penticost, Washington, Pa, offers reward for
negro man George Jones, short, about 33

417. EAM Apr 7 1809/Married Thurs 30th ult by Rev Schmucker, Joseph C.
Kellar to Miss Elizabeth Crampton, dau of Thomas Crampton, Esq. of this
co/Milton H. Sackett has lately removed from Greencastle to Williamsport, in
the Tavern Stand of Samuel Porter, lately occ by William M'Coy/William
Davis, Junr. living near Hagers Town, has taken up a stray horse and mare
/Sale of pers est of decd, William Cromwell, on Conococheague, 8 miles from
Hagers Town - G. Graff, exec/Nicholas Fritz, near Christian Lantz's mill,
has taken up a stray horse/David Fesler cautions whereas his wife Mary
Fesler, has eloped from his bed and board, without any just cause, he is
determined to pay no debts of her contracting/Charlotte Muse and William
Muse, adm of Sanford Muse

418. EAM Apr 14 1809/Married Tues 4th inst by Rev John Fenwick, William L.
Brent, Esq. of this place, to Miss Maria Fenwick, dau of Col. James Fenwick
of Welonton, Charles Co, Md/Recommended for directors of Hagers Town Bank:
Martin Kershner, Matthias Shaffner, Alexander Neill, William Fitzhugh,
Samuel Hughes, William Heyser, Jacob Zeller - for Wash Co; David Lynn for
Allegany Co; Christian Kellar for Balt/Died Wed morning last, in the bloom
of life, after a lingering illness, Miss Elizabeth Hughes, dau of Col. D.
Hughes, of this co/Erasmus Garrott, living on the Merryland Tract, offers
reward for negro named Nace, who calls himself Nace Johnson, 5 ft 8-10 inch,
likely fellow, 23-24/Catharine Gale and John Combs, adm, to sell at the late
dwelling of William Gale, decd, on Ringgold's Manor, pers prop of decd/The
horse Lovelace will be let to mares this season at George Pennel's stable in
Green-Castle - Michael Coskery. Horse certified by James M'Lanaghan, Thomas
M'Lanaghan, John Johnston/George M. Irving, joiner & cabinet maker, has
removed to shop lately occ by Mr. Steck, nearly opp Mr. Bell's Pottery, in
the Main St/Committed to jail as a runaway, negro man who calls himself
George Jones alias George Evans, says he belongs to Joseph Penticost, of
Wash Co, Pa

419. EAM Apr 19 1809/John L. Beall to open a school in Hagers Town/Mary
Helm offers reward for horse which strayed from her in Williamsport/Dividend
due on est of Matthias Knode, decd

420. EAM Apr 26 1809/Others recommended as Directors of the Hagers Town
Bank: Elie Williams, Upton Lawrence, Jacob T. Towson, and John Harry all of
Wash Co, and John B. Bell and James Scott, Allegany Co/Peter Troxell,
weaver, has taken the house formerly occ by Maxwell Welsh, Schoolmaster, a
few doors below the jail/The horse, Virgin Grey, will stand the ensuing
season at John Showman's near Harleys store and George Beltzhoover's in
Hagers Town - Isaac Griffith; certified by John Smith, Wm. Jinkins, Benjamin
Price, Loudon Co, Va/Edmund M'Coy and Robert Cheney adm of John Bond, give
notice that notes are due on the sale of pers prop of decd/John Hooper

offers reward for geldings which strayed from his tavern, 1 mile from Noland's Ferry

421. EAM May 3 1809/Robert Douglass, Hagers Town, offers reward for apprentice to the weaving bus., named Jonathan Shupe, about 5 ft 9-10 inch, 18 years of age, brown hair inclined to curl, full face, ruddy complexion, can speak English and German tolerably well/Bolting cloths - to be sold unusually low - Alexander Neill

422. EAM May 10 1809/House to be sold now occ by subscriber, Christian Fechtig, next door to Matthias Shaffner/Sale at late dwelling of Jeremiah Chapline, 2 miles from Sharpsburg, pers est of decd, negroes, two stills with tubs, and other - Elizabeth Chapline/Francis M'Namee, 4 miles from Sharpsburg, has taken up a stray mare/Jacob Hewitt, living near Mount Aetna Furnace, has taken up a stray colt/Benjamin & P. Jobson to sell tract, 117 1/4 a., 1 1/2 miles from Hancock-town/Thomas Shaw has lost a red morocco pocket book/Casper Keller, Keeper of the Work House, offers reward for those involved in breaking into the Work House in Hagers Town from which three women of ill-fame, by the names of Sally Fisher, Eliza Hamilton & Peggy Glen made their escape

423. EAM May 17 1809/Married Thurs evening last by Rev Rahauser, Jacob Kershner, to Miss Mary Kershner, dau of Philip Kershner, of this co/Married Sun evening 1sat by Rev Bower, Richard Geary, to Miss Margaret White, both of this town/John Seitz has opened a House of Entertainment in Hagers Town at the sign of the Duck in Market St. /New Hat manufactory in the house formerly occ by Conrad Coffroth - Abraham Force

424. EAM May 31 1809/Elizabeth Nesbitt, Jonathan Nesbitt and Martin Myer, adm of Peter Nesbitt/Barton Bean, living near Gen. Sprigg's Mill has taken up a stray mare/George Troutman, Boonsborough, intending to move from this place, to requests settlement of accounts

425. EAM Jun 7 1809/Samuel Frederick, on Philip Starn's farm, 7 miles from Hagers Town, offers reward for missing horse

426. EAM Jun 14 1809/John Creager, saddler, has removed to house formerly occ by his father, Henry Creager, in the Back st, within three doors of Abraham King's Blacksmith Shop opp shop of Jacob King, Wagon maker

427. EAM Jun 21 1809/Committed to gaol of Wash Co, Negro man named James Brown, 23-24, 5 ft 6-7 inch; says he belongs to Mr. Biggs, who was taking him to Carolina and that he was formerly prop of John Sutton on the Eastern Shore, Md/Mrs. Halfpenny, midwife, has moved from Williamsport to house of Mrs. Kreps, in Hagers Town, 2 doors below the shop of George Kreps, Gunsmith, in the Back St/Charles Ridenour, living near Charleton's Gap, has taken up a stray horse/Mary Helm and John Ashberry, adm, requests person indebted to est of Thomas Helm, late of Williamsport, decd, to make payment

428. EAM Jun 28 1809/Kessinger & Emmert have commenced bus. in the new brick house lately occ by Peter Artz - Summer Goods/New store - Kausley &

The Maryland Herald and Hagers-town Advertiser

Graff have commenced bus. at the stand formerly occ by Henry Middlekauff, hatter, next door to George Binkley's store - Dry Goods & Groceries

429. EAM Jul 5 1809/Married Sun evening last by Rev Rotroff, George Hawken to Miss Margaret Kreps, dau of George Kreps of this town/Died Sun morning last at his res near Newcomer's Mill, after a lingering illness, Richard Williams, in the 72nd year of his age/Jacob Huyett and Daniel Huyett, exec of Margaret Snider

430. EAM Jul 12 1809/Elizabeth Rahp and Matthias Shaffner, exec of John Rahp, to sell stone house in Hagers Town, opp the Bank, late prop of decd

431. EAM Jul 19 1809/Died last evening, after a lingering illness, Mrs. Catharine Hawken, mother of Christian Hawken of this town, in the 90th year of her age

432. EAM Jul 26 1809/Died Mon morning last, Miss Elizabeth Martini, dau of George Martini, of this town, in the 21st year of her age/Married Mon evening last, by Rev Schmucker, George Smith, Painter & Glazier, to Miss Elizabeth Dussing, dau of Philip Dussing, all of this town/Susanna Robey, living on Chews Farm, has taken up a stray mare

433. EAM Aug 2 1809/Anthony Stake, Williamsport, has taken up a stray horse

434. EAM Aug 9 1809/Fulling & dying 2 miles from Daniel Kershner at the Cross roads - Isaac Hershey, John Gibboney, Jun.

435. EAM Aug 16 1809/Samuel Spicklar, 5 miles from Hagers Town, offers reward for missing horse/Benjamin Cushwa gives notice to purchasers at the sale of John Berry's prop that their notes are due

436. EAM Aug 23 1809/Jacob Mong, near Trindle's mill, has taken up a stray mare/John Mazabach offers reward for horse stolen out of the stable of Henry Shaffer, in Funks-Town

437. EAM Aug 30 1809/William Hammett, living near Col. Hughes's Furnace, has taken up a stray steer/John Reynolds to apply for relief from debts/John Schwingle, 3 miles from Hagers Town, offers reward for negro woman, named Kate, 28-30/Patrick Quinn, Waynesburg, Franklin Co, Pa, offers reward for missing horse/David Fesler cautions the public not to harbor or trust his wife, Mary Fesler, as she has without any just cause, eloped from his bed

438. EAM Sep 6 1809/Married Sun evening last by Rev Rahauser, Sebastian Fink to Miss Mary M'Clure, both of this town/Joseph W. Lawrence, 6 miles from Fred Town, offers reward for negro boy Jacob about 18; has a sister in Balt/John Resley and David Cushwa, adm, to sell at late dwelling house of George Resley, decd, 2 miles from Hancock-town, pers prop of decd/Benjamin Laight, Hagers Town, offers reward for apprentice to bricklaying bus., named George Pinkler, about 19, 5 ft 7-8 inch, dark hair, stoop shouldered, talks quick, good well digger/Sale at Henry Evey's plantation on Bever Creek, 1 mile from Peter Newcomer's Mill, horses, cows, &c.

439. EAM Sep 13 1809/Christian Fechtig, Hagers Town, offers reward for apprentice to shoemaking bus., named John Kinckle, about 20, 5 ft 9-10 inch, sandy hair, walks lame/Dissolution of partnership of Joseph Perrin and Henry Sweitzer/Chancery sale for creditors of James Chapline

440. EAM Sep 20 1809/James Prather to sell by virtue of a deed of trust to him by Thomas Ford, at Daniel Harbine's Tavern, Big-Spring, tract called Ford's Neck/Chancery sale of lands in Allegany Co, prop of John Fitzhugh

441. EAM Sep 27 1809/Sale in Hagers Town of part of pers est of Samuel L. Chew, formerly of Queen Ann's Co, decd, 40 negroes - Benjamin Chambers, Atty for Thomas M. Forman, adm of Col. S. L. Chew, decd/Susanna Foutz, Jacob Foutz and Jacob Alter, exec, to sell plantation of Frederick Foutz, decd, 213 a.

442. EAM Oct 4 1809/Married last evening by Rev Rotroff, John Hawken to Miss Hannah Long, dau of John Long, of this co/David Middelkauff and Ann Hughes, near Hagers Town, offer reward for negro man Sam Baltimore, aged 50-55, and his wife Lucy, about 30, and Charles Bowman, 35-40/Chancery sale of land on which Norman Bruce formerly lived and whereon William Bayly lived a few years since and was conveyed by Walter Mackall to Philip B. Key - James S. Morsell, Trustee/Dissolution of partnership of Michael Kessinger and George Emmert/Benjamin Swingle and Peter Light, exec, to sell at house of James Amos, 4 miles from Williamsport, pers prop of Philip Swingle, decd/Samuel & John Perry or George Shiras, Pittsburgh, to pay reward for negro man Ned, who ran away from subscribers from Stotler's Tavern, west end of the dry Ridge, Bedford Co, Pa, on his way from Frederick Town to Pittsburg. We purchased Ned in Frederick Town jail

443. EAM Nov 1 1809/Died Thurs morning last, after a short illness, Mrs. Christiana Beard, wife of Major John Beard, of this co, in the 49th year of her age/J. Dietz, book-binder, continues his bus. at the 2nd door above the dwelling of Rev Rahauser in the Back St/Daniel Rench, 1 mile from Hagers Town, offers reward for missing steers/John Ashburg, living on Ringgold's manor, has taken up a stray mule/Isaac Bechtel to sell plantation whereon he now lives, on Licking creek, 379 a.

444. EAM Nov 8 1809/William Davis, jun., living on Henry Lewis's place, about 3 miles from Hagers Town, to sell 145 a. 5 miles above Wiliamsport, adj land formerly occ by Walter Macall, decd/Geo. G. Ross, offers reward for horse which strayed from farm of Dr. Pindell

445. EAM Nov 22 1809/Jesse Rockhold, living on Robert M'Kee's plantation, near the Penn line, about 5 miles from Hagers Town, has taken up a stray horse

446. EAM Nov 29 1809/Married at Huntingdon, Pa, Tues the 14th inst. by Rev Johnston, Daniel Huyett of Wash Co, Md, to Miss Mary Swope, dau of Peter Swope, merchant, of that Borough/Tobacco manufactory, 2 doors above James Ferguson's store, now Kennedy's, in Hagers Town - A. M. Waugh/Frederick Kehler, in Funks-town, intends to broach the two first barrels of wine of his own cultivation on 21 Dec and to sell the same by the quart/Charles

Davis, 1 mile from Hagers Town, offers reward for missing mare/Jonathan Kershner has applied to the Court of Common Please of Franklin Co, Pa, for the beneift of the insolvent laws

447. EAM Dec 6 1809/Married Thurs last by Rev Rahauser, Ludwick Zeigler, to Miss Catharine Lantz, dau of Geo: Lantz, late of Wash Co/Chancery court, Allegany Co, case of Moses Robinett agnst Robert Britt and John Britt, heirs at law of Robert Britt, decd, and John B. Beall and Josiah Beall of Thomas exec of Josiah Beall of Josiah agnst the same, to sell real est of Robert Britt, decd, so much as necessary for payments of costs and debts of the original suits at law agnst Sarah Britt, adm of the aforesaid, as stated in the bills of the complainants, and admitted in the answers of Robert and John Britt by their guardian; land within three miles of Cumberland on Evitt's Creek - Beal Howard, Trustee/Wendel Schechter, exec, to sell log dwelling in Franklin st adj George Martini's, now occ by John Greiner. On the premises are a blacksmith shop, stable and pump of excellent water/Josiah Price cautions persons from taking assignments on notes given to George M'Cullough of Allegany Co/John Heffner and John Baker, exec, to sell plantation, agreeably to will of Albertus Heffner, decd/Apprentice to the tayloring bus. wanted - Henry Deihl

448. EAM Dec 13 1809/Varle's map of Wash and Fred Countries (3rd edition) now available at $4.00 per copy/George Hawken, Gunsmith, has lately commenced bus in shop next door to John Kausler, 3rd door below Bank/Sale by Peter Troxel of plantation whereon he lives, 5 miles from Isaac Bechtel's mill/Jacob Barnett, Jun. & Henry M'Laughlin, trustees for the sale of the real est devised by Doctor Henry Schnebly to the heirs of Elizabeth Barnett, to sell plantation 1 mile from Lantz's Mill on Antietam, 300 a.; Henry Barnett who lives on the land will shew it; also a tract of 150 a. on Potomack river; Mr. Hon who lives on the land will shew it

449. EAM Dec 20 1809/Henry Startzman, 2 miles from Hagers Town, offers reward for stolen horse/George Graff adm of William Cromwell gives notice that notes on the sale of pers prop of decd are due/Wm. Heyser to sell brick house which has been occ as a tavern for about 12 years on corner of Court house square in Hagers Town, now kept by George Smith/Milton H. Sackett adm of John Keefer, to sell pers est of decd at house of decd, in Williampsort/Henry Fiery, 10 miles from Hagers Town, has taken up a stray bull

450. EAM Dec 27 1809/Married Tues 19th inst. by Rev Rahauser of Emmittsburg, Frederick Eyler to Miss Margaret Williar, dau of Andrew Williar, of Harbaugh's Valley, Frederick Co/Sale of plantation on which John Cunningham now lives, 1 1/2 mile from Rev Kennedy's Meeting house in Franklin Co, Pa, 222 a. - John Findlay, Archd. Baird, Robert Johnston, exec of Dr. Robt. Johnston, decd/Elizabeth Yakle and Henry Yakle adm of Jacob Yakle

451. EAM Jan 3 1810/Sat last, Edward Brann committed to jail of Wash Co, charged with murder of Elizabeth Murphy, a child about 10 or 11 years old, near M'Pherson and Brinn's Iron Works about 4 miles from Sharpsburgh/Sale in pursuance to order of Orphans' Court of Wash Co, the right which Jacob

Rohrer, decd to lands directed by will of decd, to be sold in Pa and Va
-George Nigh, Agent for the Exec/Sale of Paper mill, grist and saw mill, 50
a., on Antietam Creek - apply to George Miller or John Julius/Gera South
offers reward for William Downey, apprentice to the boot & shoe making bus.,
about 20, 5 ft 8-9 inch/John Holtzman to apply for relief from debts/A
distribution of assets in the hands of Mary Knode, surviving adm of Matthias
Knode/Chancery case - petition to record deed William Good executed to
Joseph Chapline

452. EAM Jan 10 1810/Henry Lewis to sell at the Coffee house in Hagers
Town: (1) house occ by John Buchanan; (2) apartments above office of Geo: C.
Smoot now occ by Adam Leopard; store now occ by Messrs. Kausler and Grove

453. EAM Jan 17 1810/Died on Thurs evening last in this town after a severe
illness, Mrs. Rosanna Heister, relict of late Gen. Daniel Heister, in the
58th year of her age; remains deposited in the family vault by side of her
husband, near the German Reformed Church in this town/P. Edwards has come at
this time with the view of making his future place of res (in Hagers Town),
to open a school/Benjamin Steel, stocking weaver to carry on bus. at his old
stand opp dwelling of Henry Middlekauff/Chancery sale of real est of John T.
Goff, decd, by James C. Goff/Wm. O. Sprigg adm of Thomas Sprigg, to sell
pers est of Thomas Sprigg

454. EAM Jan 24 1810/Died in the vicinity of this town, Mon evening last,
Mrs. Julian Crumbauch, widow of late John Crumbauch, in the 81st year of her
age/Christian Hager and Philip Wingart, exec, to sell pers est of Rosanna
Heiser, decd/Jacob Kessinger exec of George Kessinger

455. EAM Jan 31 1810/Nathan Cromwell, living on the premises, to sell
plantation whereon he now lives, 8 miles from Hagers Town, 3 from Hoffer's
mill; apply to Jacob Zeller near the premises or to the subscriber/Henry
Welty having become the proprietor of all the outstanding debts contracted
at the Carding and Spinning Factory in Hagers Town, intends to leave this
place, request persons indebted to pay dues/William Blakemore, adm of Thomas
Ford/George Graff adm of William Cromwell

456. EAM Feb 7 1810/Married Thurs last by Rev Rahauser, Jacob Chambers, to
Miss Joanna M'Mahon, both of this co/Married Sun evening last by Rev
Rahauser, Jacob I. Ohr to Miss Elizabeth Boerstler, dau of Dr. Christian
Boerstler, of Funks-town, Wash Co/Samuel Ringgold and William S. Compton,
Trustees of William Haddaway, to sell at the farm on which William Haddaway
lives, negroes and other/John Buchanan, Trustee, to sell lands for the
payment of the debts of the late John Rench, decd, part of real est of said
Rench, adj lands of Messrs. Charles Carroll, John Hager and Jacob Rench.
Land will be shewn by Jacob Rench

457. EAM Feb 14 1810/Married Thurs last by Rev Bower, John Hall of
Chamersburg, Pa, to Miss Harriet Miller, dau of William Miller of this
co/Married in Harford Co, Md, Sunday 28 Jan last by Rev Allen, William
Allinder of Wash Co, Md, to Miss Mary Foster, dau of Jesse Foster/Michael
Horsh to sell at his plantation, 1 1/2 miles from Hughes's Furnace, horses,
etc./James Sterrett to sell tract, 406 a. in Wharton Township, Fayette Co,

Pa/Edmund M'Coy, on Antietam Creek, near Sharer's mill, has taken up a stray shoot (shoat)

458. EAM Feb 21 1810/Died suddenly at his res near West Conococheague on Thurs evening, 15th inst, Jacob Seibert, an old inhabitant of this co/Mrs. Ann Rawlins returns sincere thanks to those who have favored here with the care of their children and informs them that she has employed an assistant - Eliza Rawlings, Hagers Town/Meadow Ground for sale - Samuel Rohrer/Committed to gaol, a negro man who calls himself William Pane; and says he belongs to Mrs. Priscilla Courts of Charles Co, Md, about 23, 5 ft 9 inch

459. EAM Feb 28 1810/Died Mon 12th inst. Mrs. Margaret Clarke, consort of George Clark, Esq. of Green-Castle, Pa/Committed to jail of Cumberland Co, negro man who calls himself James Smith, says his master is of the name of Robert Smith, and lives on Antietam Creek in Md, near the confluence of Beaver creek/Chancery case - William and George Oethers vs James Dimmitt and John Compton - to obtain decree for the conveyance of lots westward of Fort Cumberland that James Simmitt contracted to convey to complainants/Sale a/George Foutz to sell at res of Frederick Foutz, decd, 4 miles from Hagers Town, horses, cows, cattle, grain, furniture, wind-mill, &c./Samuel Rohrer request payment of ground rent in Rohrer's addition to Hagers Town/Henry Shafer has on hand a quantity of ground plaster Paris

460. EAM Mar 7 1810/Sale at dwelling house of subscriber near Peter Baker's Old Farm, horses, &c. - Edward Hays/Sale of 800 a. of land in Berkeley Co, Va, known as Meadow Branch - Jacob Schnebly, John Schnebly and David Schnebly, exec of H. Schnebly. The land will be shewn by John Myers, the tenant/Charles Worland will sell his dwelling in Hagers Town and quantity of saddler's work, furniture, a trooper's uniform with sword, pistols and holsters complete, and other/John Ebert has commenced the comb making bus./Room for rent with the use of the kitchen and cellar in house where he now lives - Jacob Yakle

461. EAM Mar 21 1810/Sale by Edmund Tarlton, living on the plantation of late Major I. Taylor, decd, of horses, cows, furniture and other/Henry Seibert and John Cushwa, adm, to sell at the late dwelling of Jacob Seibert, decd, about 2 miles from res of John T. Mason, pers est of decd, negroes and other

462. EAM Mar 28 1810/Died Sun last in this town, after a lingering illness, William Clagett, Esq., Assoc Judge of the 5th District of Md, remains interred in Prot Epis burial ground/George Rench adm of George Scott to sell 56 negroes at res of decd, Boonsborough/George Graff, adm of Rachel Cromwell/Michael Hauser adm of Robert T. Cary to sell negroes jointly with George French adm of George Scott/Joseph Little, plough & wagon maker, has removed to shop next door to the dwelling of Charles Gelwicks/Thomas Malone offers reward for mare which strayed away from Messrs. Dunn & King's Iron Works, in Path Valley, Franklin Co, Pa/Jacob Shool has commenced carrying on Rope manufactory on the premises formerly occ by Jonathan Hager, opp house of Gotleib Zimmerman, Pump-maker in Hagers Town

463. EAM Apr 4 1810/Married Thurs 22d ult by Rev Blit, Samuel Snavely, of Wash Co, Md, to Miss Margaret Benter, dau of David Benter of Lancaster Co, Pa/Married Sun evening 25th ult by Rev Rahauser, John Scoggins to Miss Catharine Matzabaugh, both of Funks-town, Wash Co/Two steers about 5 years old each, were lately sold by Otho Sprigg, to Messrs George Doyle & Jacob Kaelhofer, which weighed, exclusive of the hides and gut tallow, 2397 lbs./George M'Namee to sell at Stull's Old Mill near Hagers Town, 2 milch cows and furniture/David Zentmoyer, Franklin Co, Pa, offers reward for German indented servant man named George Brant, about 25 years of age, 5 ft 6 inch, brownish hair, a weaver/Bolting cloths - John & Hugh Kennedy

464. EAM Apr 11 1810/Married last evening by Rev Rahauser, Samuel Woltz, Clock and Watchmaker, to Miss Catharine Bowman, all of this town/Williams-port Market will open in a few days under regulations similar to those of Hagers Town (list of regulations given)/William Armor, tailor, has commenced bus. in house lately occ by George Hammer/Peter Troxell, weaver, has removed to house lately occ by George Hammer/William Woltz, cabinet maker, has removed to shop lately occ by William Reynolds/P. Artz & G. Emmert to keep a constant supply of flour at their store/Williams-Port market to open Apr 18th - John Langley, Jacob T. Towson, Daniel Weisel, Thomas Edwards - Comm'rs/Thomas Shuman having declined keeping Tavern, requests settlement of accounts

465. EAM Apr 18 1810/Married Thurs evening last by Rev Rahauser, Dr. Arnold Ferdinand Hanenkampf, to Miss Margaret Umrickhouse, dau of Peter Umrick-house, of this town/John Ramsey, Junr., living near the Burnt Cabins, Dublin Township, Huntingdon Co, Pa, offers reward for stolen mare/David Wilson, saddler, had commenced bus. at shop occ by Charles Worland/Samuel Young adm of Jacob Nickle

466. EAM Apr 25 1810/Died Wed morning 18th inst. at Col. David Schnebly's after a lingering illness, Mrs. Susanna Orndorff, widow of the late John Orndorff in the 39th year of her age, leaving 4 small children/Jacob Knode, living in Funks-town, offers reward for stolen mare/Peter Nigh, 3 miles from Hagers Town, offers reward for stolen mare/Dancing - James Robardet at Samuel Bayly's/E. M'Laughlin continues to keep school/Philip Embich has commenced blue dying in Washington St, Hagers Town, next door to Peter Bell, Potter and near Major Martin Kershner's/Sale of tract in Wash Co, about 2 miles from Booth's mill, 150 a. - Henry Welty, Jacob Welty/Sale of planta-tion 7 miles from Hagers Town - Patrick Sweeny, Joseph Sweeny

467. EAM May 2 1810/Wm . B. Williams adm, to sell pers est of Thomas Williams, decd, near Williamsport/John Hunter, in Hancock-town, to sell Negro girl, about 18/Conrad Smith continues wool carding at Isaac Hottman's mill, formerly John Allison's, half a mile of Greencastle/A. Withney, to act auctioneer/Jacob Shimer to sell at the farm where he now lives, 1/2 mile from Col. David Schnebly's, horses, cows, &c./Jacob Moyers and Martin Funk have erected a wool carding machine at Martin Funk's near the widow Funk's mill, half a mile from Martin Baechtel's fulling mill

468. EAM May 9 1810/Married Sun evening last by Rev Rahauser, Henry Diehl, to Miss Catharine Shank, dau of George Shank, all of this town/Died Wed 2d

inst, after a tedious illness, in the 64th year of her age, Mrs. Margaret Alter, wife of Frederick Alter, of this town/Chancery case - Nathaniel Rochester and Frances Monahan vs Mary and Margaret Sharkey, to obtain sale of real est of George Sharkey, decd for payment of his debts. George Sharkey died seized of lot No. 83 in Hagers Town and indebted to complainants as exec of Timothy Monahan. George Sharkey at the time of his death left the defendants as his only children, who are minors and res out of state of Md/Henry Wertz, Jun. Bedford, Pa, to sell real prop in borough of Bedford: (1) tavern occ by Tho: Moore, at the sign of the Rising Sun, corner of Pitt and Julian Sts; also house near the corner of Pitt and Julian sts, commonly known by the name of Martin Pleiffer's house; and other prop

469. EAM May 16 1810/Sale of house where he now lives - George Kreps, Hagers Town, next door to Christian Stemple's, opp William Brazier's/Peter Miller now carries on the blue dying bus. next door to Mr. Brunner's Tavern in Funks-town/House and half lot for rent in this town, opp Col. A. Ott's - Henry Snyder

470. EAM May 23 1810/Died Thurs night last, after a lingering illness at his farm on West Conococheague, Henry Ankeney, Esq., in the 50th year of his age/George M. Irvine to sell furniture (described)/George Miller has cotton & wool carding and spinning machines in operation at the Old Paper Mill, near Hagers Town/Persons are forewarned agnst carrying away and from the sand bank near the New Paper Mill - Henry Miller, Moses M'Namee

471. EAM May 30 1810/Tavern for sale in Hagers Town, opp German Luth Church no occ by Michael Kapp/Hagers-Town Hotel taken by S. Bayly, lately occ by Mrs. Heister, where he has opened a House of Entertainment/Philip Pitry has re-commenced the making of gun powder at his powder mill, half a mile from John Sherer's mill, 5 miles from Hagers Town/Peter Smith, Hagers Town, offers reward for missing cow

472. Jun 6 1810/Died in Balt on Mon 28th ult, James Kendal, late a clerk of the Bank of Balt and formerly Deputy Clerk of Wash Co/John Scoggins, saddler & Harness maker, has commence bus in Funks-town, in house lately occ by Frederick Grosh, 2 doors below the dwelling of Henry Shafer, nearly opp Jacob Brunner's tavern/Jacob Smith, Constable in Conococheague Hundred, has lost a red morocco pocket book/Conrad Hogmire adm, to sell negro girl and boy, prop of Mary Magdalena Hogmire, decd/Geo: Smith requests settlement of accounts/George Bowart has now on hand at his brick yard a large quantity of good brick/Two negro men for hire - Eli Williams

473. Jun 13 1810/Nathaniel Dickson has taken up a stray mare/David Westeberger has lost a red morocco pocket book/Thomas Mulhall, Funks-town, offers reward for misisng cow/Daniel Bragonier, cautions agnst fowling or hunting on the Big Spring farm, near Hagers Town/Abraham Ditto, living near Conococheague adj land of John T. Mason, 8 miles from Hagers Town, offers reward for negro woman Dinah, about 35

474. Jun 20 1810/Married Thurs last by Rev Shafer, James Murra to Miss Margaret Baker, dau of Maurice Baker of this co/Married Tues last by Rev Rahauser, Samuel Rohrer to Miss Magdalena Rohrer dau of late Martin Rohrer

of this co/Lands for sale at the house of James Amos, about 3 miles above Williamsport, tract whereon James Amos lives, 300 a., the other adj land of Peter Middlekauff, 151 3/4 a. - Wm. Bayly/Peter Newcomer, Jun. living on Beaver Creek, 6 miles from Hagers Town, offers reward for mare which strayed from the plantation of Thomas Scott near Mercersburg/Jacob Coons, Sen., Berkeley Co, Va, to sell tract of 130 a./William Yates, Esq., living near Hancock-town, has taken up a stray mare

475. EAM Jun 27 1810/Catharine Rohrback adm of John Rohrback/Patrick Campbell, near Mercersburg, Franklin Co, Pa, offers reward for stolen horse /Partnership of Samuel Ringgold and C.G. Boerstler has been dissolved /Nathaniel Dixon has taken up a stray mare

476. EAM Jul 18 1810/Dissolution of partnership of Samuel Ringgold and C. G. Boerstler; persons indebted to them, either by store, mill or smith accounts are requested to come forward; Mr. Boerstler will continue bus. at the former stand, next door to John Hogg, and 2 doors above Mr. Sackett's Columbian Inn/Otho Sprigg offers for sale 598 1/2 a., 3 miles from Hagers Town; call on subscriber at George Beltzhoover's Tavern/Those indebted to firm of Perrin & Sweitzer are requested to settle accounts - Joseph Perrin and Henry Sweitzer/Wm. O. Sprigg adm of Thomas Sprigg/Alexander Tims has lost a silver watch

477. EAM Jul 25 1810/Riflemen - Attention! Members of the Hagers Town Volunteer Rifle Company to meet in front of the Captain's Quarters - David Tutwiler, 1st Sergt/Sale at dwelling house where he now lives, Wash St, Hagers Town, of negroes, sheep, road wagon, windmill, ploughs, harrows, and other - William Belch

478. EAM Aug 1 1810/Married Thurs last by Rev Rahauser, John Schnebly, junr. to Miss Susanna Kershner, dau of Major Martin Kershner, of this town/John P. Herr, Hagers Town, notifies persons not to trespass on his garden/Sale of corner house and lot opp dwelling of Col. Adam Ott, late the prop of Abraham Bower, decd; apply to Henry Snyder, next door to William Brazier in Hagers Town, to to subscriber, Conrod Coffroth in Greencastle.

479. EAM Aug 8 1810/Brigade Orders - 8th Regt of the 2nd Brigade of Militia to parade on the 15th, the 10th Regt on the 22d, and the 24th Regt on the 29th Sep next. The Troops of Horse commanded by Captains Williams and Asbury to parade with each Regiment, under the command of their Field Officer, Major Tilghman - Samuel Ringgold, Brig. Gen. 2d Brigade, Md. Militia/Sale at the subscriber's res, about 3 miles from Hagers Town, horses, milch cows, cattle and other - George Nigh/Michael Kapp to sell tavern in Hagers Town, opp German Luth Church, now occ by him/Wm. B. Williams seeks to hire distiller/Bernard Wisenall offers reward for apprentice to the carpenter's trade, Edmund Beall; deliver to Harpers Ferry - Bernard Wisenall

480. EAM Aug 15 1810/Daniel Kershner to sell at his res at the Cross Roads, 4 miles from Hagers Town, horses, cows, cattle, and other

481. EAM Aug 22 1810/Rosanna Able, adm of Joseph Able/R. Pindell to sell several lots, including: (1) farm 4 miles from town adj lands of late Gen. Sprigg and Wendel Gilbert/Mary Senger to sell at the late dwelling of John Senger, decd, adj plantation of John Baker, 4 miles from Waynesburg, Pa, pers prop of decd/Partnership of Jeremiah Williams and Elisha W. Williams, George-town, is dissolved/Thomas M'Namee, on Antietam, 1/2 mile from Hughes's Iron works, to sell horses, cows, windmill and other/John Weitzel, Hagers Town, offers reward for apprentice to the Hatting bus. named Peter King, 19-20, 5 ft 5-6 inch, yellowish complexion, light hair, speaks slow /James Garrett to sell dwelling house where he now lives next door to Samuel Hughes, esq., adj lots with Jacob Tutwiler, Potomack st, Hagers Town; also an excellent outlet near the Poor-house, adj Mr. Irwin and Mr. Bomgardner /Meeting of Officers and Privates of the 8th Regiment of Md. Militia, at Jacob Kershner's Tavern on Conococheague - David Schnebly, Lieut. Col., 8th Regt

482. EAM Aug 29 1810/Married last evening by Rev Rahauser, John Herr, to Miss Catharine Boroff, both of this co/John Hammond, living near John Shafer's mill has taken up a stray horse/William Blakemore adm, to sell negro girl, late the prop of Abigail Ford, decd/Daniel Hefflebower to apply for relief from debts/Officers and privates of the 24th Regt to meet at my quarters - John Reynolds, Major, Commandant 24th Regt/Colonels and Major commandant of the respective regiments of the 2d Brigade, will note that the 8th Regt will parade on the 15th, the 10th on the 22d, and the 24th on the 29th of Sep next - Tho: B. Pottenger, Brigade Major/Hugh Sands to apply for benefit of act for relif of insolvent debtors

483. EAM Sep 5 1810/Sale at dwelling house of Henry Ankony, decd, near St. Paul's Church, on the West side of Conococheague Creek, 9 miles from Hagers Town, pers prop of decd - Susanna Ankony and Henry Ankony, exec/John Ardinger adm, to sell house in Williamsport, prop of Christian Ardinger, decd/George Tabb to sell tract in Berkely Co, Va, 413 a., adj William Porterfield, Esq. and Thomas Shearer on the west/John Lynch, living near Williams-Port, who intends removing to Kentucky, to sell house in Williams-port on Salisbury st

484. EAM Sep 12 1810/Married Thurs evening last by Rev Shafer, Major John Beard, of this co, to Miss Sally Harry, dau of late Jacob Harry of this town/Christian Hager, exec, to sell 128 a., 2 1/2 miles from Hagers Town, prop of John Hager, decd/Henry Arnold, Hagers Town, offers reward for apprentice to weaving bus. named Henry Hess, 20-21, about 5 ft 6-7 inch, much addicted to lying, fond of low company/George Doyle, Hagers Town, to sell house where he now lives, nearly opp Hagerstown Bank; also house opp Baltzer Bowman's Distillery/Lau. A. Washington, desirous to move to the Kenahwa to live, offers for sale tract on which he lives joining town of Winchester, Fred Co, Va, 612 a./Benjamin Burd to sell tract in Dublin township, Bedford Co, Pa, 1000 a. - Benjamin Burd

485. EAM Sep 19 1810/Joseph Miller, 7 miles from Martinsburgh, Berkeley Co, Va, offers reward for negro man, named Ben, about 30/Peter Rench to apply for relief from debts

486. EAM Sep 26 1810/Sale at the dwelling of Mary Edwards, decd, Hagers Town, next door the house occ by Casper Keller and formerly by Rev Schmucker, all pers prop of decd - John Combs, adm/Anthony Varner, living at John T. Mason's Mill, on Little Conococheague, wishes to employ journeyman cooper, who is master of his trade

487. EAM Oct 3 1810/David Miller has lost a saddle between Jacob Kershner's Tavern and his farm, 1/2 mile from Col. David' Schnebly's/Sale of tract in Berkeley Co, Va, 413 a., adj William Porterfield and Thomas Shearer - George Tabb

488. EAM Oct 10 1810/Peter Seibert, appointed Major of a Battalion in the 24th Regt, of the militia of this state, in Wash Co, vice John Beard, resigned/Ezra Slifer, Boonsboro', has arrangements for the reception of flour, for storage/George Grundy, trustee, for William Lee, to sell lots in Hagers Town, one tract known as Retreat, patented by William Lee, 307 a. and other /Chancery sale of real est of Henry Elenbaugh, decd/John Cellar, exec, to sell at res of John Miller, decd, near Daniel Schnebly's, pers prop of decd

489. EAM Oct 17 1810/Committed as a runaway, mulatto man who calls himself Ellick Howard, about 24, 5 ft 7 inch/Sale of house formerly owned by Henry Cake, horse and chair with harness complete, furniture - Christian Artz /Negroes for sale - William S. Jobson, Williams-Port/Jacob Schnebly, Hagers Town, offers reward for negro man Richard, sometimes calls himself Richard Johnson, about 35

490. EAM Oct 24 1810/Joseph Swearingen, appointed Brig Gen. of the 9th Brigade, Fred Co, vice Hon. Roger Nelson, resigned/Sale of plantation of George W. Stoud, decd, 3 miles of Parkhead Forge - Emanuel Franz/Sale of tract in Jefferson Co, Va, 2 miles above Harpers Ferry - John Morrow/Peter Little, living at John Welty's, 1 mile from Capt. John Barr's Mill, offers reward for stolen horse/Samuel Himmaker, living at Miller's Mill, formerly Swingley's, has taken up a stray mare/Philip Shouse, living about 2 miles from Mr. Booth's Mill, offers reward for missing hourse/Geo. Brumbauch offers 400 a. for sale in Harrison Co, Va/Sale of tract of 225 a. in Randolph Co, Va, adj lands of Thomas Rinehart - John Sleigh

491. EAM Oct 31 1810/Wanted - journeyman saddler - John Scoggins, Funkstown/Reward offered for negro man Harry, 35, hired to subscribers, living 1 mile from seat of Samuel Ringgold; he was hired through Edward Aprice of St. Mary's Co, Md - Peter Malott, Michael Malott, Daniel Malott/Anne Thum and Jacob Foutz, adm of Baltzer Thum, to sell at res of decd, 1/2 mile of Nicholas Ridenour, 1 1/2 mile from Hoff's Tavern, at the Cross Roads, pers est of decd/Chancery sale of house in Cumberland, mortgaged by Richard Echles to Dennis Corbert - Hanson Briscoe, Trustee/P. Humrickhouse & son seeking journeyman blacksmith/Sale of dwelling of Jacob Friend by same; also pers prop/Peter Miller continued dying bus. and coverlet weaving at his dwelling in Funks-town/Wanted - apprentice to saddling bus. - Michael F. Mayer, Hagers Town

492. EAM Nov 7 1810/New store - Perrin & Booth - Dry Goods/Bar iron on hand - Kausler & Graff, Hagers Town/Distiller wanted - John Downey, near Charles-

town, Jefferson Co, Va/William Dixon, 4 miles from Hagers Town, offers reward for negro man Bob, about 20/Cheap goods - John & George Harry - assortment of hardware and cutlery, paints, groceries & liquors/Renting prop 2
miles from Greencastle, merchant and grist mill, now in the tenure of Abraham Litter; also farm occ by Jacob Houser adj above mills - Eleanor Johnston
/Sale at dwelling of Abraham Moyer, decd, 1 1/2 from Hagers Town, pers prop
of decd - J. Schnebly, adm/Peter Smith, Hagers Town, offers reward for milch
cow/Edward Hampton forewarns persons from asking assignment on bonds given
to Ovid Flint, formerly of Wash Co

493. EAM Nov 14 1810/No additional items

494. EAM Nov 21 1810/Sale of tract, 180 a., agreeable to will of John
Flora, decd, in Upper Antietam hundred adj lands of Ludwick Protzman and
George Fishach - Frederick Fishach, exec/John Stonebreaker, 3 miles from
Hagers Town, offers reward for negro man, name Joe, 35-40 yrs of age/15
negroes for sale; apply to Peregrine Palmer at Gen. Samuel Ringgold's

495. EAM Nov 28 1810/Married last evening by Rev Schaeffer,
Baltzer G. Goll to Miss Mercy Beall, both of this co/Ch. Carroll cautions
person from hunting within his inclosures/R. Douglas gives notice that notes
given at sale of Hugh Stewart's prop are due/Coverlet, Carpet & Plain weaving - R. Douglass, Hagers Town/Tavern to be rented in Hagers Town, opp Luth
Church, now in thhe occupation of Michael Kapp - Jacob Tutwiler

496. EAM Dec 5 1810/M. Shaffner gives notice that notes given to Michael
Gunfare at his public sale and notes given to William Burrows, are due
/Tavern stand for sale, Bedford Co, on Pa line, known as Martin's Tavern -
Benjamin Martin/Andrew M'Coy of Wash Co insolvent debtor, to be discharged
from imprisonment/George Clevidence, whose plantation is near Hughes's
Furnace, has taken up a stray barrow

497. EAM Dec 12 1810/John Collier, living on Ringgold's Manor, has taken up
a stray horse/Flaxseed wanted - G. & M. Stonebreaker

Hagers-Town Gazette, weekly, established May 16, 1809, published by William
Brown. The last issue located is that of June 15, 1813, vol. 5, no. 214.

498. HGM May 23 1809/Sale of Mills & farm on Antietem Creek, within a mile
of Hagers Town, in the fertile valley of Conococheague, with never failing
streams, Antietem and Marsh Run, at the junction of which are built the
mill, saw mill and distillery, with water sufficient nearly the whole year
to drive four pair of stones, besides the saw mill; a 2 stry brick dwelling
house, 56x33 ft, stone spring house, stone barn 80x36 ft, with stabling
underneath capable of holding a very large stock, between 20 and 33 acres of
natural meadow, well set with blue grass and timothy, about 400 a. in the
midst of fine wheat settlement. Apply to John J. Stull and O.H.W. Stull

499. HGM May 30 1809/Sentence of death was yesterday pronounced by the
honorable Judge Buchanan, on Thomas Burke, who was found guilty at March
court last, for committing a rape on a child between the age of 10 and 11

years/Married at Fred. Town on Sun eve last by Rev David Martin, William W. Hite, to Miss Margaret Tilt, both of this place/A.M. Waugh candidate for sheriff/Phinehas Reed, Alleghany Co, to apply for relief from debts

500. HGM Jun 6 1809/No additional items

501. HGM Jun 13 1809/Meeting of the American Blues in front of my quarters Sat next at one o'clock, P.M. in uniform, without valises and halters - each member to be provided with three rounds of blunt cartridges. O.H. Williams, Capt./Hagers Town volunteer Rifle Company to meet at G. Smith's, Columbian Hotel, opp market house - Thos. Post, Capt./Daniel Keedy and John Keedy, exec of David Furry, Wash Co

502. HGM Jun 20 1809/portion missing

503. HGM Jun 27 1809/Hagers Town Volunteer Rifle Co to partake of a dinner at Mr. Smith's ball room on the 4th of July - Daniel Hughes, Jun. Sec./The American Blues will parade in front of Capt. O.H. Williams's quarters on 4th of July and dine at Sergeant Strause's that day - Geo. G. Ross, Secr'y/Drawing of Boonsborough Church at the house of Capt. Peter Conn, in Boonsborough

504. HGM Jul 4 1809/James F. Tong, Allegany Co, offers reward for apprentice boy to the millwright bus. named Daniel Cresap, aged upwards of 18 yrs, about 5 ft 7 inch, fair complexion, light hair; had on pair of olive velvet pantaloons, round about of brown frieze, broad cloth waistcoat and a new wool hat; it is supposed he went to Baltimore, intending to go to sea in company with his brother, and some of his acquaintances/George Smith, Justice of the peace, certifies that Jacob Mogmer, living on Sample's manor, about 6 miles from Sharpsburg, has taken up 2 stray mares

505. HGM Jul 11 1809/Isaac S. White, Sheriff, Hagers Town, offers reward for Thomas Burk, who broke jail last night, sentenced to be hung for having committed a rape on the body of Catharine Maria Brawner - said Burk is between 35 and 40 yrs, about 5 ft 6-7 inches, dark hair, strong black beard, black eyes, had on black broad cloth coat, light Marseilles vest and thickset pantaloons/Partnership of Peter & Matthias Miller and William A. Beatty of the firm of William A. Beatty & Co, hatters, is dissolved

506. HGM Jul 18 1809/Died at his farm in Franklin Co Wed eve 18 inst, Colonel Robert Peebles, aged about 80, old Rev patriot, member of state (Pa) legislature. On the night of his death 47 of his sheep were killed while standing under a tree struck by lightning/Died Fri morn last at 1 o'clock, after a long and painful illness, in 61st year of his age, Benjamin Ogle, formerly governor of this state/Sharpsburgh Independent Blues to meet - John Blackford, Capt

507. HGM Jul 25 1809/John & Joseph McIlhenny, have just rec'd and are now opening at their old stand, directly opp Mr. Brumbaugh's Tavern an elegant assortment of dry goods, Hagers Town/All persons indebted to Hogg & Irwin, Williams-Port, are requested to make immediate payment/Grand Exhibitiion of Attack and Defence with the broad & small sword at Mr. Strause's New room

508. HGM Aug 1 1809/Benjamin Galloway candidate for Gen. Assembly/Chancery case: Edward M'Carty vs John Keller's heirs – ordered that James Reed, trustee to sell land to satisfy the sum of $1900.18 due to Edward M'Carty, reserving to the widow of John Kellers, decd, her right to tract – decree rendered by the county court of Hampshire.

509. HGM Aug 8 1809/Thos. Crampton certifies that James Colbert of Wash Co, near Antietum iron works, has taken up a stray mare/Frederick-Town, Md. On Fri last came in the Georgetown stage to Mr. Cookes' Tavern, in this town, a Mrs. Jones and two gentlemen, one was Mr. H. Howard from Washington; the other was Mr. Isaac Smith of Alexandria; the woman left a trunk at Mr. Cooke's to be forwarded on to Winchester, Va, but before the Winchester stage arrived on Sunday, Mr. Cooke had to go in the room where the trunk was left, he found there was a very disagreeable smell.... a dead infant wrapped in woman's apparel was found. It has since been reported that a Mr. Jones of Alexandria was married at Mr. Holtzman's tavern, in Georgetown, on the 18th inst. to a woman who was in a very pregnant state, she is supposed to be the same that left the trunk. She went on to Winchester on Saturday last.

510. HGM Aug 15 1809/Elie Williams has a small farm for sale 1 mile above Williams Port, whereon Daniel Bowman lately lived, about 150 a.

511. HGM Aug 22 1809/Riflemen to meet in front of the Columbian Inn Sat next – Thos. B. Hall, Capt/In consequence of the resignation of Capt. Post, an election for officers was held and following elected: Thos. B. Hall, Esq. – Capt; George Harry, 1st Lieut; Thomas Keen, 2nd Lieut; Mr. Tutwiler, 3rd Sergt; Mr. Shaw, 4th Sergt/Died in 44th year of her age, Mrs. Sarah M'Mahon, wife of William M'Mahon, of Cumberland/Christian & John Hennyberger have commenced the cabinet making bus. at the corner house of the widow Stump, opp bldg of Henry Middlekauff, Hatter, and next door to Col. Adam Ott /Matthew Vanlear, at his farm near Williams Port, has taken up 2 stray cows/John Crampton of Wash Co, manager for the subscriber, a Justice of the Peace, living on the road, leading from the Trap (Newtown) to Antietum iron works brought before me a trespassing stray gelding – Thos. Crampton/John Good certifies that Daniel Paner, near Sharpsburgh, has taken up a stray horse

512. HGM Aug 29 1809/John V. Kelly continues to carry on the fulling and dying bus at the fulling mill of Martin Baechtel, near Hagers Town/Petition to straighten road leading from Hancock Town to the Pennsylvania line, between Samuel Graves and Jeremiah Stilwills/Matthew Brown, Montevino, formerly Amelung's old Glass Works, to sell lands at the old Glass Works called New Bremen on Big Bennett's Creek

513. HGM Sep 5 1809/Died at his farm adj Boonsborough Sat morn, 2d inst after a severe illness, George Scott, formerly one of the assoc. Judges of Wash Co Court and for many years a Justice of the Peace/The Washington Hussars are ordered to parade in front of the Washington Tavern, Williamsport on Sat morn at 8 o'clock precisely, in order to meet the 8th Regiment at Kershner's Tavern – At Zeigler's store on Sat Sep 23d at 9 o'clock to meet the 10th Regiment – and on Fri Sept 29th at the Forks of the Sharps-

burgh and Opeckon Roads, near Dr. Schnebly's farm at 9 o'clock to meet the 24th Regiment at Hagers Town - Tho: Kennedy, Sec'ry

514. HGM Sep 12 1809/Upton Lawrence cautions persons from cutting down and destroying his timber/Ordered that the two troops of cavalry commanded by Capt. O. H. Williams, and Capt. John Ashbury, parade with the 8th Regiment on 16 Sep, under their field officer, Major Frisby Tilghman - Tho: Sprigg, Brig. Gen./Washington Fall Races to be run over the Washington County Course /Thos: B. Hall to rent farm on which George Locke now resides, about 8 miles from Hagers Town, 3 miles from Ringgold's mill; apply to Dr. Harrison in Balt or subscriber in Hagers Town/Daniel Gehr candidate for sheriff

515. HGM Sep 19 1809/Co-partnership in Hagers Town of firm Kennedys & Ragan, dissolved - John Kennedy, Hugh Kennedy and Richard Ragan

516. HGM Sep 26 1809/It appears that Lieutenant Ridgway and Mr. Merrick came to my boarding house on Tues night armed with bludgeons and pistols; Mr. Ridgway struck at me with a bludgeon (long article) - William Brown, Editor. Witnessed by Samuel Bayly; others mentioned: Mr. White, Mrs. Bayly /Married Thurs evening last by Rev Rawhauser, Isaac White, of Hagers Town, to Miss Marey Rench of Wash Co/John I. Stull reports a missing mare

517. HGM Oct 3 1809/New store - Richard Ragan has now opened next door to Messrs. John & George Harry - seasonable goods/Doctors R. Pindell and F. Dorsey have taken Dr. Arnold Hanenkampf into partnership, the practice of physic and surgery

518. HGM Oct 10 1809/A young man of genteel appearance found Sat eve last on banks of Conococheague, suspended by a handkerchief round his neck, tied to the limb of a tree. We understand the young man was at Kershner's tavern, a few days previous to his death and called himself Buck/Married Tues eve last by Rev King, Dr. Michael A. Finley, to Miss Eliza Vanlear, dau of Matthew Vanlear, Esq. of Wash Co/Married Thurs last by Rev Rauhauser, Isaac Golladay, to Miss Elizabeth Shall, dau of Geo. Shall of this place /Married Sun last by Rev Bower, George Hedrich, to Miss Peggy Tyson dau of Benjamin Tyson, Esq. of Sharpsburgh/Married Thurs eve 5th inst, by Rev Ballmain, John Hanson Thomas, Esq. of Frederick town , to Miss Mary I. Colston dau of Rawleigh Colston, Esq. of Berkley Co, Va./Wm. Fitzhugh has 3 families of negroes for sale/Sam. Hughes, Jun. requests persons indebted to est of James Hughes, Wash Co, decd, to make payment immediately

519. HGM Oct 17 1809/No additional items

520. HGM Oct 24 1809/Susannah Yoast, adm of est of George Youst, to sell negroes, cattle, furniture and farming utensils

521. HGM Oct 31 1809/No addtitional items

522. HGM Nov 7 1809/Directors of Hagers Town Bank have declared a dividend - Elie Beatty, Cashier/Alexander Neill, Hagers Town, has just rec'd bolting clothes which he will sell/Eleanor Davis, exec, of est of Rezin Davis /Richard Pindell to sell at his farm about 3 miles from Hagers Town, on

road to Ritter's Ford, the stock on the farm, waggons, ploughs, harrows, etc.

523. HGM Nov 14 1809/No additional items

524. HGM Nov 21 1809/Dispute by editor with "Tadpole Editor of the Maryland Herald, Mr. Grieves/Philip Kreigh and Nicholas Kreigh, adm of William Dillihunt, Wash Co/Dry goods for sale - Price & Hussey, Hagers Town/Thos. Williams offers reward for horse stolen from one of his stables, living within one mile of William's-Port

525. HGM Nov 28 1809/Pay your Taxes - Isaac S. White, Late Sheriff and Collector, Hagers Town

526. HGM Dec 5 1809/Editor continues his attack on Mr. Grieves/Sale of 800 a. of land at Beltzhoover's Tavern, in Hagers Town, adj mill of John Baer, late the prop of Martin Baer, decd; tracts are: Belts Buckle, 600 a.; and Sweep Stakes, adj same, 113 5/8 a. - Thomas Peter, David Peter/R. Douglass certifies that William Ford, living near Newcomer's Mill, has taken up a stray horse

527. HGM Dec 12 1809/Married Tues last by Rev Rauhauser, William Reynolds to Miss Mercy Walling dau of Col. James Walling of this co/Valentine Mautter, near Hagers Town, has taken up a brown heifer

528. HGM Dec 19 1809/Married Tues eve last by Rev Bower, Elie Beatty, cashier of the Hagers Town Bank, to Mrs. Elizabeth D. Deery, all of this town/Died Wed last after a few days illness, General Thomas Sprigg, aged 62, of Wash Co/Thomas Peter, exec, to sell 50 slaves at farm of the late Robert Peter in the Sugar lands, with one mile of the Senaca Mills/Case of George Knode and wife vs Jacob Earhart & Mary his wife and Michael Kapp - Commission to value and divide the real est of Michael Kapp, who died intestate, decd. Jacob Earhart and Mary his wife are absent from the co/Case of Joseph Sprigg & wife vs Francis Taylor, John Chambers & Hannah his wife, Jane Taylor and Lucretia Taylor - Commission to value and divide real est of Ignatious Taylor, who died intestate. Francis Taylor, John Chambers and Hannah his wife are absent from the co

529. HGM Dec 26 1809/Edmund H. Turner to let farm of 200 a. of cleared land on River Potomac, bordering Licking Creek, near Parkhead Forge, Wash Co; apply to subscriber living at said Forge/Sale of lot within 3 miles of Hagers Town adj prop of Isaac Bear and Thomas M'Cardle - St. Leger Neal, living near the premises/Sale of mulatto man; apply to Henry Middlekauff, Hagers Town, or subscriber near Sharpsburg, Adam Myers

530. HGM Jan 2 1810/Sebastian Hartle offers reward for horse missing from Cook's Tavern

531. HGM Jan 9 1810/Clover seed for sale - C. Artz & G. Gehr, Hagers Town

532. HGM Jan 16 1810/Died Wed eve last in 58th year of her age, Mrs. Rosanna Heister, widow of Gen. Daniel Heister, late of this place/Appoint-

ments of the Justices of the Peace for Wash Co: Thomas Crampton; Adam Ott; Samuel Ringgold; John Good; John Hunter; William Yates; Robert Douglass; Robert Smith; Josiah Price; George Nigh; Henry Ankeney; James M'Clain; Thomas Kennedy; William S. Compton; George Smith; Jacob Schnebly; Martin Kershner; Philip Mains; John Langley; John Bowles; James Prather; John T. Mason; William Gabby; Robert Hughes; Matthew Collins; Henry Locher, jun. – Justices of the Levy Court: Samuel Ringgold; Adam Ott; William Yates; Robert Smith; Josiah Price; Martin Kershner; Jacob Rench – Judges of the Orphan's Court: Elie Williams; Jacob Schnebly, Frisby Tilghman – Coroner: Charles Carroll/M. Bayly to sell '4 waggon horses and a light strong waggon nearly new/Tho. T. Lowry, Shepherds-Town, offers reward for missing horses; return to Daniel Morgan, Esq. near Shepherds Town/Sale of negro woman – W. W. Evans, near Sharpsburgh/Elizabeth Chapline adm of Jeremiah Chapline, Wash Co

533. HGM Jan 23 1810/Appointments for Allegany County – Justices of the Peace: Robert Reed; Jesse Tomlinson; William Shaw; Andrew Bruce; Benjamin Tomlinson; Aza Beall; John Rice; Thomas Pratt; George Rizer; Thomas Cresap; William Coddington; Thomas Parkenson; John Devillbess; Hanson Briscoe; Thomas Greenwell; Nicholas Gower; Thomas F. Brooke; Ebenezer Davis; Wm. H. Burnes; James Morrison; John M'Neil; Joshua Willson; Robert Armstrong; Lenox Martin – Justices of the Levy Court: Benjamin Tomlinson; Thomas Pratt; Aza Beall; Upton Bruce; John Rice; Thomas Parkenson; Thomas Greenwell – Judges of the Orphan's Court: Thomas Cresap; Hanson Briscoe; Upton Bruce/Married this morning, by Rev Rhauhauser, Peter Miller of Funks-Town to Miss Margaret Mong/Sale of tract of several thousand acres in Wash Co know by name of Semple's Manor; belonged to John Semple who mortgaged it to James Lawson and died without heirs. It escheated to the state of Md. James Lawson filed a bill in chancery to obtain a sale – Elie Williams, Wm. T. T. Mason, trustees

534. HGM Jan 30 1810/No additional items

535. HGM Feb 6 1810/Elizabeth Armstrong, Shepherds Town had sufficiently recovered from her late severe indisposition to attend again to the duties of her school/W. L. Brent intends to leave Hagers Town in 10-15 days; requests payment of debts/Elijah Lynn vs Robert Williams and Mary his wife; Hester Lynn, widow of Edmond Lynn, Elijah Lynn, Elizabeth Lynn, Catharine Lynn, Mary Vance and Abigail Vance – Commission to value and divide the real est of John Banister Lynn, who died intestate; Robert Williams and Mary his wife are absent from the co

536. HGM Feb 13 1810/Meeting of Commissioners of the Tax – J. Schnebly, clerk

537. HGM Feb 20 1810/George French, Boonsborough, adm of George Scott /Tavern to rent, 3 miles from town, formerly occ by William Kerr – John Mitchell, No.20 Cheapside, Balt

538. HGM Feb 27 1810/Married at Emmitsburg, Tuse 13th inst by Rev Rahauser, John Latchaw, merchant of Waynesburg, to Miss Polly Denison/Married this morning by Rev Bower, John Tracy to Miss Peggy M'Clary, both of Funks-town /Sale of household and kitchen furniture; also billiard table, patent lamps, hack stage with pair of horses – George Smith, Hagers Town/Price & Hussey,

Hagers Town, to let store and cellar which the now occupy; apply to Henry Lewis/Commissioners to receive subscriptions for incorporating a company for making a Turnpike Road from the town of Westminster through Herman's gap, to Hagers Town: Ch. Carroll, U. Lawrence, Wm. Heyser, Wm. Downey, R. Hughes

539. HGM Mar 6 1810/No additional items

540. HGM Mar 13 1810/Died Wed 7th inst, Mrs. Mary Margaret Post, consort of late Rev. Frederick Post, aged 77/Medicines for sale by John & Geo. Harry, Hagers Town

541. HGM Mar 20 1810/Sale at farm of Phineas Watson, formerly belonging to Michael Hager, adj lands of George Cellar, John Hager and Philip Kessaker, mare, saddle, cart and other/High bread horse May-Duke will stand for mares this season at subscriber's stable in Hagers Town - Henry Strause (pedigree attested to by Samuel Ringgold who sold the horse to Tench Ringgold and Henry Strause

542. HGM Mar 27 1810/Died 15 inst Mrs. Snyder, consort of governor of Pa /Christian Fechtig has rented the Columbian Inn and has provided himself with a complete assortment of liquor, a steady and sober ostler, with every requisite for a house of entertainment/S. Bayly has taken that large and elegant house on the public square in Hagers Town lately occ by Mrs. Heister /David Little, taylor & habit-maker, has removed from his old stand to Public Square, adj house formerly occ by late Mrs. Heister/Michael Hauser adm of Robert T. Cary/Sale of plantation in the South Mountain, Adams's Co, Pa, near Nicholson's Gap road, 200 a. - James Agnew, near the premises/The Jack, Night of Malta, will stand the ensuing season at the subscriber's farm, about 4 miles from Hagers Town and Dr. Tilghman's farm - Wm. Fitzhugh

543. HGM Apr 3 1810/Daniel Stover has commenced the bus. of blue dying & coverlet weaving, in the house formerly occ by Christian Garret in village of Mercersburg. The above bus. will be carried on as heretofore at the house of Jacob Price's near Waynesburg, where all orders will be thankfully rec'd/Christian Fechtig, boot and shoemaker, has removed to house formerly occ by Mr. White as the Sheriff's Office and taken his son Lewis into part-nership/Dissolution of partnership of Samuel D. Price and George Hussey; store and cellar formerly occ by said firm available to rent/George Hammer, Hagers Town, has removed to 2 stry brick house between present sheriff's office and Captain John Harry's dwelling where he intends to carry on the tayloring bus.

544. HGM Apr 10 1810/Christian and John Hennyberger, cabinet makers, have removed to house at present occ by Geo. Rock, opp Gelwick's Brewery, and a few doors below the jail

545. HGM Apr 17 1810/Married Thurs eve last by Rev Rahauser, Dr. Arnold Ferdenand Hanenkampf, to Miss Margaret Humrickhouse, all of this place /Michael F. Mayer, has commenced the saddle & harness making bus. in house lately in tenure of Messsrs. Kausler and Graff, next door to capt. Geo. Binkley's store, public square, Hagers Town/Samuel Hager, saddler & harness maker, had commenced in house formerly occ by Jonathan Hager, 3 doors from

Mr. Furguson's store (now Kennedys) near the Court House/Dissolution of partnership of Christian Artz and George Gehr, Hagers Town

546. HGM Apr 24 1810/Land for sale before their door of the Globe Tavern, Martinsburg, Va, 226 a., about 1 1/2 miles from said town - Philip C. Pendleton, Martinsburg, Va

547. HGM May 1 1810/Recommended as directors of Hagers Town Bank: for Wash Co: Martin Kershner, Alexander Neill, Matthias Shaffner, Samuel Hughes, Jun., William Heyser, Elie Williams, Charles Carroll - for Balt: Francis Foreman - for Allegany: James Scott/N. Rochester, intending to remove to the Genesee co in a few weeks, will sell negro boy and furniture (listed)

548. HGM May 8 1810/The meeting of the PIC NIC CLUB will in future be held at Samuel Bayly's Assembly Room - Joseph I. Merrick, Sec'ry/David Adams has erected a machine for carding and rolling wool at Daniel Bashor's mill, 1 mile from Waynesburg/Sale of log house - Philip Oyler, Sharpsburg, living on the premises/Geo: Frazier, Wash Co to apply for relief of debts

549. HGM May 15 1810/Married Sun eve last by Rev Rahauser, William Beecher, merchant, to Miss Elizabeth Herr, dau of John P. Herr, all of this town /William Tekloodt, has commenced the confectionary bus., corner of Potomac & Franklin streets, Hagers Town - deserts, cordials, ice creams/Jacob Mumma adm of Henry Mumma, Wash Co

550. HGM May 22 1810/Committee to carry out establishment of Hagers Town Academy: John T. Mason; John Bowles; William Yates; Thomas Brent; John Ragan, sen.; Matthias Shaffner; Upton Lawrence; John Kennedy; Otho H. Williams; Alexander Neill; Dr. F. Dorsey; Robert Hughes; Dr.F. Tilghman; Samuel Ringgold; Jacob T. Towson; John Ashbury; Benjamin Tyson; John Brien; Dr. Clagett; Henry Locher - R. Pindell, Chairman, Elie Williams, Sec'ry /Benjamin Yoe, taylor, has commenced bus. in Washington St, 2 doors from square and next door but one to John & G. Harry's store/A. Clagett adm of William Clagett, Wash Co/Dissolution of partnership of John Blackford & Presley Marmaduke, in the Ferry and Tavern, opp Shepherdstown/Christian Artz, Hagers Town, requests payment of debts; his attorney, Peter Artz to receive same/2d Battalion to parade companies in front of my quarters - John Reynolds, major, 2d Battalion, 24th Regt., Md. Militia

551. HGM May 29 1810/Christ. Burckhart, exec of George Burckhart

552. HGM Jun 5 1810/Agents of the Hagers Town Gazette: Boonsborough, Capt. Peter Conn; Williams-Port, Jacob T.Towson, Esq.; Sharpsburg, Benjamin Tyson, Esq.; Sheperdstown (Va.), Benj. Brown, Esq. P.M.; Martinsburgh (Va.), Mr. Levi Price; Hancock, Mr. Thos: C. Brent; Old-town, Mr. James M. Cresap/Died at Balt, on 28th ult, Mr. James Kendall, formerly an inhabitant of this town/George Smith requests payment of debts/John Harry, Hagers Town, offers reward for mulatto man, named Jim, about 25, 5 ft 4 inch

553. HGM Jun 12 1810/John Stull forwarns persons from pursuing their amusements anywhere within his enclosures, or from fishing with nets in the water

running through his farm/James H. Bowles candidate for sheriff/Robert Cheney adm of John Bond

554. HGM Jun 19 1810/The Rev. Wm. Ryland will preach at the Methodist meeting house on Sunday at 11 o'clock./Henry Middlekauff and John Julius carry on the hatting bus. at the corner of Potomac and Frankin sts, opp Col. Adam Ott's in Hagers Town/Thomas S. Lee, Frederick Co, Needwood Farm, offers reward for 2 slaves, Jim a mulatto about 21, 5 ft 6-8 inch and Charles about 5 ft 11 inch, 45-50

555. HGM Jun 26 1810/No additional items

556. HGM Jul 3 1810/Mr. Dubuisson, dentist, has arrived from Phila

557. HGM Jul 10 1810/Hugh M'Calley, living on Ringgold's Manor, has taken up a stray horse/Daniel Gehr reports stray cattle

558. HGM Jul 17 1810/Samuel Ringgold, Esq. of Washington Co, appointed brigadier general of the 2d brigade of Maryland Militia in the room of Gen. Thomas Sprigg, decd/William H. Smith, Shippensburgh, offers reward for missing horse/Sale at res of George Scott, decd, Boonsborough, of 2 negro women and cattle and furniture - George French, Boonsborough

559. HGM Jul 24 1810/No additional items - HGM Jul 31 1810/No additional items

560. HGM Aug 7 1810/Tues eve last, during the heavy rain, the barn of Mr. James Downey Jr. living on the Antietem, near the old Rock forge, was struck with lightning - the barn, together with a large quantity of grain in the straw was entirely consumed and three valuable horses killed/James Wigginton living at the Lick Mills, near Martinsburg, Va, offers reward for mulatto man, David, about 27, 5 ft 8-9 inch; return to Jacob Light in Berekly co, near Martinsburg or Mrs. Sarah Wigginton, Fred Co, near Battle-Town

561. HGM Aug 14 1810/Pay your taxes and fees - Matthias Shaffner, Sheriff and collector, Hagers Town/Camp meeting for Frederick circuit on farm of Francis Hoffman, 2 1/2 miles from Newtown (Trap), under superintendance of Rev H. Jefferson/Charles M'Calley living 3 miles from Hagers Town, adj lands of Samuel Hogmyer, has taken up a stray horse

562. HGM Aug 21 1810/Flock of merino sheep for sale - E.A. Gibbs, Hagers Town/John Wiltshire, living between Sharpsburgh and M'Pherson and Brien's iron works, has taken up a stray horse

563. HGM Aug 28 1810/Edward Harris, Market St, Balt, offers reward for horse which strayed from his farm on the York Road, 14 miles from Balt; horse was bred near Hagers Town

564. HGM Sep 4 1810/10th regiment to meet at Cary's Cross Roads - John L. Beall, Adj't, 10th Regt

565. HGM Sep 11 1810/No additional items

566. HGM Sep 18 1810/Seeking a sober industrious man who is well acquainted with shearing woolen cloth and a good spinner of wool – James Mosher, Robt. C. Long, Wm. Gwynn; apply at Lanvale, near Balt or to subscribers/George Lowery has taken up a stray cow

567. HGM Sep 25 1810/Sale of brick dwelling house now in the possession of Judge Buchanan – John Harry

568. HGM Oct 2 1810/Sale of tract near mouth of Little Cove, 3 miles from Isaac Baightles – Elie Williams/Found by my waggoner, negro Lewis, as he was returning from Balt, in company with other waggoners, 2 bags of shot; owner may claim/John Zimmerman, living near Jno. Hersheys, has taken up a stray mare

569. HGM Oct 9 1810/St. Leger Neal, Wash Co, will sell prop, mostly lime-stone, about 4 miles from Hagers Town, 252 7/8 a./Thomas Garret of Wash Co, gives notice that all debts due him will be received by Daniel Hughes, Jr.

570. HGM Oct 16 1810/No additional items

571. HGM Oct 23 1810/Married Tues eve last by Rev Shafer, Captain John Ragan, to Miss Amelia Harry, both of this town

572. HGM Oct 30 1810/No additional items

573. HGM Nov 6 1810/Otho H Williams and John Ragan, Jun., Hagers Town, have nearly completed their extensive Rope Walk, and are ready to purchase any quantity of good merchantable hemp/Thomas Shuman having taken into partnership Charles Moore, coppersmith from Balt, has just commenced the coppersmith bus. at his house in Hagers Town/William Dixon, 4 miles from Hagers Town, offers reward for negro Bob, about 20, 5 ft 9-10 inch/Samuel Hammet, 3 miles from Hagers Town, offers reward for missing fillies

574. HGM Nov 13 1810/During the heavy rain on Sat last, the Potomac and Conococheague raised to a greater height than has been known for upwards of 40 years. The bridge lately built across the Conococheague at Williamsport was entirely swept away. Mr. Towson's ware-house at Williamsport, which contained a quantity of tar and coal, was carried away; loss estimated at 1200 dollars

575. HGM Nov 20 1810/Benjamin Galloway, Hagers Town, wished to dispose of 800 a. of woodland near Potomac, between Hancock and Old Town/John B. Woltz, clock & watch maker has removed his shop into house owned by Henry Lewis, formerly occ as a store by Messrs. Price & Huffey/Alexander Neill has just rec'd a large assortment of bolting cloths

576. HGM Nov 27 1810/No additional items – HGM Dec 4 1810/No additional items – HGM Dec 11 1810/No additional items

577. HGM Dec 18 1810/Married Tues eve last by Rev Rauhauser, John M'Il-henny, merchant, to Miss Nancy Newcomer, both of this town/Sale of farm on which he now res on Antietam Creek, 300 a. – John I. Stull

578. HGM Dec 25 1810/No additional items

(Fredericktown) Bartgis's Republican Gazette. Published by Matthias Bartgis

579. RGM Feb 7 1806/Married Tues 4th inst by Rev Wagner, Jacob Houck to Miss Margaret Getzendannner, dau of John Getzendanner, of this co/John Frall offers reward for recovery of bank notes robbed from him at Daniel Burkhurts tavern on Monocacy/John Develbiss of Casper forewarns person from cutting his timber/George Rice carries on the Cabinet making bus. next door North of Conrad Shaffers tavern/Samuel Howard of Carrolls manor has taken up a stray gelding/Mary M'Clean adm of William M'Clean/Henry Poffinborger offers reward for negro man John Jackson, alias Lawyer, 24/Mill and land for sale - Jesse Matthews, where he res

580. RGM Mar 7 1806/Married Tues 4 inst. by Rev Bowers, Wm. Ross, Esq. attorney at law, of York-Town, Pa, to Miss Kitty Johnson, dau of Col. Baker Johnson, of this town/Died 3d inst Mrs. Ellis Flemming, in her 80th year, inhabitant of this co, remains interred in Episc burying ground/Bethuel Middleton, Berekeley Co, Va, offers reward for negro man generally known as Joe, but calls himself Joe Winters, about 27/James Robertson cautions that Jacob Gombier, formerly of this co, now living on Will's creek, Ohio, did inclose a bond in a letter direct to subscriber, James Robertson, which bond was drawn in favour of said Gombier and accepted by Abraham Shriver and Andrew Hed.... This is to forewarn persons from taking assignment on said bond/Henry Kolb, Hagers Town, offers reward for apprentice boy, named John Goodly

581. RGM Mar 14 1806/Henry Kolb, Frederick town, offers reward for apprentice boy named John Goodly/Henry Stoner to sell negroes, grain in the ground, coults, milk cows, and other/New Tavern - Levi Chambers, Inn-keeper, sign of the Green Tree, in George Town

582. RGM Apr 18 1806/Married by Rev Wagner, William Thomas to Miss Catherine Houser, dau of Capt Houser of this town/Benj. Ds. Penn, Montg Co forwarns persons not to trust his wife Chloe Penn as he is determined not to pay anything of her contracting/Andrew Mills, Fred Co, offers reward for apprentice, Jacob Stocks, about 22, 5 ft 5 inch, slim made, dark complexion

583. RGM May 9 1806/Joshua Fletcher, Faquier Co, Va, offers reward for negro man Tom and Fillis his wife; well acquainted with Counsellor Carter's people/Robert Bailey, Winchester, to sell farm, 215 a., Fred Co, 3 miles from Winchester/John Devilbiss forewarns person from throwing down his fences/Edward W. Duvall offers reward for horse misssing from inclosure of Benjamin Simpson, 3 1/2 miles from Fred Town/Dying for liveing - Samuel Clark, wool, cotton, linnen, silk dyer, and finisher, removed to lower end of Patrick St, near the Pence town Bridge, nearly opp Dr. Duvall's

584. RGM May 23 1806/Peter Grossnickel, near Middle-town, has taken up a stray horse/Valentine Doub, Fred Co, offers reward for apprentice named Joseph Richmond, by trade a waggon maker, about 5 ft 6inch, 10 yrs old, slim, sandy hair, very talkative/House for sale in Pence Town at house of

Lewis Gardner, decd - Lewis Gardner, Junr, and James Gardner/Jacob Smith, near Middle Town, has taken up a stray mare/Henry Lodge will sell his plantation in Montg Co, in the neighbourhood of John Wilstons

585. RGM Oct 17 1806/Stephen Elliot, Poplar Springs, offers reward for negro man, Cesar, 23, formerly belongd to Allen Banks, living near the Poplar Springs, Ann Arundel Co

586. RGM Oct 31 1806/Married Sun 26th inst., by Rev Wagner, Augustus Graham, merchant of this town, to Miss Patty Cock, dau of Capt S. Cock of this co/Jackscrews for sale - Crumbine and Wentzel, opp Dr. Bogen's, Fred Town/Saw mill for rent on Linganore near where it empties into the Monocacy - Charles Hammond/Thomas Powell has lost a note drawn by John Clark of Clarksburgh, Mont Co

587. RGM Nov 14 1806/Frederick Seaver, near Fred Town, has taken up a stray cow

588. RGM Nov 21 1806/William Jenkins & Welsh seek boys to learn the currying bus.

589. RGM Jan 23 1807/Jason Phillips in pursuance fo the last Will of John Phillips of Fred Co, to sell farm, 151 a., adj late res of said John Philips /John Flanagin cautions person from taking assignment of note given to Casper Measel

590. RGM Jan 30 1807/Married Tues 26th inst by Rev Martin, Solomon Staley to Miss Peggy Butler of this Town/Died Wed 28th inst, Jacob Hole, old inhabitant of this town

591. RF Feb 6 1807/Sale of tract, 80 1/2 a., near Matthews Mill; apply to James Wiles living on the premises/John Baker, living near the mouth of Toms Creek, offers regard for apprentice boy John Slice, bound to the blacksmith bus., about 5 ft, 18, down look, swaggering walk, dark hair/Joseph Harris forwarns person from taking assignment on note given to James Bowden/Thomas J. Hammond to apply to extend benefit of act to aid insolvent debtors/Valentine ---, guardian, to let house, formerly prop of Matthias Buckey, decd, and lately occ by Henry Cronise as a tavern/Committed to jail - negro man who calls himself Joe, about 33, says he belongs to Colonel James King of Sullivan Co, Tenn/Reward for deserter from Marine Barracks, City of Wash, Isaac Foster and George Woolger, fifers in the corps; the former was born in town of Stafford, Connecticut, enlisted 18 Jul 1804 at Washington, about 21, 5 ft 6 inch, dark eyes, dark hair and fresh complexion; the latter born in England, county of Suffex, town of Chicester, enlisted at Washington 19 July, 1806, is 22, 5 ft 6 inch, blue eyes, light hair, fair complexion, much marked with the small pox/Mrs. Whitcraft keeps tavern at her old stand in Market St/Singleton Burgee offers reward for mulatto man, Adam, about 25

592. RGM Feb 13 1807/Died Tues 10th inst, William Dearn, old inhabitant of this co

(Fredericktown) Bartgis's Republican Gazette

593. RGM Feb 20 1807/Frederick Row and George Row, exec of Arthur Row/John
Yondiss forwarns person from taking assignment on bonds given to John Snook,
now living in Ohio/Cabinet bus. - George Rice, next door north of Conrad
Shafer's tavern/Joseph Harris forwarns person from taking assignment on note
given to James Bowden/Chancery sale of real est of Joseph Black, decd, 117
a., 5 miles from Graceham - Henry Kuhn, trustee

594. RGM Feb 27 1807/Died in Calvert Co, morning of 2d inst, after a short
but severe illness, James Skinner, in the 56th year of his age, husband and
parent/Daniel Miller, 3 miles from Fred Town, 1 mile from David Kemp's mill,
will sell road waggon, horses, milch cows and other; also house in Fred Town
occ by John Miller/Catharine Doup, in Carrol's Manor, has taken up a stray
bull/John Tiffe, Montg Co, near John B. Medley's Tavern, offers reward for
negro girl Mill, about 16

595. RGM Mar 6 1807/Simon Snook to sell or rent mills on Fishing Creek

596. RGM Mar 13 1807/Henry Fout forwarns persons of trusting his wife Nancy
Fout as he is determined not to pay any contracts she may make; Henry Fout
will sell his house in Market St near the Barracks

597. RGM Mar 20 1807/Married Tues evening, last by Rev Bowers, William
Potts of Fred Town, to Miss Susanna Campbell, dau of Capt. William Campbell,
of Fred Co/Henry Fout, Fred Town, forwarns persons of trusting his wife
Nancy Fout

598. RGM Mar 27 1807/Abraham Crum to sell plantation of late William Dearn,
161 a., 6 miles from Fred. Town, adj land of Nicholas Randle/Elizabeth Fox
and Conrad Eiler, adm of Baltzer Fox/Committed to gaol of Mont Co, negro man
who calls himself Frank Butler; says he belongs to a young man living in
Fred Town, named Edward Warring who follows the tanning bus - John Fleming,
Shff.

599. RGM Apr 10 1807/Henry Hildebrand to sell farm 5 1/2 miles from Fred.
town, 109 a./Matthias E. Bartgis carries on printing bus. at Rockville, Md -
hand bills, cards, blanks/Christian Brengle to rent house where Christian
Devilbiss, decd, formerly lived/George Buckey to let stone house, with kitchen, smoak house, stable and blsck smith's shop, 6 miles from Fred Town,
now occ by Widow Buckey

600. RGM Apr 17 1807/John Richards to sell farm, 192 a., in Fred Co/Evan
Crawford to apply for relief from debts/Mary Schilknecht adm of Henry Schil-
knecht/Jonathan Wickersham, Berkeley Co, Va, to sell land, 122 a.

601. RGM Apr 24 1807/John Askins to sell plantation in Loudoun Co, Va, 3
miles from Noland's ferry

602. RGM May 1 1807/Severe hail storm - considerable damage to the house of
Daniel Burkhart at the Ferry on the Baltimore road/Henry Remsberg of Jacob
has taken up a stray gelding/George Wissinger, living on the Manor, offers
reward for apprentice boy named David Wilson, bound to the blacksmith bus.
about 15, 5 ft/William King has just moved from Liberty-Town to Fred. Town

and taken the tavern stand of Mr. Schley, lately occ by Mr. Miller/Committed
to jail, negro fellow, who says his name is Andrew Hoskins, says he is free
born in Md, served his time with William Anderson who lived near Ellicots
old mills but has since moved to Pa; age about 29/Committed to jail, mulatto
who calls himself Tom Brown, about 21; says he was purchased by John Tygart,
Howard's st, Balt; says he is originally from Washington, Pa

603. RGM May 8 1807/Married Sun 3d inst., Jacob Boyer of this Town, to Miss
Mary Knouf, of Pa/Mr. Duff, about to leave this town, intends to return in
the fall with a company of performers

604. RGM May 15 1807/Married last evening by Rev Daniel Wagner, William R.
Sanderson, hatter, of Winchester, Va, to Miss Elizabeth Leatherman, dau of
Henry Leatherman of this place/Wanted - man for fulling bus - Jacob Staley,
living about 4 miles from Fred Town/John Ringland has removed to tavern
stand where Jacob Kiler lived in Liberty Town

605. RGM Jun 12 1807/M. Bartgis offers reward for John Kyle, apprentice to
printing bus., about 17, 5 ft 7 inch, stoop shouldered, pock marcked, down
looking, writes a good hand; has been engaged as a clerk in the store of Mr.
White, in Brownsburg, Va; says his father lives near M'Connelsburg, Pa and
his mother in Brownsburg, Va; took with him blue coat, mixed coatee, both
cloth, 2 jackets of swandown, 3 pairs of pantaloons, 1 corduroy, 1 nankeen
and 1 homemade with blue strips, 2 shirts, fur hat, old shoes, and sundry
other cloths

606. RGM Jun 19 1807/Sale of plantation 5 miles from Fred. Town - Benjamin
Biggs, Abraham Haaf, John Ritchies, exec/John Myer, 1 miles from Fred. Town,
has taken up stray steers/Elizabeth Luckett, Fred. Town, offers reward for
negro man, named Jack, a joiner in the service of John Brien at the Antietum
Mills, about 25, speaks the German language

607. RGM Jun 26 1807/Ice Cream at John Hasefeldt's confectionary, may be
had during the season/Jacob Everhart, Middletown, has taken up a stray mare
/Robert Fulton exec of Robert Fulton

608. RGM Nov 26 1808/George Bready cautions not to trust his wife Margaret
who left his bed and board without any cause/Rope making - Jacob Kimmerly
and Nicholas Hoover, Fred Town/Leonard Billmyer, Fred Town, offers reward
for missing cows/Committed to gaol of Fred Co: (1) mulatto man who calls
himself John Covee, about 27; says he served his time with Mrs. Hunter,
Berkly Co, Va; (2) negro man who calls himself Bill Jones, about 24; says he
is free and was raised in Pittsburgh with General Nevell; served his appren-
ticeship with Philip Thomas to the barber bus.

609. RGM Dec 10 1808/Mon 5th inst. a duel took place at Leesburg, Va, be-
tween Dr. Peyton & Wm. Littlejohn, in which the former was killed/John
Coventry, about 10 miles from Fred. Town, has taken up a stray colt/John
M'Cann gives notice to his creditors he is to apply for relief from debts

610. RGM Dec 17 1808/A duel was fought on 6th inst in Harford Co between
Abingdon and Bell-Air by Abraham Jarrett, Esq. Register of Wills, and Henry

Dorsey, esq., Clerk of the Co. They stood at the distance of ten yards,
facing, each a brace of pistols. Both Jarret's shots took effect but
neither wound dangerous. Mr. Dorsey's first fire missed his antagonists,
his second pistol burnt priming/Hatman Lips, having rented Mrs. Kimbolls
elegant billiard tables has just received from Balt new balls, maces and cues
- 6 cents a game in the day time and 12 1/2 cents at night

611. RGM Dec 24 1808/Jacob Shroyer forwans persons from trusting his wife
Catharine as he will pay none of her debts/Joseph Hardy offers reward for
apprentice to waggon making bus. named Anthony Rencher, about 16, about 4 ft
6 inch, slim, very much knockneed, large ball eyes

612. RGM Jan 7 1809/Francis Hagan, 8 miles from Fred Town, has taken up a
stray horse

613. RGM Jan 14 1809/Cheap goods - Benjamin & Eli Ogle/David Halverstaet
and Noah Worman adm, to sell at Jacob Worman's old place, near the Sulpher
Springs, 2 miles from Jacob Landeffe's Mill, pers est of Mary Worman/Joseph
Arnold to apply for relief from debts/Philip Goodman forwarns person from
trusting his wife Elizabeth; he will sell his real and pers prop, about 3
miles from Fred. Town

614. RGM Jan 21 1809/Henry Coppersmith has taken up a stray heiffer/George
Baer offers reward for missing steer, strayed from his plantation near Fred
Town/Joseph Browning to apply for relief from debts/Saddle bags found, can
be picked up at Mr. Deveney's Store in Fred. Town

615. RGM Jan 28 1809/Benjamin Simon, 2 miles from Woodsbury, has taken up a
stray gelding/Thomas Carlton, 3 miles from Fred Town, offers reward for
apprentice boy, Zacheriah Gray, bound to the shoe and boot making bus.,
about 15, 4 ft 3 inch

616. RGM Feb 4 1809/Amelia Wolfenden has removed to the house of Elias
Boteler, decd, where she continues the millinary bus.

617. RGM Feb 11 1809/Elizabeth Philpott adm of Charles Philpott

618. RGM Feb 25 1809/Case of Herbert Otto, Abraham Otto, Tobias Hammer and
Catharine his wife, Matthias Otto, Joseph Black and Elizabeth his wife and
Henry Otto agnst William Otto, Jacob Otto, and the heirs of Peter Otto -
Commission appointed to divide real est of William Otto, decd/John M'Cann
insolvent debtor/John Cookerly insolvent debtor/Sale of real est of Chris-
tian Smith/Sale by Lanham and William Long of real est of Solomon Kephart
decd/Chancery case - Catharine Zimmerman for herself and infant children vs.
Elizabeth, Mary, John, Nancy, Henry, and Susannah Fox - Object is to obtain
decree for recording of deed. The bill states that on 6 March 1808 Henry
Fox executed to Benjamin Zimmerman a deed for tract, Chesnut Levells but not
recorded; Benjamin afterwards died and devised whole of estate to said
Catharine Zimmerman. Henry Fox is since dead leaving the defendants his
heirs/George Ovelman offers reward for apprentice boy, Clem Harding, bound
to the tanning bus./Hugh Sands insolvent debtor, discharged from custody of
the sheriff

619. RGM Mar 25 1809/Samuel Thralls offers reward for apprentice boy named William M'Kinzie, about 20

620. RGM Apr 1 1809/Sale at house of Henry Winemiller, decd, of set of tinman's tools, and furniture - Mary Winemiller and John Winemiller, adm /Zachariah Walker has lost between Fred. Town and Mr. Beads farm cord, linen and a waistcoat pattern

621. RGM Apr 8 1809/Henry Schmeltzer to sell plantation, 117 a./Sale of tract of 105 a. - Peter Summers, living on the place

622. RGM May 20 1809/John Glisan adm of Edward Bond/Samuel Dawson has taken up a stray horse/Farm for sale on Carrol's Manor - William Marshall/John Hooper offers reward for missing geldings/Abraham Rouser offers reward for apprentice boy, Martin Sack, about 5 ft 3-4 inch, about 19

623. RGM May 27 1809/Jacob Widrick to sell horses, milch cows, sheep and a waggon

624. RGM Jun 3 1809/John Hoover and Christn. Hoover, Jun., adm of Christian Hoover/Edward Purdy and Charles Purdy, adm of William Purdy/Henry Poorman adm of Yost Wyandt/Enos Noland to apply for relief from debts/Daniel Yandes, Liberty town, offers reward for apprentice boy, Joseph Knox, bound to the waggon making bus., about 16, 4 ft 10 inch

625. RGM Jun 10 1809/Married Tues 6th inst by Rev Waggoner, Samuel Young of Winchester, Va, to Miss Maria Koontz, dau of Henry Koontz, of this town /Christian Blieckingstaffer, living on the South Mountain, Fred Co, offers reward for apprentice boy named Peter Brier, 15-16, dark hair, dark complexion/John Morrison has taken up a stray mare, trespassing on his enclsures at Gen. Williams' Farm

626. RGM Jun 17 1809/Peter Ortner, Fred Town, offers reward for apprentice to hand screw making bus. named Walter Middleton, upward of 20 yrs of age, dark hair, fair complexion/John Sweningan has taken up a stray gelding /Thomas Morwood has taken up a stray mare

627. RGM Jun 24 1809/Committed to jail of Fred Co, negro boy, who calls himself John Williamson, about 17; says he belongs to Leonard Johns, near the New Port Mills, Montg Co/William Baer of Henry offers to sell 30 barrel of herrings/Sale of house in Creagers-town formerly occ as a store and tavern by Mr. Holtsman, for a number of yrs - Jacob Kuhn/Benjamin Barnhart has taken up a stray gelding/John Miller has taken up a stray mare/William Conradt offers reward for missing cow

628. RGM Jul 1 1809/Died Fri last, Edward Salmon, old inhabitant of this town/John Buckias, Fred. Town, to sell house on Market St/Joseph Miller adm of Leonard Weddle

629. RGM Jul 15 1809/Chancery sale of real est of William Lambky/Sale by William Marshall at his plantation on Carrol's manor of horses, cattle, &c. /Sale at house of William Smith in Woodsberry of land of William Craimer,

decd, 200 a., on Israel's Creek/Bazil Waters, living near Clarksburg, Montg Co, offers reward for negro man, Sam about 30/Anna Brown adm of Henry Brown

630. RGM Jul 22 1809/John Beall forwarns person from trusting his wife Elizabeth Ann Beall, as he is determined not to pay any debts of her contracting/Henry Creager, 5 miles from Fred Town, has taken up a stray colt /Henry Baker offers reward for mare missing from pasture 5 miles below Liberty Town/Frederick W. Shriver forwarns persons from trusting his wife Elizabeth as he will pay none of her contracts

631. RGM Jul 29 1809/Walter Smith has taken up a stray mare/Petition to open a road from Bridle road, at or near Joshua Harley's, from thence to John Fluck's mill, from thence to Henry and John Stembel's mill

632. RGM Aug 5 1809/Jacob Heldbrand, Merryland Tract, to sell negroes/Mills for sale, 5 miles from Fred Town - Philip Fiege/Chancery - Michael Barndollar vs George Fisher, to record deed to tract called The Resurvey on Brother's Agreement/Jacob Shoemaker, Pipe Creek, has taken up a stray mare /Sale of house of Elizabeth Colegate, near the Market House - Benjamin Stallings, Matthias Bartgis

633. RGM Aug 12 1809/Woodland for sale - John Hoffman, adm land of George Erder and Michel Zimmerman

634. RGM Aug 19 1809/Ludwick Hawn, near Union Mills, has taken up a stray horse

635. RGM Sep 16 1809/Sale of house in Fred Town, fronting Church st - Michael Loehr/Sale of farm on road to Creager's Town - Christian Garber; land will be shewn by Jacob Hoover/Persons who purchased prop at sale of Henry Runner, are informed that notes are due

636. RGM Sep 23 1809/Zachariah Zimmond, Taylor, has removed from Newton (Trap) to house of Jonathan Levy/Chancery case - Daniel Burkhart and Henry Baer vs Peter Burkhart - to convey lot in Fred Co sold by George Burkhart, decd, to Henry Baer. The bill states that George Burkhart has died, leaving Peter, George, Christopher, John and Daniel Burkhart, Mary who m Francis Mantz, Margaret who m John Slonaker and Phebe who m Christopher Burkhart, his children, and John Peltz, Joshua, Ezra and Eliza Dill, his grand children, his heirs at law. George & Christopher Burkhart, John and Margaret Slonaker, and John Peltz, are non-residents/Chancery case - Bazil Wood vs Charles Wood (res out of state)/John Winemiller, Montg Co, offers reward for negro, Isaac Dorsey, 35/Enos Noland and Joseph Browning, insolvent debtors, to be dishcarged from custody of sheriff

637. RGM Oct 7 1809/George W. Ent, Fred Town, offers reward for apprentice lad, John Kelly, about 5 ft 4-5 inch, 10 yrs of age, stout well built lad /Henry Stoner insolvent debtor, to be dischared from custody of sheriff

638. RGM Oct 28 1809/Sale by virture of deed of trust of Capt. John S. Lawrence to us Peter Shriner and Allen Talbott, of land, 200 a., 4 miles from Liberty-town

639. RGM Jan 20 1810/Married Tues 16 inst, by Rev Shaffer, Septemus Stevens to Miss Emelia Shriock, all of this co/John Frey cautions person not to take assignment on note given to Mathias Ringer/Jacob Froshour and Christian Brengle adm of Adam Froshour/Joseph Penn to petition for relief from debt

640. RGM Feb 3 1810/Chancery case - Jacob Eversole vs The Attorney General. The bill states that Charles Qus indebted to complaiant died intestate, seized of certain land to which became escheated to state of Md/John Strasburger to sell his farm, 2 miles from Liberty-town

641. RGM Feb 10 1810/John S. Miller and Fredk. Heisely exec of Gottlob Miller, to sell prop of decd, stocking looms and other/Joseph Penn, insolvent debtor, to be dishcared from custody of sheriff

642. RGM Mar 3 1810/Died at the house of John Dill, in this place, 23d ult, Mrs. Margaret M'Graw, aged 36; interred in Cath burial ground/Sale of tract, Shady Grove, prop of Christopher Ambrose, decd, half a mile from mill of Joseph Miller, 125 a. - John Getzandanner, Henry Keefer, Jacob Staley, comm. /Robt. Ritchie to apply for relief from debts

643. RGM Mar 10 1810/James Reid to sell plantation whereon he now lives, on Linganore, 130 a./Christian Weaver to sell land nearly adj Fred Town, adj lot of Christian Brengle, 11 1/4 a./Mills and land to rent, prop of late Jacob Fout, decd - Christian and David Kemp/Chancery sale of real est of Daniel Gaver

644. RGM Mar 24 1810/Frederick Traxsel has taken up a stray gelding

645. RGM Apr 7 1810/Elizabeth Philpott adm of Charles Philpott, to sell land part of tract Merryland on Piners Hill, 5 miles from Harpers ferry /Arthur Boteler offers reward for negro man, Richard Streams

646. RGM Apr 14 1810/Married 8th inst by Rev Daniel Wagner, William Barker to Miss Mary Dorff, both of this town/Died 10th inst of an apolectic, Mrs. Stickle, consort of Solomon Stickle of this place/Died George Nichols, old inhabitant of this co

647. RGM Apr 21 1810/Married Thurs last by Rev David Shaffer, Frederick Reel, to Miss Catharine Zimmerman, all of this place/Sale of house in Bentztown, late in the tenure of Zachariah Simmons - Jonathan Levy/Sale of woodland of late Stephen Shelmerdine - William Campbell, Henry Koontz, jun., Nicholas Randoll, Sebastian Graff, comm.

648. RGM Apr 28 1810/George Castle, jun. has taken up a stray mare

649. RGM May 5 1810/ Married 29th ult by Rev Higgins, Henry Barckman,to Miss Rebecca Champer, both of this co/Robert M'Croffon insoved debtor/Jacob Kiler of Fred Co, insolvent debtor/Jonathan Ballad has taken up a stray mare

650. RGM May 19 1810/L. B. Appollo, reduced through various circumstances, seeks a loan of 60 pounds/Abraham Flenner insolvent debtor, to be discharged from custody of sheriff

(Fredericktown) Bartgis's Republican Gazette

651. RGM Jun 23 1810/Joseph M. Cromwell adm of William Marshall/Chancery sale of real est of John Carter

652. RGM Jul 14 1810/Addison White defends himself in long letter to editor, Mr. Bartgis, "... astonished to see my reputation assailed ..."/G. Jacobs Sen. to sell land, 1 mile from Fred Town, 8 a./Pol Colla has taken up as a stray on his enclosures, of Mrs. Victoire Vincendiere a stray mare

653. RGM Jul 21 1810/Died Thurs morning last, Hieronimus Size, old inhabitant of this town/Ignatius Oferral, Sulpher Springs, Berkley Co, Va, offers reward for negro woman, Nelly/Sarah King, offers reward for negro man, Gerrard, who frequently calls himself Gerrard Thompson/Sale of land on Big Seneca, 800 a., with brick merchant mill, with 3 run of stones, 2 of burr, one cullin's; and other tracts -Allen Simpson, William Benson and Ninian Benson/Sarah Rhodes and Daniel Williard adm of Henry Rhodes, jun.

654. RGM Jul 28 1810/Frederick Eichelberger has taken up a stray cow/Benj. Stallings having removed to Balt, requests payment of debts/Leather lost between Joseph Kemp's Tan-yard and Fred Town/Joseph Waters, Jun., to apply for relief from debts, Montg Co

655. RGM Aug 4 1810/Died Wed 1st inst. Mrs. Coffal, in the 49th year of her age, after a long and tedious illness/Philip Shirtz of Upper Cotoctin hundred has taken up a stray mare/Edward Swany, of Upper Cotoctin hundred has taken up a stray horse/Benjamin Dubell, 15 miles from Fred Town, has taken up a stray mare/Sarah King to sell negro man

656. RGM Aug 18 1810/Persons who bought prop at sale of Jacob Staley are notified that notes are due/Frederick Linthicum to sell house in New Market, lately occ by Miss Poultney and Miss Plummer, near centre of town/Turner Banks, offers reward for missing horse/David Boyd, Fred Town, offers reward for apprentice boy to weaving bus., named Vachel Harding, about 18, 4 ft 8-10 inch/Thomas Newens has found near road from Fred Town to Harpers Ferry in John Baers wood near Fred Town, 3 heaps of clean wheat

657. RGM Aug 25 1810/Mill for sale - on Tuscaro Creek - Adam Shindler /Charles Chaney and Andrew Wickham, Fred Co, insolvent debtors, to be discharged from custody of sheriff/Valentine P. Luckett insolvent debtor

658. RGM Sep 15 1810/Married 28 Aug by Rev David F. Shaeffer, Jacob Shaeffer to Miss Elizabeth Shaeffer, all of this co/Joseph Waters, Jun. to apply to Montg co Court for relief from debts/John Hart, No. 104, North Fourth St., Phila, offers reward for Henry Haufman, German, about 32, 5 ft 8-9 inch who robbed him. He has dark complexion, dark eyes, short dark hair, high cheek bones, large mouth, thick lips/George Castle, 9 miles from Fred town, has taken up a stray bull

659. RGM Sep 22 1810/Died 15th inst, Mr. Seaver, old inhabitant of this co/Sheriff's sale of negres: Ned, Rachel, children named Nelly, Mill and Alfred, negro woman Clary and 3 children, woman Amey and land called Rock Hall in Fred Co, prop of Trammell Delashmutt, at suits of Francis Mantz, Sampson Delashmutt, use of Francis Mantz, John Whiteneck, use of Samuel

Philips, John Brunner and Jacob Grove/Enoch Taylor, 3 miles from Liberty-town, offer reward for missing horse/John Compton, insolvent debtor, to be discharged from custody of sheriff

660. RGM Sep 29 1810/James Gittings to petition for confirmation of deed given by Rebecca Brook to William Dent, for 150 a. of land called Dan, in Montg co

661. RGM Oct 13 1810/Notice from Jacob Kiler that sundry creditors of his refuse their signatures to his discharge under the insolvent laws, renders it his duty to himself and family to petition the Gen Assembly/Sale of tract, in Jefferson Co, Va, 359 a. - John Morrow/Sebastian Ramsburgh to sell at his dwelling near Newtown (Trap), horses, cows, hoggs, waggons, ploughs and all kinds of farming utensils/Elizabeth Seaver to sell on the farm occ by Frederick Seaver, late of Fred Co, decd, cows, hogs, sheep, and other /William Didenhover carries on the fulling & dying bus., 3 miles from Fred Town on Tuscarora Creek; has now erected another fulling mill

662. RGM Oct 20 1810/Charles Robinson, Jun, insolvent debtor, to be dis-charged from custody of sheriff/Chancery sale of real est of John Rusher, decd, consisting of tract Rusher's Purchase and other; Dennis Hanley living on the farm at Owens creek on the one farm and George Kale living on the other farm will shew the land

663. RGM Oct 27 1810/Peter Hawman has commenced the tayloring bus. at Creger's town/George Frederick Gentley, 4 miles from New Market offers re-ward for mulatto servant, Tilly, about 20/Jacob Frushour gives notice that Catharine has left his bed and board/Lewis Hill and Charles Robinson, Jun.., insolvent debtors to be discharged from custody of sheriff

664. RGM Nov 3 1810/Nathan Browning of Nathan, Montg co, to petition for relief from debts/Joseph Castle and Paul Clapsaddle, to be discharged from custody of Sheriff

665. RGM Nov 10 1810/Peter Crist to sell negro/Sale of estate of John Hummell at the house of John Dill, house between houses of Richard Potts, decd and George Schnertzel, in Fred town for benefit of creditors of said John Hummell

666. RGM Nov 17 1810/Hezekiah Conn to sell horses, cows and sheep/Isaac & John Mantz seeks journeymen tanners

667. RGM Nov 24 1810/Joab Waters, living in town of Woodsberry, wishing to leave the state of Md by next Fall, will sell lands on Monocacy river, 187 a. and other/George Fox adm of Jacob Becht, jun./John Williar and Jacob Williar adm of John Williar

668. RGM Dec 1 1810/Died Sun evening 24th inst. Erickson H. Stone, Esq. Attorney at Law of this place; remains interred in the Episc burial ground. Mr. Stone had only returned home, on the Wed previous to his death, from Montg Court, where he was first attacked with a disease that terminated his life in a few days,, leaving widow and orphan

669. RGM Dec 8 1810/Married 27th ult by Rev David F. Shaffer, Lewis Smith
to Miss Elizabeth Eichelberger, dau of Frederick Eichelberger, all of this
co /Married Thurs last by Rev Davidson, John P. Thompson, Editor of the
Fred. town Herald, to Miss Mary Barnhald, all of this co/Married Thurs 6th
inst, by Rev David F. Shaffer, William Bowers, of Wash Co, to Miss Rachael
Adkin, of Fred. Co/Jacob Barth to sell farm, 1 mile from Fred Town and 1/4
mile from Fout's mill, 126 a./Jacob Souder has taken up a stray mare

670. RGM Dec 15 1810/Died near this town on 4th ult, in the 17th year of
his age, Nimrod W. Hearn, after a short, but severe illness, of 6 days,
leaving an aged father and mother/Michael Motter & Frederick Stembel,
Middletown, to give current price for hides

671. RGM Dec 22 1810/Died 29th ult at his res in Ohio Co, Va, Col. George
Stricker, formerly of Fred Co, Md, at the advanced age of 78 yrs, after a
short but painful illness of 3 days. He entered Smallwood's regt as captain
early in 1776, from which he was soon after promoted to Lieut. Col. in the
German regt, raised by Md and Pa; served in 2 campaigns, when owing to some
arrangement relative to rank, in which he considered himself injured, he
retired from the army; and removed from Fred Co to place of his late res.
He was born at Winchester, Va; has left son and 2 daus/Thomas B. Jones, a
Justice of the Peace, to stop the practice of wagons passing to and from
Market through Fred Town on the sabbath, complains about the rattling of
waggon wheels and the crackling of whips, and other complaints/Susannah
Spunt, 3 miles from Middletown has taken up a stray horse/Perry Wayman,
saddler, cap and harness maker has commenced bus. at Newtown (Trap)

672. RGM Dec 29 1810/John Reitzel has commenced at the house opp George
Creager's Tavern and George Trisler's store a tobacco manufactory/Miller
wanted - David Kemp/John Remsberg, near Fred Town, has taken up a large
stray boar

673. RGL/Jul 22 1809/Lawrence Brengle, Morris Jones, Jacob Kuhn and Ezra
Mantz, candidates for sheriff/Benjamin Cecill reports stray gelding to his
plantation nr Clarksburg/Boonsbury church lottery to take place 26 Aug/Mills
for sale 5 miles from Fred town - Philip Fiege/A duel was fought on Wed last
at Centreville, between Mr. Gustavus W. T. Wright and Mr. Nicholson of Baltimore. They exchanged two shots and Mr. N. was each time wounded, but not
dangerously. The cause we are informed originated in Mr. Wright's having
spoken contemptuously of Mr. Charles Sterett Ridgely, in presence of Mr.
Nicholson, who is a relation of his/George Creager, jun, Sheriff of Fred Co,
has committed to gaol of Fred co, negro man who calls himself Charles
Thomas; appears to be about 44 yrs of age, 5 ft 7-8 inch; says he belongs to
Capt Nathaniel Beall, Montgomery Co, nr Wm. Robinson's Mill on Rock creek/S.
R. Hobbs requests creditors to meet with him, being desirous of withdrawing
petition for benefit of insolvent laws/John Baer, of Henry, has recd dry
goods and groceries/Jacob Frushour, Christian Brengle, exec of Adam Frushour
/Committed to gaol of Fred Co, mulatto man who calls himself Dick, about 5
ft 10 inch, appears to be about 34-35 yrs of age; says he belongs to Nicholas Manyweather of AA Co, about 3 miles from Carroll Manor/Andrew Schriver
certifies that John Miller brought before him a stray mare/William R. King,

(Fredericktown) Bartgis's Republican Gazette

Peter Hawman and Samuel R. Hobbs, of Fred Co, insol debtor discharged from custody of sheriff

(Frederick) Hornet, printed and published every Tuesday morning by Matthias Bartgis, at his new English and German Printing Office and Book-Store, at the corner of Market and Patrick-streets.

674. FHM Jan 7 1806/John Ludy, 1/2 mile from Middle Town, has taken up some stray sheep/James Willson, Editor of the Mirror, Wilmington, Del, offers reward for Miles G. Downes, apprentice to the printing bus., age 21 on 26 Dec 1806, stout and strong made

675. FHM Jan 14 1806/Died Mon 6th inst., Mr. John Cookerly, old inhabitant of this co/Married 7th inst by Rev Dubois, Roger B. Taney, Esq., Attorney at Law to Miss Anne Key, dau of Gen. Key, of this co/Married, Mr. J. Strider of Va, to Miss Sally Stoner, of this town/Married George Burckhart to Miss Betsy Castle, both of this co/Daniel Leatt, near the mouth of Monococy, has taken up a stray mare

676. FHM Jan 21 1806/Died Mon 13th inst, Jacob Bierly, old inhabitant of this town/A. Umstattd, Mont Co, forewarns persons from taking assignment on a note given to George Hoyle

677. FHM Jan 28 1806/Married Sun 19th inst, by Rev Wagoner, John Deal, to Mrs. Phebe Fout, all of this town/Died Tues 21st inst., Philip Dawson, son of Nicholas Dawson, Esq. of this co; remains interred in Episc burying ground of this town/Henry Lambright, Fred. Town, to sell house in upper end of Market st/Joseph Miller gives notice to purchasers at sale of prop of George Shoup's that notes are due

678. FHM Feb 4 1806/Married Sun 26th ult., Elias Boteler, to Miss Suckey Evitt, dau of Mr. Woodward Evitt, merchant of this town

679. FHM Feb 11 1806/John Frall claims to have been robbed at Daniel Burkhart's tvern on Monocacy

680. FHM Feb 18 1806/Died 12th inst, Valentine Black of this town; remains enter'd in the Presb burial ground/John Martin, Fred. Town, offers reward for apprentice to the shoemaking bus., Zacariah Jones, about 5 ft 7 inch, 19, well made, brown hair/Caleb Plummer has found a silver watch on George town road, between Clarksburgh and Montg Courthouse/Francis Hagens, Fred Co, living near the Sugar Loaf Mountain and the new glass works, has taken up a stray gelding, now in the possession of Adam Cohlenburg

681. FHM Feb 25 1806/Conrad Young, exec, requests persons indebted to est of John Thomas to make payments

682. FHM Mar 11 1806/Michael Hoffman has for sale near Creager's Town, a Negro girl/Charles Barton, 3 1/2 miles from Fred. Town, offers reward for mulatto boy named William Barton, about 15/Persons indebted to the est of Christian Osterday, senr, are requested to make payment – William Tabler,

Chris. Osterday, Jacob Osterday, exec/Benjamin Routzong, 7 miles from Middle-town, offers reward for John Beard, apprentice to the hatting bus., about 13 yrs of age, brown hair

683. FHM Mar 18 1806/Henry Gardner to sell house where he now lives in Market St/Sale of land at late dwelling plantation of William Rice, decd, 148 3/4 a. 7 miles from Fred. Town - James Rice and Mary Wolf, exec

684. FHM Mar 25 1806/Died Wed last, Nicholas Dawson, Esq., old inhabitant of this co; remains interred in Episc burial ground of this town

685. FHM Apr 1 1806/Married Sun last by Rev Wagner, Michael Buckey, to Miss Catherine Peifer, both of this town/Died Sat 22d inst., Mrs. Mary Catherine Burckhart, inhabitant of this town, in her 78th year; remains interred in the Luther burial ground

686. FHM Apr 15 1806/George Keller will sell his farm whereon he now lives in Fred Co, 123 1/2 a.

687. FHM Apr 29 1806/Died Mon 21st inst, Mrs. Elizabeth Shriner, 75 years old; remains deposited in Presb burial ground of this town/Died Tues 22d inst., John White, aged 24 yrs, son of Capt. White of this town; remains interred Thurs in Episc burying ground of this town

688. FHM May 6 1806/On Wed 30th ult, Lewis Gardner; as he was returning with his cart from Balt, about 7 miles from this town, was found dead on the road; jury of inquest brought in verdict of accidental death by the horses running away with the cart. Bruises were seen on his body, apparently received from the cart running over it. He left a wife and children

689. FHM Jun 17 1806/Married Tues last by Rev Wagner, John Crombine to Miss Sophia Weaver of this town/Marrried John Adlum, formerly of this town, to Miss Polly Cooley of Mont Co/Died Wed last in this town, Adam Ritter, formerly of Winchester, Va/Jacob Neuman adm of Joseph White/Alexander Ogle, living on the premises, to sell tract of 270 a. in Bourborn Co, Ky

690. FHM Jun 24 1806/Christopher Epting carries on the coopering bus. in all its branches at Mr. Deahis(?) Brewery

691. FHM Jul 1 1806/Adam Coblence, living in Middle-town, offers reward for apprentice lad named Dennis Hines, about 18, 5 ft 10 inch, stout, sandy hair, speaks English and German well/Henry Markwert, 5 miles from Fred. Town, offers reward for mulatto woman and child

692. FHM Jul 29 1806/Abraham Strawbridge has taken up a stray cow at his plantation, 6 miles from Fred. Town/John B. Medley, living within 4 miles of the mouth of Monocasy, Montg Co, wishing to decline bus., will sell prop where he now res, 125 a.; improvements are frame dwelling house 60 ft its front occ as a tavern, store house, kitchen, stable/Samuel Robinson seeks the whereabouts of Matthew Robinson, a printer, aged now about 24 yrs, left Harrisburgh, Pa, about 4 yrs ago; last accounts were received from him when he was in Virginia, about 2 yrs ago

693. FHM Aug 5 1806/Lewis Herring, Newtown (Trap), offers reward for negroes, Antony, about 32, and Bet, about 19/Jacob Firestone requests those indebted to him to make payment

694. FHM Aug 12 1806/Christian Reich offers reward for mare missing from yard of John Campble in Woodsbury/Jacob Maltz, 3 miles from Liberty Town, has taken up a stray mare

695. FHM Aug 19 1806/"Samuel Burgess of Caleb is a mean fellow unworthy of notice, like the canker worm, his tongue preys upon honor and honesty... he has said things for the purpose of bringing upon me, the hatred of a beloved uncle, to injure me in my trade... he has (brought) lies and slanderous burthen from my native country, to my adopted one.... He has propagated a scandalous report relative to my denying my own hand writing, in Ann-Arundal to my brother, for the purpose of destroying the confidence of my connections here." - West Burgess.

696. FHM Sep 2 1806/Chambersburg - August 12 - Wed last, Charles Martin, living on the plantation of Simon Eaker, in Antrim township, and a John M'Farlan, of Washington Township, fell victims to the imprudence of entering a well on the place of Mr. Eaker, infected with fixed air. Mr. Martin left a wife and 4 small children

697. FHM Sep 9 1806/Paul Trit forwarns persons from trusting his wife Catharine, as she has left his bed and board/Daniel Walter, Montg Co, near Conrad's ferry, offers reward for negro fellow, Isaac, about 22; sometimes calls himself Isaac Greenfield and other times Isaac Walter/John Waltz, living near Liberty Town, has taken up a stray horse

698. FHM Sep 23 1806/Thomas Benson, Montg Co, near Medley's Tavern, offers reward for negro man, John, about 38/Nathaniel White, living on the premises to sell 312 3/4 a. in Berkley Co, Va

699. FHM Oct 7 1806/Edward Hagthrope, Balt, offers reward for 2 apprentices to the shoe making bus., one a white boy, Patrick Conelley, about 18, 5 ft 5 inch, light hair and a French Mulatto boy, native of St. Domingo, named John Christian, about 18, 5 ft 5 inch; left Balt with a drover headed toward Frederick

700. FHM Nov 11 1806/Christian Rowzan to sell plantation whereon late Philip Jacob Shaffer, decd, lived, 234 a., 4 miles from Middle Town

701. FHM Nov 18 1806/Married 11th inst by Rev Wagner, John Cromwell to Miss Catharine Gephart, dau of John Gephart, all of this town/Married same day by Rev Jasinsky, John Peltz to Miss Elizabeth Markworth, of this place

702. FHM Dec 2 1806/Wm. Aubery has for sale quantity of hempseed at George Baer's store/Samuel Brayfield has taken up a stray heiffer at his plantation near Buck's Town/William Dearn forwarns persons from trusting his wife Margaret Dearn, as he is determined not to pay any debts of her contracting

(Frederick) Hornet

703. FHM Jan 6 1807/Died 29th ult, Henry Fout, aged 81 yrs and 10 months, old inhabitant of this co/Henry Stembel, living in Middle Town, offers reward for apprentice boy named Jacob Herring, bound to the hatting bus., about 5 ft, 19 yrs of age, swaggering walk, freckled in the face, bowlegged

704. FHM Apr 14 1807/Married Tues 7th inst. by Rev Wagner, George Creager, senr, Esq., late sheriff of this co, to Miss Mary Apler, dau of Jacob Apler, at the Sulphur Springs

705. FH Apr 28 1807/If Phillip Summers and Elizabeth Summers, grand children of Phillip Beamer are alive, they are requested to call upon Henry Beamer, Fred Co, as there is a dividend of a legacy left them by their grandfather/Mary Schilknecht adm of Henry Schilknecht

706. FHM May 26 1807/Married Sun 17th inst by Rev Higgins, William Salmon to Miss Sally Davis, both of this co/Married Thurs last by Rev Wagoner, Adam Zealer, to Miss Rebecca Levy, all of this town

707. FHM Aug 30 1809/Jacob Beard, near Fred. Town, has taken up a stray mare

708. FHM Sep 6 1809/George Zimmerman has taken up a stray horse/Emanuel Colclasier, 3 miles from Fred. Town., offers reward for black boy bound to the blacksmith bus., named William Bowers, about 5 ft, 16 yrs old/Charles Stevenson offers for sale plantation on road leading from Westminster to Petersburg, 248 a./Sale of land of 300 a., called Well's Invention, 4 miles of Newtown - William B. Lamar/Christian Keefer, near Fred. Town, offers reward for missing mare

709. FHM Oct 11 1809/Seeking Nancy and Joseph Hutchison, heirs of their uncle, Joseph Hutchison, who died intestate, who are entitled to share in estate, being sought; also Rachel Duffield who res some yrs ago with a Joseph Wood

710. FHM Nov 1 1809/Chancery sale of tract granted to Daniel Gaver, decd, called the Land of Promies, 220 a., on Catoction Creek, 6 miles from Middle town on which Henry Werlder(?) now lives; George Marker living near the premises will shew the land; apply to Samuel Duvall - Roger Nelson, trustee

711. FHM Nov 22 1809/Michael Myers adm of Bernart Gilbert, to sell negroes, horses, cows, hogs, wagon and geers, ploughs and harrows, grain, hay, beds and bedding, house clock and a watch, and furniture/Mary Schilknect forwarns persons from taking assignments on bonds that her husband Henry Schilknect gave to Jeremiah Chaney, exec of William Chaney for purchase of a tract.

712. FHM Nov 29 1809/Married 21st inst by Rev Rawhauser, from Hagerstown, Miss Elizabeth Wagner, of this town, to Rev Frederick Rawhauser of Emmittsburg/Married Thurs evening last by Rev Schafer, Miss Catherine Myers to William Adams/Died 21st inst., Nicholas Hauer, in the 40th year of his age, after a lingering and painful illness/Died Thurs last, Mrs. Mary Reihl, consort of Frederick Reihl, after a long pulmonary complaint/Died 18th inst, Gottlob Miller, in the 73d year of his age/Charlotte Remsberg adm of Jacob

Remsberg, to sell furniture/John Scott exec of George Dixon/Henry Stein-
fifer, near Union Mills, has taken up a stray horse

713. FHM Dec 20 1809/Married 7th inst by Rev Frederick Rauhauser, John
Johnson to Mrs. Heart, late widow of Jacob Heart of this place/Married 12th
inst by Rev Jefferson, John Walker to Miss Charlotte Stuart, dau of Mr.
Stuart, of this co/Married 14th inst by Rev David Shaffer, Daniel Fairman,
to Miss Catharine Keplinger, all of this co/Married 14th inst by Rev Shafer,
Silas Englis, Editor of the late Republican Advocate to Miss Mary Hauer, dau
of late George Hauer, of this place/Married 14th inst by Rev Frederick Rau-
hauser, John Brunner, to Miss Catharine Brunner, dau of John Brunner, all of
this co/George Batson forwarns persons from trespassing on his premises
/Henry Kaufman, boot & shoemaker has removed to house formerly occ by Daniel
Stouffer, Potter/Chancery case - James M'Neely, Martha M'Neely and Letitia
M'Neely agnst Richard Hill. Bill states that Richard Hill executed to John
M'Neely a deed for part of a tract called The Addition to Brooke's Discovery
and said M'Neely having died the said deed was not recorded. Said M'Neely
died intestate, leaving the petitioners, his children, and heirs at law (In
the same issue is a similar chancery case involving same complainants and
Isaac Hill/Chancery case - Jacob Stemmel and others agnst Raphael, John,
Robert, William, Edward and Prudence Logsdon and Margaret Love and Ellis and
Honour, Ellis his wife, heirs of John Logsdon, decd. Object is to obtain
decree for recording a deed for 179 a. of tract called Bedford and part of
Logsdon's amendment/Nicholas Muffar has taken up a stray horse

714. FHM Dec 27 1809/2 pages missing/Hezekia Harris, Montg Co, 15 miles
from Fred. Town, has taken up a stray bull

715. FHM Jan 3 1810/John Brown cautions that Mary Brown has eloped from his
bed and board, 23d Dec, inst/John Spohn, Clarksburg cautions persons from
taking assignment on notes given to Lawrence Snyder

716. FHM Jan 10 1810/Catharine Keller adm of Adam Keller/Chancery case -
Joseph Swearingen vs John Van Swearingen, Thomas Van Swearingen and others -
bill to obtain decree for paying to complainant sums of money due to him
from Thomas Van Swearingen, out of the proceeds of the sale of land and
mills, sold by John Van Swearingen, to Henry and John Stembel. Van Swearingen was possessed of interest in said land and mills, and devised same to
John and Thomas Van Swearingen; the said John Van Swearingen procured title
to be made to Isaac Van Swearingen for said lands and mills who conveyed
them to said John Van Swearingen, who sold same to said Henry and John
Stembel

717. FHM Jan 17 1810/Died 26th Dec, Mary Winnifred Delashmutt, aged 16 yrs,
wife of Trammell Delashmutt/Peter Coblentz adm of Philip Keller

718. FHM Feb 7 1810/Chancery case - Daniel Miller vs John & Alexander
Mitchell, Elias B. Caldwell and Peter Rowman. Object of the bill is to
obtain a conveyance for part of lot No. 70 on Patrick st. The bill states
that Alexander Mitchell on 15 Mar 1803 executed bond of conveyance for same
to Peter Rowman, that said Mitchell since died without conveying same and by
his will appointed Elias B. Caldwell of City of Wash, his exec; that said

Mitchell left John Mitchell, res in Scotland, and Alexander Mitchell, of Wash Co, Md., his only children

719. FHM May 2 1810/Died 26th ult., Mrs. Beall, consort of William M. Beall, Post Master of this town

720. FHM May 9 1810/Married 29th ult by Rev Higgins, Henry Barckman, to Miss Rebecca Champer, both of this co

721. FHM May 30 1810/Married 22d inst., by Rev Simon Goodwin, Dr. Jacob Baer, of this place, to Miss Elizabeth Chinewith, dau of John Chinewith of Berkly Co, Va

722. FHM Jun 6 1810/Died 30th ult Michael Miller, inhabitant of this town, in the 41st year of his age, after a tedious and severe illness/Died at three o'Clock yesterday, Thomas M'Elderry, Esq., one of the Senators in the State Legislature/Elisha Falconer, to sell farm on Bush Creek, 2 miles from New Market, 144 a.

723. FHM Jul 4 1810/Adam Hoffman, Catorus(?) township, York Co, Pa, gives notice that he was indebted to George Weber, on the account of his wife, Amelia Hoffman, the sum of 25 pounds which sum belonged to Amelia as her legacy, after mother's decease, and has been for some yrs due to her. George Weber who moved to the South Branch, Morefield, Va, if alive is requested to call for same - Adam Hoffman, 6 miles from Hanover

724. FHM Jul 11 1810/Married Thurs 28th ult., at Phila, by Rev Helmut, Rev David F. Shaffer, of this town, to Miss Elizabeth Kreps of Phila/Married Sun 2d inst., by Rev Martin, John Bigham to Miss Sarah M'Intire, both of this co

725. FHM Sep 19 1810/William Springer, Fred. Town, offers reward for apprentice named Elias Butler, bound to the Hatting Bus., about 16, 4 ft 5 inch, well made

726. FHM Sep 26 1810/Chancery case - Daniel Miller vs John and Alexander Mitchell, Elias B. Caldwell and Peter Hawman. The bill states that Alexander Mitchell on 15 March 1810 executed a bond of conveyance for a lot on Patrick st to Peter Hawman. Said Mitchell since died, without conveying the same, and left Alexander Mitchell one of his children who it is said, res out of the state of Md. Peter Hawman on 21 Aug 1807 assigned said bond to complainant

727. FHM Oct 17 1810/Died at Barnstable, Va, 23d ult, in his 83d year, Joseph Otis, Esq., son of late James Otis, esq of Barnstble, and brother of distinguished statesman and lawyer of same name/Died at Balt on 28th ult in 47th year of his age, Joseph Spear, merchant of that city

728. FHM Nov 21 1810/Christian Kemp adm of Trammell Delashmutt, to sell at his (Kemp's) dwelling, 4 miles from Fred. Town, near David Kemp's Mill, pers est of decd

Republican Advocate

729. RAM Nov 29 1805/Married Tues last by Rev John Dubois, Monsieur, J.J. Dugas of the house of Dugas and Mitchell, merchants of Balt, to Miss Louisa Morris of Fred Town

730. RAM Jan 10 1806/Commission for division of real est of Elias Lefever, decd, under act of Assembly, to Direct Descents: Jacob Smith and Catharine his wife, Elias Lefever, Dan'l Lefever, Peter Lefever, and John Lefever, agnst Jacob Lefever, Christian Lefever, & Geo. Lefever

731. RAM Jan 17 1810/Married George Burckhartt to Miss Elizabeth Castle, both of this co/Christian Hersheay, Wash Co, gives notice that he purchased from Ignatius Macatee of Fred Co, a negro girl, but said Macatee has previously given bill of sale for same girl to another person/Died Mon last, after a short but severe illness, Frederick Birely, inhabitant of this town; remains interred in German Luth. Burying Ground/Died suddenly, and unexpectedly, the mother of the Editor of this paper, Priscilla Scott, in her 60th year by an appolectic stroke/Chancery case - Philip Bishop & Barbara his wife, Christ. Gorman & Mary his wife, Anna, Barbara & John Evey, agnst Jacob Stoner & Barbara his wife, Eph'm Evey, Jacob Rorer & Elizabeth his wife, Chris. Evey & others. The bill is to obtain decree to sell real est of Christian Evey, of Fred Co, decd, for purpose of dividing proceeds thereof among the heirs. Jacob Evey, eldest son of said Christian, elected to take real est aforesaid at a valuation by commissioners, under act to direct descents, but died before he obtained title. Defendants Jacob and Barbara Stoner, Ephraim Evey, Jacob Rurer and Elizabeth his wife and Christian Evey res out of the state of Md

732. RAM Feb 21 1806/Thomas Elder adm of Guy Elder/Casper Mantz adm of Charles Philpot Taylor/James Rice and Mary Wolf, exec of William Rice to sell tract of decd, 148 3/4 a./Henry Stoner gives account of John Frall who submitted advertisement that he was robbed at Daniel Burkhart's tavern. Stoner says that Frall came to the house of Mr. Burckhart in company with a number of waggoners, very much intoxicated, and behaved in rude manner. John Kreps, constable, being at the house at the same time, by way of amusement to himself, played a few tunes on the violin, whereupon the said Frall began to dance like a maniac and the wagoners joined in with him; whereas Frall and the waggoners began to quarrel. Frall as a means of shewing his consequence, repeatedly pulled out handfulls of small money, swearing that he could buy the whole of the waggoners. Ludwick Kesselring, 4-5 miles from Taney Town, has taken up a stray gelding/J. Dorsey, Trustee, to sell real prop of Nathaniel or Nathan Clary

733. RAM Feb 28 1806/Died Sat last in this town, Mrs. Charlotte Boyer, in 47th year of her age/William Hunter adm of Chudley Mathews/Sale of tract known as Pleasant Valley, adj New-Market, 229 1/2 a. - George Davis, Jonathan Davis, Sarah Davis, Mary Davis

734. RAM Mar 7 1806/Duel Wed last 3 weeks took place in vicinity of Annapolis, between Matthias Hammond, son of Major Philip Hammond, of Anne Arundel Co and William Hammond Marriot, who are related to each other. Two shots were exchanged on each side and Mr. P. Hammond, at the fourth fire, received his antagonist's ball in the right groin but is likely to recover/Married

116

Tues evening last by Rev George Bower, William Ross, Esq., of York, Pa, to Miss Catherine Worthington Johnson, dau of Col. Baker Johnson, of Fred. Town, Md/Died - Jacob Troxell, after a short illness, juror at the late Fred. Co Court, and was attacked whilst in town. A few days after his return home, he expired/Philip Hauptman, Fred. Town, offers reward for Samuel Holtzman, apprentice to the cordwaining bus., about 17 yrs of age, 5 ft 3-4 inch, dark complexion, down look

735. RAM Mar 14 1806/Jacob Appler cautions persons from purchasing from John Winter, who lives somewhere on Pipe Creek, Fred Co, a deed for any land contained in tract, The Deeps

736. RAM Mar 21 1806/Died Tues last by a relapse into a severe indisposition which he had laboered under for a long time, Nicholas Dawson, Esq., inhabitant of this co, in the 56th year of his age; remains interred in Episc burying ground of this town/Catharine Horn to sell two houses in town of Berlin

737. RAM Mar 28 1806/Died in this town Sat 22d inst. at the house of her son George Burkhart, Esq., Mrs. Catharine Burkhart, relict of George Burkhart, decd, in the 78th year of her age; she had 11 children, 75 grandchildren and 25 great-grand children/Died Tues evening last at his farm on Linganore, after a long indisposition, John Hammond, in the 60th year of his age, kind father and indulgent master

738. RAM Apr 4 1806/Elizabeth Johnson adm of Thomas Johnson/Christpher Brandt adm of Charlotte Boyer

739. RAM Apr 11 1806/Cumberland, Md Apr 1st, 1806 - Fire about 4 o'clock broke out in kitchen of Capt. Harry, reached his dwelling house

740. RAM Apr 18 1806/Married same day John Myerheffer to Miss Elizabeth Grover/Married at Pittsburg, 3d inst., Philip Bier to Miss Patience Elliott dau of William Elliott of that Co/Died in Balt, James Winchester, Esq., Judge of the U.S. for the Dist. of Md./Daniel Buzzard, near New Market, offers reward for missing horses /Sale of house adj Woodsborough, prop of Adam Creager decd - Solomon Creager and Christian Creager, exec

741. RAM Apr 25 1806/Married Thurs evening at George-Town, by Rev Balch, Benjamin Hodges, merchant of Upper Marlborough, to Miss Kitty Murdock/Mary Troxall adm of Jacob Troxall

742. RAM May 2 1806/Mr. Gardiner of this town killed Wed about 9 o'clock, coming from Balt, by his cart that was loaded, running over him. His body was found about 7 miles from this place/Jacob Pentz forewarns persons from hunting, shooting, fishing or going through any of his inclosures

743. RAM May 23 1806/Silas Bailey and Jesse Starr, exec of John Starr/Sale of negroes, horses, hogs, 1 milch cow and other, all pers est of Mary Price, decd - George Price, Joseph S. Smith, adm

744. RAM May 30 1806/Married Tues evening 13th inst., Dr. Peregrine War-field, of Anne Arundel Co, to Miss Harriot Sappington, dau of Dr. Sapping-ton, of Liberty Town, Fred co/Married Sun evening 18th inst. by Rev Daniel Wagner, John Fritchie to Miss Barbara Hauer/Married Tues last, Elie Philips to Mrs. Catherine Stallings

745. RAM Jun 27 1806/Chancery case - John Milller vs. Jacob Miller, Abraham Miller, Henry Shoemaker, and Elizabeth his wife, George Miller, Conrad Lech-lider, Elizabeth Lechlider, Geo. Lechlider, Catharine Lechlider, and Magde-lina Lechlider. The bill states that John Miller, the complainant's father on 16 Apr 1787 sold to complainant and the defendant Jacob Miller, a tract called Brookes's Discovery on the rich lands, in Fred Co, 190 a. Jacob Miller on 30 Mar 1791 transferred to the complainant all his title to said land. John Miller, the father, died in 1804 without having conveyed the said land to complainant, leaving the following representatives, that is to say, the complainant, Jacob Miller, Abraham Miller, George Miller, Elizabeth Shoemaker, wife of Henry Shoemaker, Conrad Lechlider, Elizabeth Lechlider, George Lechlider, Catharine Lechlider and Magdeline Lechlider. The said Lechliders are infants and they and said Jacob and George Miller res out of the limits of the court/Married Sun inst. by Rev Wagner, John Rigney to Miss Sophia Heisely, dau of Frederick Heisely, Esq. all of this town/Solomon Glisson and William Stallings adm of Andrew Miller/Chancery case - Jacob Brotzman vs Frederick Holtzapple, Abraham Rodwick and Catharine his wife and others, heirs and devisees of Frederick Holtzapple, decd/ Object of bill is to obtain decree for conveyance of several tracts. The bill states that Frederick Holtzapple, decd, by his last will directed his real and pers est to be sold by his executors, and that Henry Miller and Peter Grossnickle the exec, sold the same to the complainant. Henry Miller one of the exec hath died without having conveyed the said land. Frederick Holtzapple, Junr, Abraham Rodwick and Catherine his wife, res out of the state of Md

746. RAM Jul 11 1806/Thomas Castle son of Thomas has taken up a stray horse

747. RAM Aug 15 1806/William Cramer hast taken up a stray gelding/John Mitten, living in Westminster Town, has taken up a stray horse/Apolonia Shealy adm of Andrew Shealy/Beene Smallwood Pigman, Atty at Law, has opened an office in Fred. Town

748. RAM Aug 29 1806/Married Sun night last, William Fout to Mrs. Magdalena Adams/Married Tues night John Sponceilar (?) to Miss Elizabeth Lambrecht /Long editorial against election of Philip Barron Key who allegedly said that Patrick Magruder had a strong heart but a weak head

749. RAM Oct 10 1806/Dissolution of partnership of William M. Smith and Matthew Steene/Mary Orr adm of Joseph Orr

750. RAM Oct 24 1807/Died yesterday morning at 4 o'clock, Louis Buchanan Smith, eldest son of General Smith

751. RAM Nov 21 1806/Married last evening by Rev Wagner, Oliver Cromwell to Miss Harriot Gebhardt/Chancery case - Benjamin M'Kain vs Samuel Caldwell. Object is to obtain decree for recording deed executed by said Samuel Cald-

well to Benjamin M'Kain on 2 Apr 1803 fo land devised by Alexander M'Kain to said Benjamin M'Kain

752. RAM Nov 28 1806/William Moreland exec of Charles Quay/Westall Ridgeley cautions that his wife Sarah, has left his bed and board

753. RAM Dec 12 1806/Jacob Neff adm of George Miller/John Ramsburgh adm of Philip Charles Smith/J. Browning adm of James Hall

754. RAM Dec 19 1806/Married Sun evening last by Rev Wagner, J. Bausman, of city of Balt, to Miss Elizabeth Birely, of this town

755. RAM Jan 30 1807/Those subscribers to the Republican Advocate who are indebted to John B. Colvin, late editor, will please settle their dues with B.S. Pigman, Atty

756. RAM Feb 6 1807/Ran away from the office of the American, yesterday morning, after neglecting to serve a great number of subscribers to this paper in his usual round, John Brown, carrier of the American for Old Town, nearly 16 yrs of age, about 4 ft 10 onch, flaxen hair, fair complexion, red and full cheeks, face is rather round than long, son of George Brown, miller in vicinity of Fred. Town

757. RAM Apr 10 1807/Married Tues evening last by Rev Wagner, George Creager, Senr, Esq., of this town, to Miss Margaret Appler, of Fred Co/Nicholas Holtz adm of Magdalen Storm/Peter Slyder near Taney Town has taken up a stray gelding

758. RAM Apr 24 1807/Married in Balt on 16th inst., William Baltzell, merchant, to Miss Mackenheimer, dau of Major Mackenheimer, all of that city/Ann Lynn adm of John Lynn/William Clark has taken up a stray mare/Catharine Delawter adm of Jacob Delawter

759. RAM May 22 1807/Married Sun evening last by Rev Higgins, William Salmon of Pleasant Valley, to Miss Sarah Davis of New Market

760. RAM Jun 11 1807/Margaret Fout, Jacob Smith, George Smith adm of Jacob Fout

761. RAM Jul 2 1807/Benjamin Hall adm of Francis Hall/Meshech Browning, Clarksburgh, adm of John Holmes and Mrs. Mary Holmes

762. RAM Jul 16 1807/Died Tues evening last in 23d year of her age, Miss Elizabeth Shellman, dau of Jacob Shellman of this town/Agreeable to last will of Henry Rempsberg, decd, of pers prop - Peter Kemp, exec

763. RAM Jul 23 1807/Died Tues last at his house in vicinity of this town, in the 79th year of his age, George Baer, sen/Chancery sale of real prop whereon William Hall res, in the case of Thomas Burgee, Senr, agnst William Hall - Joab Waters, Trustee/George Markle and Valentine Bowlus adm of George Markle

764. RAM Jul 30 1807/George Phelps, New-Market, offers reward for apprentice boy to the carpenter and joiner's bus., named Hezekiah Warfield, about
5 ft 3 inch, dark hair, brown eyes, dark complexion

765. RAM Aug 20 1807/Deserted from Recruiting Rendezvous at Fred. Town,
Richard W. Leyster, private of the U.S. army, native of Fred. Co, Md, 28 yrs
of age, 5 ft 8 1/2 inch, fair complexion, grey eyes, light hair, by occupation a blacksmith; enlisted in Fred. Town;; said he had been enlisted by
Capt. Peter Shoemaker and regularly discharged at the elapse of the term of
his enlistment, has since that period res near Liberty Town, engaged in the
blacksmith's bus. - John R. N. Luckett, Lieut/Benjamin Hall adm of Francis
Hall

766. RAM Aug 27 1807/Died Sun evening last, Juliana, infant dau of Abraham
Shriver, Esq., of this town

767. RAM Sep 10 1807/Jonathan Levy has taken up a stray mare/Sale of ne-
groes of late Samuel Nicholls - Prisscilla Nicholls and Samuel Nicholls adm
/Sale of plantation 1/2 mile of main road leading from Middletown to Hagers
Town; apply to John Birely, living on the premises or Lewis Birely, at
Zimmer- man's paper-mill

768. RAM Sep 17 1807/Died at Fort Adam on 28 July, Capt. Benjamin Lockwood
of the 1st regt of Infantry, after a short and severe illness/Sarah Shipley, intending to retire from public bus., will let the Fountain Inn; apply
to her or to Thomas Shipley, near New-Market/W.R. King has removed from
Liberty Town to Fred. town to tavern stand of Mr. Schley, lately occ by Mr.
Miller

769. RAM Oct 8 1807/Married Sun evening last, by Rev Daniel Wagner, Jacob
Brunner, to Miss Margaret Doll, dau of Joseph Doll, all of this town/Died
Mon evening last in the vicinity of this town, William Darnall, in the 30th
year of his age/Died 1st inst. at Montg Court House, Mrs. Rebecca Wilson,
consort of Thomas Wilson, Esq. of that place and dau of William M. Beall,
Esq. of this town

770. RAM Oct 29 1807/Died at Norfolk, on board the U.S. Frigate Chesapeake,
Lieut. Benjamin Smith, 1st Lieut of that Frigate/Died at Balt Sat night,
after a long and painful illness, Lieut. James S. Higinbothom of the American navy, in the 25th year of his age

771. RAM Nov 5 1807/Died at Annapolis on 21st ult., Mrs. Elizabeth Kilty,
consort of the Hon. William Kilty, of that place/Nicholas White, Fred. Town,
has found a silver watch on road from this place to Middle-Town

772. RAM Nov 26 1807/Married Thurs last in Old Town, Allegany Co, by Rev
Jacobs, James Hughes, merchant of Balt to Miss Rosanna Fetter, dau of Daniel
Fetter, merchant of the former place/Married Tues evening last by Rev Wagner, Leonard Storm, to Miss Elizabeth Santer, both of this town/Died Fri
evening last after a short illness, in 66th year of her age, Mrs. Margaret
Schley, consort of Capt. George Jacob Schley, of this town/Died Monday morning last, Tobias Bantz, infant son of Henry Bantz of this town/Michael Frack

has taken up a stray mare/Daniel Beall adm d.b.n. of James Beall (of Robt.) and adm of Margaret Beall to sell his dwelling plantation and all pers est of James Beall and Margaret Beall/Chancery case - Michael Walter vs heirs of Henry Myers, decd

773. RAM Jun 2 1808/Died at Phila on 24th ult, James Reynolds, M.D./Died at Balt, 29th ult, Nathaniel B. Wylie, printer, in the 27th year of his age /Died at Balt, Allen Dowell, printer/Margaret Reid adm of Hugh Reid

774. RAM Aug 4 1808/Frederick Rudy adm of Peder(?) Rudy/Jesse Cloud, Taney Town, offers reward of one cent and a chew of tobacco for indented servant girl, named Loveas Albaugh alias Sally Bower, aged 11 yrs

775. RAM Aug 11 1808/Richard L. Head adm of Christian Butts/Tobias Belt, Merryland Tract, offers reward for mising gelding

776. RAM Aug 25 1808/Michael Myers adm of John Rusher

777. RAM Sep 15 1808/John Thomas and Henry Thomas adm of Gabriel Thomas to sell pers est of decd at his at plantation near road leading to Noland's Ferry, 2 miles below Buckey's town/Hugh Lemmon offers reward for horse/Sale of tract near Bards Town, Nelson Co, Ky, by order of the creditors of William Springer - William C. Hobbs, trustee

778. RAM Sep 22 1808/Francis B. Sappington adm of Charles Marchant

779. RAM Oct 27 1808/John Glisan, Liberty Town, has taken up a stray bull /Sale of farm near Trammellsburg, now the prop of heirs of Lindsay Delashmutt, decd, 200 a. - Trammell Delashmutt, John Briscoe

780. RAM Nov 17 1808/William Geisendorffer, Fred. Town, has taken up a stray cow

781. RAM Dec 8 1808/George Household, Balt, has lost his trunk in stage office at Fred. Town, distined for Balt/John Glisan adm to sell at late dwelling of Edward Bond, decd, adj Liberty Town, several items (listed)

782. RAM Dec 15 1808/Married Sun 20th ult by Rev Wagner, George Dorff to Miss Mary Weaver, dau of Christian Weaver, all of this place/John Lookenpeale adm of Malachi Bonham

The Independent American Volunteer, published by William B. Underwood

783. IAM Wed Jul 22 1807, vol. 1/Died Tues evening 14th inst, in 23d year of her age, Miss Elizabeth Shellman, dau of Jacob Shellman, of this town /Died Sat last in the 60th year of her age, after a long and painful illness, Mrs. Anne Hoffstedtler, consort of Henry Hoffstedtler, old inhabitant of this town/Died yestrday in the vicinity of this town, George Baer, senior, in the 79th year of his age/John Liester, near Westminster, has taken up a stray horse/Aaron Cunningham offers reward for horse stolen from stable of Conrad Shafer, in Fred. Town

The Independent American Volunteer (Frederick)

784. IAM Aug 19 1807/Jacob Arnold has taken up a stray gelding

785. IAM Aug 26 1807/Died Tues 21st ult., Miss Mary Watson, of Fayette Co, in the 65th year of her age, having lived in a state of celibacy - Kent pap.

786. IAM Sep 2 1807/Thomas Elder, on Owen's Creek, near Graceham, offers for sale a negro girl, about 18

787. IAM Sep 9 1807/To petition Gen Assembly for road to Wash Co through Middle creek Valley, from Fred. to John Bruner's Mill to John Main's to Daniel Gaber's to John Hoover's passing Hughes's coaling ground to the Cross Roads, at Hughes' Town - Henry Leatherman, Conrad Shafer, Henry Kuhn, Seth Clark

788. IAM Sep 30 1807/Farm for sale, 3 miles from Middletown, 185 a. - George Main

789. IAM Nov 4 1807/John Peak has taken up a stray gelding at his res near the Old Glass Works

790. IAM Dec 2 1807/Thomas Maxwell forwarns persons from taking assignment on note given to Samuel Musgrove, junr, given for a negro boy, which by the will of said Musgrove's grandfather is to be free at age 16

791. IAM Jan 6 1808/Peter Trett, living about 12 miles from Fred. Town, has taken up a stray gelding

792. IAM Jan 20 1808/Joseph Miller exec of Jacob Warenfels/John Yandes, living in Woodsbury, offers reward for apprentice lad named Casper Hardy, a waggon maker, about 5 ft 7-8 inch, upwards of 18 yrs old, slim made, a good look

793. IAM Feb 3 1808/Married at Leesburg Thurs 21st, John Newton, Printer, to Miss Harriet M'Cabbe, of the same place/Died in this town, Mon 25th ult, Mrs. Catharine Bayer, aged 75 yrs

794. IAM Feb 10 1808/Richard Brooke adm of Josias Clements

795. IAM Mar 2 1808/Died Fri morning, 19th ult, between hours of 5 and 6, after a short warning, Amos Thomas, in the 59th year of his age; served as an officer in Rev War

796. IAM Mar 16 1808/Sale of waggon horses, milch cows and other - Michael Late, 9 miles from Fred. Town, 5 miles from Newtown Trap/I inform the public that some time ago Benjamin Biggs did come to Conrad Dottero's house and made mention that if he did not withdraw the suits he had agnst his brothers, he would receive considerable damage in future; and since that time the said Mr. Dotterer has had three barns burnt. I caution all persons agnst offending William Biggs, Frederick Biggs and Jos. Biggs, for said Biggs have taken Mr. Dotterer's rails, &c. - Jacob Grace/Martha Dorsey and Barick Hall adm of E. J. Dorsey/James Allnutt, Mont Co, near the Sugarland,

The Independent American Volunteer (Frederick)

offers reward for Negro man Clem who calls himself Clem Bolin Chaney, about 6 ft, 32 yrs of age

797. IAM Apr 6 1808/Land for sale in Harrison Co Va, 8-9 miles from Clarksburg - James Drummond/William Dydenhover, Montg Co, offers reward for apprentice to the fulling bus., named Greenbury Wilson, about 18, 5 ft 8 inch, well mad lad; had on brown coat and pantaloons

798. IAM Apr 13 1808/Married Tues last, John M'Cann, merchant of this town, to Miss Nelly Burgess, dau of John Burgess, Esq. of Montg Co/Jacob Grace now declares the previous statement about Benjamin Biggs to be false, that he was perverted to say such, that Biggs is an honest man, useful member of society - witnessed by Alexander Fulton, John Hyder. It is observed (by whom?) that Jacob Grace was seduced by Conrad Duttorow to make the false statements/Andrew Mills has taken up a stray mare

799. IAM Apr 20 1808/Married Sun 10th inst by Rev Wagner, Thomas Gitzendanner to Miss Catharine Baer, dau of John Baer, all of this co/Charles G. Righter, hair dresser and wig-maker, lately from Norfolk, has opened a shop opp Mr. Nelson's Office/Jacob Widerick has taken up a stray mare

800. IAM Apr 27 1808/Died Mon 18th inst, after a lingering illness, in the 19th year of his age, Henry White, son of Captain Nicholas White/George Rhodes has lost a red morocco pocket book between Mr. Hildrebrand's house on the Harper's ferry road and Fred. Town

801. IAM May 4 1808/James Gatton exec of James Gatton/George Tice offers reward for apprentice lad to the tailoring bus., named Joseph M'Dade, aged 18-19, about 5 ft 3-4 inch, well set, down look, freckled face; had on a blue coat striped Bennet cord vest, small corded pantaloons/Samuel Potinger, living aobut 15 miles from Fred. Town, has taken up a stray mare

802. IAM May 11 1808/John Bell, living near Gen. Williams's ferry, offers reward for missing mare

803. IAM May 18 1808/Jacob Schlifer offers reward for Jacob Reinecker who stole items from his house. Reinecker says he was born in M'Collester, Pa; has black complexion, one of his eyes hurt. He was employed for a month /Christian Harding forwarns persons not to take assignment on notes given to Alexander Montgomery, living in Liberty Town/Daniel Shoun, near New-Town Trap has taken up a stray mare/John Creager has taken up a stray gelding /George Weterich, 7 miles from Fred. Town, has taken up a stray mare

804. IAM Jun 1 1808/Abraham Grushon has taken up a stray mare

805. IAM Jun 15 1808/Died Sat evening, 4th inst, near this town, Michael Connolly, a native of Ireland, a young man; remains interred in Roman Cath burial ground/Andrew Tucker forwarns persons from trusting his wife Betsy Tucker, as she has left his bed and board/William Jenkins, Fred. Town, offers reward for apprentice boy, by trade a mason, named William Riggs, about 15 yrs old, 4 ft 6-7 inch, dark complexion; took an old brown coating doublet

806. IAM Jun 29 1808/This is to certify that the subscribers have accepted a fire engine constructed by John Achman and now will raise money for such purpose. It throws the water through a tube 3-4ths of an inch diameter, 1-- feet distance, and through a hose of 1-4 feet in length with a tube of 1/2 inch diameter, the additional distance of 70 feet. - Henry Bantz, Jacob Madtert, Francis Mantz, Peter Burckhart, Henry Steiner, George Creager, sen., Lewis Weltzheimer/John Swearingen has taken up a stray mare/Fred. Wm. Shriver and Jacob Shriver forwarns persons from fishing or hunting in their inclosures

807. IAM Jul 13 1808/Married Tues evening by Rev David Martin, Job Hunt to Miss Mary Ann Boyd, all of this town/Ned Boos forwarns persons from trusting his wife Diny Boos, as she has left his bed and board/Michael Irvin seeks information on William Thompson who came to this country from Ireland in 1806, supposedly living at Pittsburg, Pa/William Williams has taken up stray mares

808. IAM Jul 27 1808/Robert Fulton, offers reward for horse stolen from John Scholl's, about 5 miles from Fred. Town/George Barrall, living near Mr. Hobbs' Mill, Bath Creek, offers reward for stolen mare/Daniel Golligar, Liberty town, offers reward for apprentice lad named John Swedner, bound to the hatting bus., about 5 ft 3 inch, about 18, stout made/Died on 18th inst., Charles Philpott, Esq. of this co, occasioned by a fall about 4 days previous, by which one of his arms was broken - a mortification soon took place/Died in this co, Miss Priscilla Tillard, dau of Col. William Tillard /Died at his res near Liberty, on 16th inst, John Wagner, in the 75th year of his age

809. IAM Aug 3 1808/John Adams, Fred. Town, offers reward for missing horse /John Fose, 5 miles from Fred. Town, has taken up a stray cow

810. IAM Aug 10 1808/Catharina Remsperger has taken up a stray colt/Jacob Harbach has taken up a stray gelding

811. IAM Aug 24 1808/Jacob Getzendanner of Gabriel will sell at the plantation where he now lives, 3 miles from Fred. Town, horses, cows, and other /Charles Wilkes offers reward for missing mare/Abraham Grushon, near Creager's town, offers reward for yellow boy named Yok, about 18, 5 ft 2-3 inch/John Crist, 6 miles from Fred. Town, has taken up a stray horse

812. IAM Aug 31 1808/Michael Hardman, Jun., near Delaplain's Mill, Pipe Creek, offers reward for Joseph Disberry, apprentice to the blacksmith bus. /Jehu Hughes offers reward for information on villian who shot a mare of his

813. IAM Sep 14 1808/Hooper's Tavern Races - near Hooper's tavern, 1 miles from Noland's ferry - John Hooper, Andrew Havener

814. IAM Sep 21 1808/Benedict Joy, Carrolls Manor, offers reward for 2 apprentice boys bound to the blacksmith bus., Daniel Barckmon, about 19, well looking lad, and Carlton Taneyhill, about 19, very much pockmarked

815. IAM Oct 12 1808/Adam Stone has taken up a stray colt/Christian Getzandanner, Rockville, intending to remove to the Mississippi Territory, offers a farm for sale where he lives, 2 1/2 miles from Rockville, 420 1/4 a.

816. IAM Nov 2 1808/Thomas Hawkins, exec, to sell agreeable to last will of Erasmus Gitting's late of Fred Co, a tract of 121 a. (Mrs. Jane Gitting's has the use of the tract during her life)

817. IAM Nov 23 1808/John Valentine gives notice that he will pay no debts contracted by his wife Esther Valentine, who having absconded from his house

Variations in spelling are shown in parentheses.

ADAM (Adams) Cornelius; Jacob; James;
    John; John - near Newcomer's Mill
AGER Samuel
ALBERT John; George
ALLEN William
ALLINDER (Allender) Richard; William;
    William - care of Thomas Shuman
ALLISON Andrew
AMOS James
ANDERSON James; John - blacksmith
ANDREW Mr.
ANKENY (Ankony) Henry, jun; Miss
    Polly
ANSHITZ Jacob; Mr. Funks-town
ARMSEY Thomas
ARMSTRONG Catharine; Hugh; John; John
    - care of Gen. T. Sprigg
ARNEL Mary - near Funks-town
ARNOLD David - care of Thomas Garret
ASHBERRY (Ashburry) John
ASHKITTLE James
ATKINSON Thomas
AULT Henry; William, William - care
    of Mary Sullivan
AVEY Christian; Henry; Michael;
    Samuel

BABMAN Jacob
BAECHTEL Martin
BAER Mary, widow
BAILEY Major Robert
BAKER Col. Joshua; Jacob; Elizabeth -
    care of Morris Baker; John - 6
    miles from Hagerstown; Maurice;
    Mrs. Elisabeth; Mrs. Eliza B.;
    Samuel
BALLENT Miss Nancy - prop of Gen.
    Thomas Sprigg
BALSH L.P.W.
BALTZER Anthony
BANER John
BANKS Thomas
BAPTISTE Monsier - care of M.
    Lasenore
BARBER William
BARNES Col. John; John - care of
    Jacob Dunn; Miss Sally; Thomas
BARR Christopher; Jacob; John; Miss
    Ann; Mrs. Barbara

BARTLETT John; John - care of S.
    Ringgold
BARTON John; Will; William - near
    Stephen Barton's
BATTORFF Michael
BAUGHMAN Andrew
BAYLY John; Samuel
BEALL James - care of William Hughes
BEAN George; John
BEARD John; Major Jacob; Mrs.
    Catharine - care of Samuel Miller;
    Richard; Zacharias
BEATTY Martin
BEESE George
BEGOLE Upton
BEIZLEY Benjamin - Chews Farm
BELCH James
BELL James; James - care of Wm.
    Hughes
BELTZHOOVER Elizabeth; Maria
BENCIL Bazil - near Booth's mill
BENDER Melchior
DENNETTE Aquilla
BERGER daniel
BERNHART Henry
BERRY Richard; John G.
BETZ Caty; Ludwick - care of Mr.
    Shuman; Mrs. Mary; William
BEVINS Leonard
BINKLEY Jacob; Michael; Michael -
    care of Geo. and John Binkley
BIRD Job
BIRELY John; Lewis - care of Geo:
    Brendle
BLACKMORE George
BLEAKMORE Mrs. Catharine; William
BLIZARD Capt.
BOBY (or his heirs) John
BOHANIAN Jesse
BOND George; Mrs. Nancy
BOOTH John; John - Delamere Mills;
    Miss Hannah
BORAFF Adam
BORCKERT John - Big Spring
BORGER Daniel - near John Barr's Mill
BORING John
BORRERS Douglas
BOVESON Widow
BOWER Mrs. Rosanna; Widow - 7 miles
    from Hagerstown

BOWMAN Benedict; Henry, senr; Isaac – near John Shafer's Mill
BOWSER Henry
BOYD Walter
BOYER (Boyar, Boyers) Israel; Jacob; John – Paper maker; Philip; Philip, junr
BRADSHAW Miss Mary Ann
BRADY James
BRANDSTATTER (Brandsteter) Andrew – at John Barr's Mill
BRANNAN (Brannen, Brannon, Branon) James; James – care of P. Means; Sarah; Sarah – care of Daniel Harbine; Sarah – care of J. Baechtel
BREADENBAUGH Miss Betsy
BREATHED James; Francis
BRENDLINGER Frederick
BREWER (Breward) Edward; Joseph; Gustavus
BRINHAM John; Miss Sally
BROMET Michael
BROTHERS Mr.
BROWN Alexander; David – care of C. Carroll; Eli; Jacob – care of Beby Bovison; John; John – 5 miles from Hagerstown; Michael; Valentine
BROWNING Joseph
BRUMPARGER Benjamin – care of Christian Bowartz
BRUNEN Widow – care of Philip Mains
BRUNNER Peter
BRYAN Joseph
BUCHANAN Jesse; Joseph – care of John Cushwa
BUCKITT Daniel – 7 miles from Hagerstown
BURAS Richard – Ringgold's Manor
BURD Benjamin
BURGESS Mrs. Elizabeth – care of Adam Shryock
BURK Thomas – care of I. S. White, Sheriff
BURKHART Jacob
BURNS Patrick
BUTERBAUGH David – care of Henry Buterbaugh; Henry; Mrs. Christina – care of H. Buterbaugh
BUTLER Alexander; Miss Charlotte – care of Mr. Huhn; William – at

Gen. Tho. Sprigg's; William – a black man
BYARD Chrisly; Christopher – care of Mr. King, Wagon maker
BYER Jacob
BYERLY John – care of George Brendle

CAMERON James
CAREY Martha
CARR Miss Eliza
CARRICO Mr.
CARROLL William
CARROW Thomas
CARTER Bennett
CASEDY Edward
CEASER Philip – Semple's Manor
CELLARE Mrs. Margaret
CELLARS John; Mrs.
CHACE Thomas
CHADBURN John
CHAMBERS Vincent W.; James
CHANEY (Cheney) Jeremiah; Mr. adminstrator of estate of Mr. Chaney, decd.
CHARLSTON Mr.
CHASE Mrs. Letetia
CHOPPERT Mr.
CHRISMER Anthony or his wife
CHRISTIAN Daniel – near Boonsboro Daniel
CILMORE Francis
CLABBAUGH Miss Margaret – care of John Shaffer
CLAGETT (Claggett) Benjamin; Mrs. Nelly
CLARK Elizabeth; Edward
CLAY Henry, Esq.
CLAYTON Daniel
CLEAPSADLE Mr.
CLEMENTS Mr. F.
CLEMMONS Leonard
CLINE George; Andrew – near Fiery's mill
CLOVES Matthias; Mrs. Susanna
CNODLE Samuel
COALE Joseph A.
COFFMAN Jacob; Henry – care of Michael Kapp
COGGINS John
COGLE Benjamin
COLE George – Schoolmaster
COLLAS Monsier Paul

COLLIFLOWER George
COMBS Coleman - care of Robert
  Douglass Coleman; John - care of
  Robert Douglass
COMMENS Jonathan
COMPTON Miss Margaret; Miss Susan B.;
  William; William S.
CONNER Frederick; Mrs. Elizabeth -
  near Jackes' Furnace; Peter - care
  of Jacob Renner
COOK John - Innkeeper
COON Elizabeth
COOPER Charles - blackman; Samuel
COPY Augustus - care of John Cook,
  Inn-keeper
CORD Michael - on Mason's Farm
CORWIN Oliver
COSSELL Miss Mary
COUARDER Charles; John
COULTER Charles
CRAGUL Jothen
CRAILING John
CRAMPTON Thomas
CRAWFORD George
CRAYLY John - care of Wm. Willis
CREAGER Mr. - saddler Mr.
CREPS George; John Jun. - near Big
  Spring
CRICK Jacob - Big spring
CROMER Samuel
CROUS Peter
CRUMBAUGH Conrad
CUMMINS Jonathan; Jonathan - care of
  Mr. Fernsler
CURTIS William John - Antietam
  Ironworks
CUSHWA David; John
CUTSHAW Miss Jenny
CYBERT Mrs. Anne - care of David
  Harry

DAILY John - care of Philip Clein
DAVIDSON Mrs. Sarah; Robert; Thomas
DAVIS Col. Samuel W.; John; John -
  care of Frederick Fishach; Mrs.
  Catharine; Mrs. Catharine - care
  of David Schnebly; R. C. Richard -
  care of Samuel Ridenour; William
DAVISON Mrs. Susannah
DAWSON John
DAY John - care of Michael Knode
DAYOR Jacob

DEITZ Jacob I. - Bookbinder
DELANEY (Delany) John E.; John
  Edward; Samuel
DELEHUNT Thomas
DENNIS Valentine - about 20 mi from
  Hagerstown
DICK John; Mrs. Susanna
DICKSON Isaac
DIEL George
DIERNER Peter
DIETRICK Jacob D.
DIETZ T. T. - book-binder
DINER Joseph
DITTO Abraham
DOCHINS Michael
DOGOOD Joseph
DOLL Peter - near R. Iseburn's Tavern
DONALDSON Hezekiah; Hezekiah - near
  Funks-town; Mr.
DOOSINGER Philip
DORNBAUGH Jacob
DOUDS Andrew - care of S. Hughes
DOUGHERTY Samuel; Samuel - care of
  Tavern-keeper, Big Spring
DOWLAR Richard
DOWNEY Miss Betsey
DOWNS James
DOYLE Theodore; George
DRURY Thomas
DUHAMEL Rev Charles
DULHEUER Henry
DUNN Jacob
DUNTEN Elijah

EAGLE (Eacle, Eakle) George; Mrs.
  Rachel
EASON William
EASTER Conrad
ECKLEBERGER David - Parkhead-forge
ECLE William
EDWARDS Benjamin; Benjamin - Chew's
  Farm; Benjamin - Ringgolds Manor;
  Patrick; Mrs. Elenora; Thomas -
  care of E. Palmer
ELLICOTT Ely Williams
EMBICH Christopher
EMMARY Miss Margaret
ERECH George
ERHART Frederick
ERLIBACH Mrs. Ann Maria
ERMENTROUT Lewis
ESPECH Jacob

EVERSOL David

FABURELLE Francis
FACKLER Maria - black woman
FASNACHT Henry; John
FAWCETT John
FEIGELE Peter
FERGUSON William
FERNSLER Michael
FERREE Cornelius
FESLER David
FIELD John
FIERY Henry; John
FISCHACH George
FISHER Henry - Funks-town
FITZJERLES Master - care of Mr.
   Brumbaugh
FLEGEL George - care of George Krebs,
   Gunsmith
FLETTER Jacob
FLORA Jacob
FOGLEY Jacob - care of Jacob Rench
FOLK Casper
FOLTZ John - care of Mr. Strouse
FORD Robert
FORRESTER Doctor Alexander
FORSTER Jeremiah
FOSTER George; Jeremiah; Mrs. Sarah
FOUTS (Foutz) David; Mrs. Susanna
FOX George - South Mountain
FRANCIS Adam
FRIEND Jacob
FRUM David
FUNK Jacob jun.; John; Samuel - near
   Newcomer's Mill

GAADIG Geo.
GABBY Margaret
GABRIEL John Jun.; Josiah care of
   John Gabriel
GALE William
GALLOWAY Harry - care of Mr. Prather
   Harry; Samuel
GANSINGER Abraham
GARDNER Wine
GARRETT Thomas
GARVER Isaac; Jacob
GASSAWAY John T.
GATEWOOD Mrs. Mary
GEAR John
GEARHART Mrs. Sophia - widow
GEETING Rev George Adam

GEHR Capt. Daniel
GEISSER Michael
GEITAN Benjamin
GELWICKS John
GERLACH Henry; Trangott
GERLINGER Jacob
GIBBS Edward; Edward A.
GIBSON Robert - care of James
   Ferguson
GILBERT Mrs. - near the Cave; Wendel
GLENN Thomas; Thomas, senr.
GLESSAN Thomas, jun.
GOBLER George
GOLDSMITH Joseph - care of G.
   Beltzhoover
GOOD William, Jun. - near Boonsboro
GOODDEN Elenor
GORDE Jim
GORDON Patrick - care of A. Clagett
GOWER Adam
GRAHAM Joseph - taylor; Victor
GRAY Samuel
GREENWOOD Benjamin
GRIEVES Thomas
GRIFFITH Daniel; George; Henry;
   Silvanus
GRIMM Alexander
GROFF Joseph
GROSH Frederick - Funkstown
GROVE Joseph
GUEDING Rev George Adam - care of
   Christian Newcomer
GUILLON V.
GUSHWA David; John
GWYNE John E. - care of M. Conn,
   Boonsborough

HABLITZEL William
HADDAWAY William W. - Ringgold's
   Manor
HAFFNOR Jacob - care of Mr. Hager
HAGER Jonathan
HAIRBAN Mr. - Innkeper, Nicholson's
   Gap, care of A. Ott, Esq.
HALL John; William
HALLBERT William - near David
   Schnebly's
HAM George; William
HAMILTON Abner
HAMMETT John; Samuel; William
HAMMON (Hammond) Michael; Philip

HANDSBY Frederick - care of Jacob
     Smith; Ludwick - care of Jacob
     Smith
HANES Jacob
HANNAN Thomas
HARDEN John Close
HARLIN Joseph - care of James Hughes
HARMAN William
HARMISON James - near Dr. Jackes
HARR Philip - taylor
HARRISON John; Thomas
HARRY Mr. Druggist
HART Samuel; William
HARTLE Bastian
HARTLY William
HARTMAN Jacob - care of H. Strause
HASSON William - care of J. Rohrer
HAUN Adam; George; Henry - care of
     David Kauhn
HAUSER Isaac
HAVNER Mrs. Barbary
HAWKEN Christian
HAWKER Jacob - near the Welch Run
HAWLING John
HAYES Levin; Maurice
HEATHERINGTON John
HEBB James
HECKLY Henry - near Hagerstown
HEDGER Mrs. Aimy
HEFLEIGH (Heiflich) John; Peter
HEILBRUNER John; John - care of Mr.
     Miller
HEISTER Rosina
HELL Valentine
HELLER Geo.
HELMICK Mrs.
HELTER George - near Fiery's Mill
HENDERSON Lieut. Henry
HERMAN William
HERR Rudolph; Rudolph - 10 mi from
     Hagerstown
HERSHEY John, jun
HESAW George - Herman's Gap
HEST Jacob
HEWET Jacob
HIDE Jacob
HIESTAND Jacob
HIGHLAND William
HIGHT Mrs. Hannah
HILDEBRAND Conrad
HILL David; John H.
HIMERS Andrew

HINDSMAN Joseph
HINES Jacob
HOCKMEYER Widow Daniel
HOEVELMAN John
HOGGINS Samuel
HOGMIRE Jonas; Col. Jonas
HOMES John
HOONE John
HOOVER Peter; John
HOPKINS George - a man of color
HORINE Adam
HORNBAKER Philip
HOWARD Mrs.
HOWER Anthony
HOWSER Christly - 5 miles from
     Boonsboro; Isaac
HUBER George
HUDSON Thomas
HUGGINS Samuel
HUGHES isaac
HUNT William
HUNTER Samuel
HURLEY Moses
HUTCHISON Andrew

IMMON Miss Catharine
INGRAM Mrs. Rachel
IRWIN Andrew; James - care of Jacob
     Dietrick

JAMES Elie
JOBSON Benjamin; Miss - at Mr.
     Ringgolds
JOHNSON Baker - care of Robert
     Johnson; James; John
JOHNSTON John; John - care of Jacob
     Rench; James; Miss Docas; Sarah
JONES Jacob; Jonathan
JUNGMAN John

KARNS Abraham; Miss Susan; Mr.
KARRICK Hugh
KEAGY Abraham
KEATON Thomas
KEITH Miss Mary J.
KEIZER Michael
KELHOFFER Jacob
KELLER (Kellar) Casper; John
KELLY John - fuller; William - care
     of Col. Rochester
KEMP Miss Mary
KENDLE (See Kindle) Barbara

KENNEAR William
KENNEDY George
KEPNER Mary
KERSHNER Jacob; Jacob - blacksmith;
    Jonathan
KERSLEY Miss Elizabeth Tarr - care of
    John T. Kersley, sen.
KESSINGER Jacob
KEY Hugh
KIEFER (Kieffer) Martin
KINDLE (See Kendle) William; William
    - care of Wm. Willis
KING Abraham; Richard
KINKLE Conrad
KISACKER Simon
KITCHEN Henry
KITZMILLER Jacob; John; Mrs.
    Elizabeth
KLENCK George
KLICK Jacob
KLINE Henry - near Hagerstown
KNODE Henry - care of Paul Warner;
    Jacob - Funks-town
KNODEL (Knodle) George - miller;
    Samuel
KNOPS Adam
KORTSMAN Anthony
KREPS George; George, junr; William
KRICK Jacob
KROH Martin
KUNTZ John

LAFRESSELLIERE George - care of Mr.
    Carroll
LANCASTER Joseph
LANDIS Henry
LANE John; Samuel
LANSDALE William M.
LATSHAW Joseph
LAUMAN John - care of David
    Westeberger
LAUTENSHLAGER Henry
LEACH Jepthath
LEFFLER Elizabeth
LEGGET (Liggett) James
LEITER Jacob; Christian
LEWIS Isaac; William - hatter
LIGHTER Jacob
LITTLE Miss Mary; Newson - care of
    Barton Carricoe
LOCKE (Lock) George; George - care of
    P. Binkley; William

LONG Isaac; James; John
LORD Geain
LORSHBAUGH John; Miss Polly
LOWE George; Nicholas
LOWMAN Henry
LOWRY John
LUCAS Theodore
LYLE Mrs. Catharine; Robert -
    Paper-maker
LYNCH Miss Cordelia

M'CALLEY James - care of Mr.
    Heighness; James - Hughes's Iron
    Works
M'CALLISTER James
M'CANN Archibald
M'CAULEY (M'Caully) Hugh; James;
    William
M'CLAIN, James, Esq.
M'CLEARY Elizabeth
M'CLELLAND Alexander
M'COY Daniel; Daniel - living at
    Swope's Mill; James; James - care
    of Col. Rezin Davis; Joseph
M'CREA John
M'DILLON Miss Susanna - Funks-town
M'ELROY Neal
M'FARLAND Isaac Y.; Isaac - care of
    S. Ringgold
M'GINNIS John
M'HILL Gamiel
M'ILROY Neal
M'INTOSH Joseph
M'KEAN Mr. - tanner
M'KEE Hugh; Robert
M'KEGNEY John - care of Col. Schnebly
M'KIERNAN (M'Kernan) Francis;
    Laurence
M'KINNEY Samuel - care of Stephen
    Barton
M'KINSEY Mrs. Christiana - care of
    Samuel Martin
M'KISSECK James
M'KOWN John - care of R. Douglass,
    Esq.
M'KOY John
M'LEARY Mrs. Elizabeth - Funks-town
M'LUNG William
M'MECHAN James
M'MILLIA Archibald - care of R. Beard
M'NAMEE Job; Moses
M'PHERRIN Mrs. Rebecca

M'PIKE Jesse
M'QUIN Michael
M'RACH John
M'ROBERTS Andrew - care of Samuel
 Martin; Andrew - care of W.
 Compton
MACKEY Miss Rachel - care of Mr.
 Wagoner; Mrs.
MAGRUDER Cristian; Christian - care
 of Col. Rochester; Miss
MAINS Philip; Thomas
MALOTT Daniel
MANESCA Mr.
MARIANTZ Jacob - care of Thomas
 Crampton; John - care of Thomas
 Crampton
MARKER Christian
MARSTELLER George; Mrs.
MARTIN George; Nicholas; Stephen
MASON George - hatter; John T.;
 Jeremiah; John Thomson
MATHEWS Michael
MATTINGLEY Gabriel I.
MAURER John Andrew
MEIER Andrew
MELLINGER Henry
MELTON Philip
MELVIN Daniel W.
MERKLIN Henry
MEYER Henry; Jacob; Jacob - Wine
 Gardener; Martin
MEYERLY John - care of Adam Leopard
MEYERS Jacob - near Fiery's Mill;
 Samuel
MEYLIN Christian
MIDDLEKAUFF Henry
MILES Henry - at Hughes's Furnace
MILLER (Millar) Catharine; Daniel;
 David - care of Geo. Stonebreaker;
 Elizabeth; John - son of Geo.
 Miller, decd; Miss Catharine; Mr.
 - tanner; Peter - merchant;
 William; William - care of Mr.
 Alter; William - weaver
MISERS George
MITCHEL David - care of H. Arnold
MONEHAN James
MONG Jacob; Peter
MOORE (More) Benedict; John; John -
 care of S. Miller; Joseph -
 cooper
MORELAND Daniel A.

MORGAN William
MORGENTHAL John
MORRISSON Hugh; Hugh - care of John
 Newson, junr.
MORROW Frederick; William - care of
 H. Arnold
MORTAN David
MOTES Jacob
MOURLAND Daniel A.
MOUTAUD Daniel A.
MUCK Adam
MUFFETT Miss Polly
MUIR Adam
MULLAND (Mullen) Daniel; Mary
MUNN Martha
MURE James
MURPHY Christopher; James -
 blacksmith
MUSE Sandford
MYARS Martin
MYER (Myers) Jacob; Jacob - care of
 Andrew Kline

NATHAN A.M.
NEAD Major Daniel; Matthias
NEAL (Neal, Neill) Dorio; Elisabeth;
 John; Jonathan; St. Leger
NEEDY Miss Margaret; Mrs. Margaret
NELSON Mrs. Catharine; Mrs. Catharine
 - care of David Middelcauff Mrs.
 Catharine
NESBETT (Nesbit, Nesbitt) Elizabeth;
 Nathaniel
NEUSHWANGER Abraham
NEWCOMER Andrew; Christian; Christian
 - 2 miles from Hagerstown; Henry -
 care of Petery Shryock; Jonathan;
 Peter; Rev Christian; Samuel
NEWKIRK Henry
NEWSON John
NICHOLS (Nichol) George; Jacob;
 William - care of A. Ott
NIE John; Philip
NIELL Conrad
NIGH George
NISBITT (Nisbett) Jacob; Nathaniel
NOONEN James
NOTTINGHAM Enoch; Enoch - care of
 Edward Hughes
NOWELL Mrs. Priscilla
NULL Benjamin - care of H. Shaffer

O'NEAL (O'Neill) Charles - Delamere Mills; Paul
OAKES John
ODERFER John
OLIVER (Olliver) John; Mrs. Betty
ORMSTON Ralph; Ralph - at Booth's Mill
ORNDORFF John; Mrs. Susanna
ORR Thomas; Thomas - care of Henry Arnold
ORVEN Henry
OSTER John
OTT Adam, Esq.; Benjamin; Benjamin - near Sharpsburg
OWENS Joshua - care of R. Hughes
OWINGS Francis

PACHEL Martin
PAGE John, jun.
PALMER Bartley; Jacob
PARSONS Daniel
PASKIL William
PATRICK Catharine; Isaac R.; Mrs. Easter; William
PATTERSON Joseph; William P.
PEACOCK Cornelius
PEAK Bennet
PECK Andrew; J. A.; John H.
PEIFER Michael
PELLY Joshua
PENCE Jacob
PENCIL Bazil
PETER David
PHILIPS Abraham; John; Plunket - schoolmaster
PICKET John
PLEAGHER John - on Jacob Lantz's place
POFF Jacob - shoemaker
POFFENBERGER Henry
POST Mrs.
POWERS Thomas
POWLES John
PRATHER Henry; James; Mrs. Ruth - near the North Mountain
PRATT Thomas - care of Elijah Cheney
PRICE Col. Josiah
PRIEST Stephen
PRITNER John - care of H. Kaelhofer
PUTERBAUGH Henry

QUANTRILL Thomas

RACK F.
RAIURES John
RAMER Benjamin; Frederick
RANCKIN Barbara - care of Christian Newkommer; James - care of Dr. Downey
RAPE John
REED Hamilton C.; James
REEDER Hanson
REICHARD Daniel
REIDENOUR (Ridenour) David; George; Jacob; John
REINULL Daniel
REITZEL John
REMANS William B.
RENCH Jacob; John; Margaret; Otho; Peter
REPLOGLE Henry
REYNOLDS John; Loyd; Lucy; Major John; Mrs. Lucina - care of John Booth; Willim M.; William - near Booth's Mill
RHODES William
RICE John
RICHARDSON William
RIGHT Absolom
RINGGOLD Tench
RIPLEY Jacob
RIPPEL Philip
RISHER David
RITTER John
RIVER Jacob
ROBARDET James
ROBERTS Robert
ROBEY Mrs. Susannah; Susanna
ROBINSON John; John - care of William Robinson; William; William W.; William - care of C. Newcomer
ROBISON John; John - care of William Robison; Robert - care of John Cook
ROCK George
ROCKWOOD Easter
ROGERS Edmund; Philip
ROHRER John M.; Mrs. Veronica
ROLAND John
ROLINGS Charles - care of Mr. Hughes
ROLLIN Charles
RONK Mrs. Barbara
ROOTES Thomas, Esq.
ROWLAND Henry; Isaac
RUDISILL Michael

RUSH Frederick
RUSSEL (Russell) Arthur; John;
   Joseph; Miss Kitty
RUTROFF Philip
RUTTER Edmund; Isaac

SAINTMIRES (See Sentmeyer) John
SAMER Vincent
SANDERS Henry
SANNER Mrs. Lydia; Vincent
SAYLOR Michael
SCANDS Hugh
SCHISSLER Hermansler
SCHLENKER Daniel
SCHMIDT Jacob - care of J. Barnett
SCHNEBLY Adam; Daniel; Henry
SCHNIVELY Henry
SCHWIER Nicholas
SCOTT Archibald G. - care of Geo. M.
   Irving; Samuel - care of William
   Hughes Samuel
SEIBERT Jacob
SENTMEYER (See Saintmires) John
SHADDOWES Robert
SHAFFNER Philip
SHALL Samuel
SHANBARGER (Shanabarger) Michael;
   Peter
SHANE Henry
SHANEBIER (Shanabier, Shanebiere)
   Michael; Michael - near Funks-town
SHANK Christian
SHAW John; Thomas
SHEERER Thomas
SHEETS Widow
SHEKAP care of Christian Fechtig,
   Tavern-keeper Michael
SHENEFELD William
SHENK Henry - near the Big Spring
SHICK Lawrence
SHIELDS Samuel, Esq.
SHILCOUP Michael
SHILLING John - care of Jacob Bruner
SHIMER Jacob; Jacob - at Col.
   Hughes's
SHIRLEY Robert
SHNELL John; Mrs. Rachel
SHOLL David
SHONOG John
SHOOFE Adam
SHOOK Daniel
SHOUP John

SHOWMAN Michael
SHRIVER John - care of Matthias
   Shaffner
SHUEY John
SHULL George
SHUPE (Shupe) Daniel; Peter
SHUY John
SIBERT Ann - care of David Harry
   Anne; Elizabeth; Peter - Beaver
   Creek, near Hagerstown
SIEGMUND Jacob
SIMMONS Mrs. Margaret
SIMPSON John
SIPHART Elizabeth
SLAGLE John - near Booth's Mill
SLEIGH Henry - care of John Sleigh
   Henry; John
SLUSHER John
SLYTHE William
SMALL John
SMITH Abraham; Capt John - Harbaugh's
   Gap; Capt Robert; Christian;
   Isaac; Jacob; Jacob - 8 miles from
   Hagerstown; John; Oliver Peter;
   Robert, Esq.; William; William -
   bookseller;
SMUTZ Abraham
SMYTH William - at John T. Mason's
   Esq.
SNEAD Charles
SNEIDER Abraham; Miss Alley
SNELL John - Antietam Forge
SNEYDER Anthony - Innkeeper; Jacob
SNIDER A.; Ann; George - near the Big
   Spring; Jacob
SNIVELEY (Snively) Casper; Mrs. Eve
SNYDER George - on Potomac; Jacob;
   Jacob - near Hagerstown; Michael -
   near John Shafer's Mill
SPEEN James
SPEER John
SPEICE Daniel
SPESSERT (Spessard) David; Peter
SPITZNAGLE (Spitznagel) Jacob;
   Leonard
SPRIGG John; Michael C.; Samuel
SPRINGER Emanuel; Henry; Joseph; Mrs.
   Anna
SPRUCKMAN Solomon
STAIRBUCK Mrs. Nancy
STANTON Elizabeth
STARLAPPER Anthony

STARLING William
STARRETT (Sterrett) James; James –
   care of Peter Rench
STARTZMAN David
STEEL Benjamin
STEFFE (Steffy) Andrew
STEICKLEATHER Peter
STEPHENS Evan
STERLING William
STERN Philip
STEWART (Steward) Daniel – hatter;
   George – Ringgolds Manor; John;
   Moses; Posey
STIKELETTER Peter
STILES Jacob – care of David Harry
STIMEL Albert – care of John Conrod
STINE Henry; John – tobacconist
STONE Esq. E.R.H.; William
STONEBREAKER Michael
STONEKING Henry
STONER David
STOOFER Jacob – near Newcomer's Mill
STOR Jacob
STOUT John
STOVER Frederick; Jacob – tanner
STRADLY Ayres
STRONG David
STULL Capt. Daniel; Daniel
STURR Jacob; Mrs. Elizabeth
SULLINS Richard; Richard – near
   Sharpsburg
SULLIVAN Mary
SUMMEY (Summy) Christian; Samuel
SUTTER Peter
SUTTON Mrs. Mary
SWALES Jacob
SWANAGIM Mrs.
SWAYER John
SWEARINGEN Col.
SWEENY Patrick
SWEITZER Henry
SWINGLEY Benjamins; Leonard – care of
   Rev Rahauser
SWOAP Peter
SYBERT Henry

TALBOTT (Tolbott) John
TALMAN John
TAYLOR James
TEAS John; John – care of Alexander
   Clagett
TEEL Christian

TEITER Daniel – care of John Schnebly
TENLEY Thomas
THOMAS Alexander; Andrew – care of A.
   Waugh; David; Elias; Greigert;
   Philip; Ranatus; Stephen
THOMPSON (Thomson) Andrew – care of
   A. Waugh; Elick; Mathew
THOT Barton
TICE (Tise) Peter; Michael
TILLINGTON James
TITES Thomas
TITJON Christian
TOBY Michael
TODD David – of Kentucky
TONG William
TOUSEY Thomas
TOWNSEND Mr.
TRABINGER Christopher
TRAP Stophel
TRESSLER Jacob
TROUP Adam; Henry
TROXELL David
TROXLER David
TRUMPOWER Leonard
TURNER Edmund H.; Jacob
TYLER Samuel

UTTO Henry

VAN WYCK William
VARLE Charles

WACHTEL (Wachtell) John; Mr. –
   cooper; Zellars
WAGONER Frederick – care of Thomas
   Shuman; John
WALLING Miss Mercy
WALTY John
WARFIELD Billy
WARNER Widow
WASHABAUGH David
WASON John; John – care of A. Johnson
WATKINGS Horatio
WATSON Mrs. Catharine – care of P.
   Watson; Mrs. Christian; Walter
WATT Archibald S.
WAUGH Archibald M.
WEAGLY John
WEBB George; Samuel
WEIS John
WELTY (Walty) Jacob; John
WENGER Philip

WENTLING Jonathan – near Boonsboro
WERNER Peter
WERT Herman
WESTENBERGER David
WEYANDT Christian
WHETSTONE John – near the Big Spring
WHITE Isaac S., Esq.
WHITINGTON John of James
WHITMORE John
WIGANT Christian – near Hess's Mill
WIGENOR Michael
WILKINSON Thomas
WILLIAMS Conrod; Elisha; Robert;
    William B.
WILLIPHKILL Elizabeth – care of
    William Reynolds
WILLIS Andrew; Jacob; William
WILSON David; George; Isaac; James;
    Major Richard; Mrs. Elizabeth;
    Nathaniel; Phebe; Samuel; William;
    William – care of D. Hughes; Zadoc
WILY Joseph
WINTER (Winters) Benjamin; Jacob;
    John
WISEHART Jacob
WITMER John
WOLF Michael; John
WOLFORTH (Wolford, Wolfert, Wolfarth,
    Wolfard) Henry
WOLGAMOT (Wolgamood) Jacob; Mr.;
    David; John; Mr.
WOLTZ Otho
WORD John
WORK Alexander
WORKING Jacob
WORLAND Charles
WRIGHT William
WYANT Christian
WYINKLIN Widow

YACLE (Yakle, Yeckel, Yekle)
    Catharina; Henry – 10 miles from
    Hagerstown; Findley; Jacob; Jacob
    – care of John Cook, Inn-keeper;
    Jacob – 9 miles from Hagerstown
YONTZ Conrod
YOST George; Philip – Mount Etna
    Furnace
YOULGOMOOD John
YOUNG George; Henry; Isaac; P.C.;
    William – care of George Young
YOUNGMAN Daniel

ZACHARIAS George
ZEIGLER (Zigler) Frederick; William
ZELLER Adam; Jacob
ZILLHART Frederick
ZIMMERMAN Abraham; Michael; Michael –
    care of Leonard Broadstone
ZITTLE Michael
ZOPFY S. – care of George Brumbaugh
ZUCK Jacob

APPENDIX B - Letters remaining at the Fredericktown Post Office, 1806-1810

Following are names on letters that have not been picked up at the post office. Note that spelling is that of the sender who may have only heard the name. Variations in spelling are given in parentheses. Because of the poor quality of the print and the reduced size of print these names were oft times difficult to read. Many were impossible to read and omitted.

ADAMS Peter - care of Daniel Howard; William
ADLUM Richard
ALBAUGH Christian
ALBURT Jacob
ALEXANDER William
ALLEN William
ALLISON Henry
APPLER Jacob
ATON David
ATOR David
AUD Joseph
AULL Joseph

BAGENT John
BAKER Conrad; Widow - care of Benjamin Werters; John - care of Mr. Simmons
BALSER John
BALTZELL (Baltzil) George; Jacob; Michael
BALY Widow
BARR Robert R.
BARRICK Jacob
BARTGIS M.
BAYLEY William
BEALL W. M.
BEARD Jacob
BEATTY John M.; Lewis A.; Thomas
BEAVER Jacob
BECKENBAUGH (Beckenbough) Jacob
BEEMESTEFFER George
BELL John - 4 miles from Town; John - care of Mrs. Campbell; Thomas
BELTZELL Dr. Jacob
BENNETT Robert
BENNYSTERSER Peter
BEYER John
BLACK Andrew
BLAIR Mr.
BLANDS Catharine - care of George Baer
BOAH Eliza
BOLAY Elisabeth
BOMGARDNER Jacob
BOONE Robert

BORSTER Burton
BOSS Rebecca M.
BOUGH Frederick - at Blackford's Works
BRANDT Christopher; Rosana
BRANEY John - care of Mr. Walin
BRENGLE Laurence
BRINKMAN John
BRISCOE John
BROOKE Basil
BROOKOVER Thomas
BROWN Dr. Richard; James R.; John H.; Joseph D.; Samuel
BRUBECKER John
BRUNER (Brunner) Jacob, jun.; John - Carroll's Manor; John - near town; Valentine
BUCKEY (Bucky) David; George; George - tanner; Jacob
BUDD Rev Thomsa L.
BUFF Solomon
BUFFARD Philip
BUFFON Benjamin - care of Daniel Miller
BULL John
BURCH Thomas
BURCKHART Christipherf
BURFON Benjamin
BURGESS Miss Elizabeth
BURKHART Christian; John
BURKITT Henry
BURNS Dominick
BURWELL Robert C.
BUSSON Benjamin
BUTLER Richard
BUTTERINU Maria
BUTTS Christian; Henry
BUTZEN's widow of William
BUZARD Daniel
BUZZARD Solomon

CACOE(?) Jacob
CALCLAZER Elizabeth
CAMPBELL Colonel; Elizabeth
CAPPART Catrharine
CARBERRY Gen. Henry

137

CARLINGTON Thomas
CARNAY Patrick
CARNEGY William
CARROL Charles
CARY Robert
CASTLE John; John — care of H. Swann
CAYWOOD John
CHARLES Mary — Johnson's Glassworks
CHARLTON Elizabeth
CILENCE Ritched
CLANCEY John
CLAPPER Frederick
CLARK William
CLAUBAUGH James
CLEMENTS William
CLOPPER Nicholas
CLOYD David
CLYNE Mary
COCHE Samuel
COCHRAN James
COFFMAN Henry
COLCLASTER Mary
COLE Elizabeth — care of George Cole; George; George — schoolmaster
COLEGATE John; Nancy; Richard
COLLER Jacob, jun.
COLVIN John B.
CONRADE Henry
CONSTANTINE Edward
COOK (Cooke) Edmond; John
COOKERLY Jacob
COOMES Baalis; Sarah
COONS George
COOPER James; Robert
COPPERSMITH Henry
COWLEY Thomas
COX William
COYLE Hugh
CRAMER Solomon
CRAVEN H. Luckett
CRAWFORD Samuel
CREAGER Henry; John
CREBLE Elizabeth; Margaret
CRIST Peter
CRUM Abraham
CRUMPARKER John
CUMP George
CURTIS Daniel; William
CURTS Easter — care of George Leipley
CUSHMAN Charles
CUST Peter

DADE Rev Townsend
DAREFMAN Jacob
DARLINGTON Thomas
DARNALL Major Henry; William
DARNEY Patrick
DARR Jacob
DAVIS Elie S.; Ignatius; J. S.; Joseph; Reuben; Richard; Solomon; Thomas
DAVY Henry
DAWSON Nicholas; Samuel
DEAN (Deane) James; Robert; Thomas
DECKER Elyas
DEHEAULME Madam
DELASHMUTT Tremmel
DELEHAY Thomas
DER (Derr) John; John Morton; Martin
DEVILBISS John; George of John
DIBLER Joseph
DIGGES Edward
DILLON Mary
DODD Robert
DODEL Robert
DOLL Conrad, senr
DOMMER(?) Jacob
DORFF Jacob
DORSEY Deborah, care of John L. Dorsey
DOWSON Samuel
DREWRY Miss Rebecca
DURANG John
DUTTRO Peter
DWIER Jane

EADOR Polly
EARLY John — care of Col. McPherson; Sarah
EBERLE John — care of Christian Rhor
EBERTS Christian; George; Jacob
EDMONSON (Edmunson) Robert
EGLEBERGER John
ELLIS Joseph, sen.
EMERSON John
ENGLE Peter
ENGLES Pere
ENGLISH Joseph
ENSEY Polly
EPTING Frederick
ETTINGER John
EVANS Joseph; Thomas
EVERDING Christian
EYFENNOGGLE Solomon

FABRIETZE Henry
FARLING Samuel
FINDLEY Connolly
FIRESTONE Jacob
FISH Bartin
FISHER Elisha; John
FITZPATRICK Joseph
FLANAGAN (Flanigan, Flannigan) John;
    Malichie
FLEMING Polly
FOLER Henry
FORD William
FORKER James F.
FOWLER Sadoc
FOX George; Jacob
FRAFFOU Thomas
FRONK John
FUNDENBERG Walter; Walter - care of
    Jacob Cronise
FUNSTON John

GANT Edward
GARDNER Isaac
GAUGH Abraham - printer of the
    Herald; Christopher; George; John
GEBB Frederick
GERMYER Franz, care of Mr. Potts
GETZENDANNER (Getsendaner) Henry;
    Jacob - at M'Pherson's Mill; John;
    Mary
GIBBONS Thomas
GILBERTS Jonathan
GILLMORE William, junr
GLANCE Frederich, senr
GOSLIN Ambrose
GRAFF (See Groff) Francis - miller;
    Sebastian
GRASON Jane - at Mr. Butlers
GREENWALD Christian
GREEVELL John
GRESS Robert
GRIFFIN John, miller
GRIFFITH Abraham
GRIM Christopher
GRIMES Cornelius
GROFF (Groffe, also see Graff) David;
    William
GROSHUN Abram
GROSS Charles
GRUBER David
GRUENEWALT Christian
GUILLOU Josephe; Mrs. Faure

GUNDERMAN C.L.C.
GWINN Jacob
GYPS Mr.

HAFF Abraham
HALL Elizabeth; Major John S.; Mrs.
    James
HALLER Michael
HALLYBURRON Loudon
HAMBLETON John; Sally
HAMMOND Nathan; Susannah
HANE Ludwick
HANEM Peter
HARBAUGH John
HARDEN Richard
HARDESTY William
HARDING Elias; Lewis; William
HARDMAN Michael
HARE Everard; Rebeccah
HARKIN Patrick
HARRIS Mrs. Rachel
HARRISON Benjamin; Samuel
HARTMAN Elizabeth - care of Henry
    Koffman
HARTZ Francis
HASE Frederick C.
HASFELUT John
HAUCK John
HAWER Nicholas
HAWMAN Peter
HAYDEN Jesse
HAYES George - care of Geo. B. and
    Richard L. Head
HEAD John; R. L.; Richard; Richard
    Lee
HEAM Daniel
HEARN Daniel
HEBRICK Joseph
HEDGES Andrew - care of Geo. Creager;
    William
HEFFNER Michael; Michael of John
HEMPHILL Thomas
HENDERSON Archibald; James
HENRY Steel; William
HIEM Andrew
HILL Christian
HILLAD Christian
HILMON Henry
HINES Adam
HISELEY Mr.
HOBBS Basil N. - Editor of Fred Town
    Herald; William C.

HOCKERSMITH Jacob
HODGES Robert A.
HOFF Garrott
HOFFMAN Henry; Jacob; John,
  blacksmith
HOLLAND Samuel
HOLLARD Joseph
HOLLEN William
HOLLING John
HOLODAY Nancy
HOLTER George
HOLTZ Michael
HOSKINS John
HOUCK John - near Frederick Town
HOUCKS John - chair maker
HOUK John
HOUSER Jacob
HOUX George J., jun.
HOWARD Charles; Dorcas; Mrs. Darkey;
  Samuel
HUFFARD Miss Susannah
HUFFART Daniel
HUFFMAN Francis
HUGHES John; Levy
HULL John; Peter
HUNT John W.
HUNTER John

IJAMS Thomas M.
ISENNAVGAL Michael

JACKSON Henry; James
JACOBS Maria; Michael
JAMES Noah H.; West
JAMISON Baker S.; Leonard; Samuel
JARBOE Rapheal
JEFFERSON Hamilton
JINKINS David
JOHNSON Baker; Benjamin; Casandra;
  Eleanor; Lt. John; Richard;
  Thomas; Thomas W.
JOHNSTON Benjamin
JONES Allen; Benjamin; Car.(?);
  Elizabeth; Jacob; Simon; Thomas
JORDEN John

KAHN Henry
KANTNER Adam
KARKIN Patrick - care of Thmas Conner
KEETS(?) Mrs.
KEIFFER Mary

KELLENBARGER George - care of Mr.
  Kemp
KELLER Conrad; Henry
KELLY Henry
KEMP Christian; Margaret
KENNEDY Nathaniel
KEPERS Mary
KESLER (Kessler) Matthias
KIBER George
KIGHER Conrad
KING William
KINNER Alexander - care of George
  Baer
KISINGER George
KLINE Henry; Mrs. Mary, widow
KOPPERSMITH Mr., Constable
KORBMAN Barbara
KRAYMER Adam
KRIEGER John
KRUNE Jacob
KUFS Jacob
KUMLER Jacob
KYCKMAN John
KYSINGER George

LAIR Henry
LAMBRIGHT Philip
LANGDON Polly
LARKEIN John
LATE Jacob
LAURENCE John; Otho
LAWSTATIN Peter
LEACH Edward
LEAPLY John
LEATHER (Lether) George
LEDDY Andrew
LEE Washington
LESHORN (See Lushhorn) Conrad
LEVY Valentine
LEWIS William
LINDSEY Oliver
LINK Thomas
LINSEY Oliver
LINTON Mary Ann
LITTLEJOHN Wm. M.
LIVERS Judah - care of B. Ogle;
  Thomas
LOTT Catharine
LOW (Lowe, Lows) Jacob; Maria;
  Phillip
LOWERS Peter - La. Sprigg

LUCKET (Luckett) John R.N.; Lawson;
    M.B.; Mountjoy B.; P.; Philip H.;
    Thomas H.; Thomas M.
LUCUS Garrot
LUSHHORN Mary
LYLES Rebecca
LYNCH Barney

M'ATEE James
M'CLAIN Joshua
M'CORMICK Daniel
M'CUTCHIN John
M'DANIEL Joseph
M'DIVIT John
M'DURMETT Hugh
M'GROCHY Rev
M'KATEE Eliza
M'KINNICK George
M'KINTIRE Eliza
M'PHERSON Robert
M'SHPLLEY Robert
MACKUBIN John C.
MAGRAW Mrs. W.
MAHONEY Barnabus
MALSBY Benjamin
MANARY John
MANE John
MANTZ Francis
MARKE John
MARKIN Patrick
MARKLE John
MARKY John
MARSDEN(?) A.
MARSH Andrew - care of Mr. Pence
MARSHALL William
MARTIN George; Isaac; Jacob; James;
    John, senr; M. S.; Rev Daniel
MATHERS Captain Philip
MATTHEWS (Mathews) David; J.; James;
    Jesse
MAYER John
MAYFIELD Thomas
McCORMACK John
McCREARY William - joiner
MEAGER Johanes
MEAM Gilbert
MEASLE Eleanor
MEHANEY Stevin
MELTON Phillip
METZ Jacob; William
MEYNARD Elizabeth
MICHAEL William

MICKLE John
MILLER George, Fishing Creek; Hester
    Ann; Jacob; Jacob - Innkeeper;
    John; Jonathan; Peter
MINTHAN Cornelius
MOBLEY Lewis
MONTGOMERY Alexander; John; Joshan
MOORE Abraham
MORNINGSTAR Michael - care of Peter
    Christ
MORRIS William
MOSSBURY Daniel
MOUNT Thomas
MURPHY James

NAGLE Sebastien
NEAL Elizabeth
NEIL (Neel) John; John - taylor
NELSON Arthur; Henry, care of J.
    Schley; Roger; Thomas
NESMITH Ann
NEWMAN Robert; Robert - care of Mr.
    Colvin
NIEGORE Robert
NOLAND Loid; Thomas; William
NORRIS Edmon; Samuel
NUS Michael - weaver

ODER John George
OGLE John; Peter
ONGLEBARGER George
ORBOUGH Enoch
OTTNER Peter
OWINGS Edward

PALMER Henry
PARKER Barzilla
PATTERSON Joseph
PEASE Jacob
PELLY Joshua
PELTZ John
PENN Nackey
PERRY William
PETTY Jesse
PHILLIPS (Philip) John; Joseph; Miss
    Amelia; Samuel
PITZEL Henry
PLUMMER Jearum; Phillip; Yate
POFF Fany
POOL William
POTTS William
POWELL Thomas

PRICE George
PRINGLE George
PYOTT James

RAGON Basil
RAMSBURG Geor.
RAMSOUR (Ramsower) Henry; Susan
RASZOR Mr.
RAYMOND Stephen
READ (Reat, Reid) James; Rev James;
    James – care of David Martin;
    Robert
REP Adam
REST James – care of George Bentz
REYNOLDS John H.
RHODES (See Road) Maria
RICE John
RICHARDS John – Cooks Mill
RICHARDSON Davis; William
RIDGE Cornelious
RIDGELY Jacob
RIGGS heirs of John – care of Mr.
    Boyer
RIPLEY Jacob
RITCHIE Robert
RITTER J.; Jacob
ROAD John
ROAR John
ROBBY Loyd
ROUZER John
RUNNER Daniel
RUSHER Magdalena
RUSSEL Mr.
RYAN(?) George

SAPHRON Mary
SAUNDERS Walter
SAYLOR Adam
SCHEACHI Francis
SCHLEIGH Jacob
SCHOLLE Christian
SEDWICK Benjamin C.; George S.
SHAFER Philip
SHAHON James
SHINDLER Adam
SHIRLEY Joseph
SHOCK Joseph
SHOOK Solomon – care of George
    Creager
SHOOLS Cathninah
SHOTS Margaret
SHOUN Elizabeth

SHOUND John
SHOVER Peter
SHRANTZ John Frederick
SHRIVER Isaac; Jacob; Philip
SHUH Walter
SHULTZ Catharine; David
SIMMONS John H.
SIMPSON Benjamin
SMELSE Henry
SMITH Christian; Elias; George – care
    of George Buckey; Jane; John; John
    – at Mr. Blackford's; Joseph; Mary
    – care of Jacob Sholman; Matthias;
    Robert
SNUKE Simon
SNYDER Gorge; Mary; Rev Parson
SOCKMAN Marton – care of Mr. Waggoner
SOWER Mr.; Peter
SPEELMAN John
SPOHN John
SPRIGG (Spriggs) Capt. Thomas;
    Lethania; Otho; Thomas
SPRINGER William
STAFFORD David B.
STALLINGS William
STEINER Hannah
STENSON E. – care of John Campbell
STEPHEN Jacob
STEPHENS James
STEPLER Elisha
STEUART John; John – book binder
STEWART James; Posey
STOANBRAHER Sebastian
STOCKER John
STONE E.R.H.
STONEBREAKER (See Stoanbraher)
    George; John
STOOE Adam
STORM Leonard
STOUFER (Stowper) Daniel; Henry
STRAFER Mikel
STULL Adam; John
SUMAN Ellen
SUMMERHILL James
SUMMERWELL William
SURGART John
SWANN Henry
SWARTZ George
SYKES Nathaniel

TABLER Christian
TALL John; Nancy

TANNER Richard
TARLTON Jeremiah; R.
TEELM Robert
TEMPLIN Richard
TERREY Samuel
THOMAS Daniel; Edward; Eleanor;
    Jacob; Levy; Nathan; Otho H. W.
    Lucket; R. B.; Samuel Junr Samuel
THOMPSON Eleckias; John P.; Josias
THRIFT John, Junr
TICE (See Tise) George
TIDEY James
TIDY James
TISE (See Tice) Michael
TOOLE Francis
TOUP Catherine
TRISLER George
TROUT Jacob; John
TRUNDLE David
TUNCLIFF William
TURNER Charles
TYLER Comfort; Dr. John

VAEGELLS John
VANHORN Jesse
VARLE Mr.
VEATCH Hezekiah
VEREMILLION Levi

WALLIS Mr.; Samuel
WANTICE George
WARD William
WARFIELD Henry; Henry R.
WARNER John
WARRING Edwrd G.
WATERS Benjamin
WATT Andrew
WAYNE Isaac
WEAVER Jacob; John
WELLER Henry
WELSH Rev John
WENRIG Johannes
WHADMAN Conrad
WHEELER Hanson; Mr. - student under
    Dr. Martial
WHIP Jacob
WHITE Elisha; James; John; Joseph;
    Richard
WHITMORE Sally
WHITTINGTON John of Jas.
WICKRICH George
WILBEHN Jacob

WILEY William
WILLIAM Harrshman
WILLIAMS James
WILLIAMSON James H.
WILLIS Henry
WILTH Samuel
WINEBREME Phillip
WIREMAN John
WITHERS Sara
WITMAN Abraham
WOOLF Valintine
WRIGHT Isaac; Joshua

YOUNG John; Thomas
YOUS John

ZACHARIA Matthias
ZEBELY James
ZIM Samuel
ZIMMERMAN George; Nicholas

INDEX

(to paragraph numbers NOT page numbers)

Single Names

INDEX

(to paragraph number, NOT page number)

BELWOOD Henry 114; James K. 31; John
  136; Ninian 240, 653; Robert 295;
  William 240, 653
BENSON Thomas 698
BENTER David 463; Margaret 463
BERGER Jacob 100
BERRY John 282, 394, 435
BESSER Henry 300
BEVERLY Robert 197
BICKETT James 135
BICKNELL Esau 317
BIER Philip 740
BIERLY Jacob 676
BIGGS Benjamin 61, 83, 210, 606, 796,
  798; Frederick 796; John 137;
  Joseph 796; Mr. 427; William 796
BIGHAM John 724
BILLMYER Leonard 608
BINCKLEY Jacob 317
BINKLEY George 268, 366, 374, 375,
  376, 395, 428, 545; Jacob 318,
  320, 385; Philip 268, 290, 366
BINNS Charles 199
BIRELEY Lewis 416; Elizabeth 14, 754;
  Frederick 14, 731; Jacob 3; John
  767; Lewis 14, 767; Widow 209
BISCOE James 64, 69
BISER Daniel 93
BISHOP Barbara 731; Philip 731
BLACK Elizabeth 618; Joseph 593, 618;
  Valentine 680
BLACKFORD Benjamin 40; John 271, 366,
  506, 550
Blackford's Ferry 398
BLAIRE Lewis 292
BLAKEMORE William 455, 482
BLESSING Abraham 137, 188; George 137
BLIECKINSTAFFER Christian 625
BLIT Rev 463
BOARD John 285
BOARMAN Raphael 135
BOERSTLER C. G. 475, 476; Christian
  335, 456; Elizabeth 456
BOGEN Dr. 586
BOMGARDNER George 411; Mr. 481
BOND Edward 622, 781; George 343;
  John 420, 553; Thomas 210
BONHAM Malachi 782
BONTZ Henry 7
BOOS Diny 807; Ned 807
BOOTH John 277, 372
BOOTH's Mill 265

BOREOFF Adam 337
BORING Mill 273
BOROFF Catharine 482
BOTELAR Arthur 137; Elias 99; Susanna
  99
BOTELER Alexander 12, 299; Arthur
  645; Edward 210; Elias 616, 678;
  H. 339; Henry 85
BOWART George 472
BOWDEN James 591, 593
BOWE Jacob 332
BOWEN Richard 376
BOWER Abraham 297, 478; George 10,
  64, 198, 309, 734; Mrs. 385; Rev
  96, 257, 261, 270, 284, 297, 301,
  303, 317, 352, 365, 381, 391, 403,
  408, 412, 414, 423, 457, 518, 528,
  538, 580, 597; Sally 774
BOWERS William 669, 708
BOWIE & HERSEY's Mills 355
BOWLAS Jacob 294, 353
BOWLUS Valentine 763
BOWLER Peter 412; William 412
BOWLES Henry 137; James 355; James H.
  552; John 312, 339, 532, 550; Mary
  298, 336; Samuel 295, 298, 336
BOWLING James 380
BOWMAN Baltzer 484; Catharine 464;
  Charles 293, 442; Daniel 267, 317,
  510; John 267
BOWSER Henry 285, 297, 319; Isaac 412
BOX James 367
BOYD David 656; Elisha 131; Mary 261;
  Mary Ann 807; Walter 57, 261, 301,
  304, 312, 353, 399; William 261
BOYER Charlotte 733, 738; Jacob 603;
  Michael 1, 164; Philip 93; R.M.
  37; Thomas 147
BOYLES Charles 1
BRADFORD John 24
BRADLY Patrick 230, 231
BRADY John 68
BRAGONIER Daniel 473
BRANDNER John 404, 410
BRANDT Christian 143; Christopher 738
BRANHAM John 352
BRANN Edward 451
BRANT George 463
BRAWNER Catharine Maria 505
BRAYFIELD Jane 76; Samuel 76, 702
BRAZIER William 469, 478
BREADY George 608; Margaret 608

M'KAIN Alexander 751; Benjamin 751
M'KALEB John 129, 210, 212; Joseph
110
M'KEAN Alexander 72
M'KEE Robert 445
M'KENNEY James 349; John 349
M'KIERNAN Michael 301, 328
M'KIGNEY John 360
M'KINNY Charles 256
M'KINSTRY Joseph 224
M'KINZIE William 619
M'KUBEN Zachariah 75
M'LANAGHAN James 418; Michael 173;
Thomas 418
M'LAUGHLIN E. 466; Henry 448
M'LENAHAN James 385
M'LIND Catharine 380; Samuel 286,
311, 380
M'MAHON Joanna 456; Sarah 511;
William 511
M'MASTERS John 365
M'MECHEN David 102
M'MEEKEN William 230
M'NAIR Samuel 60
M'NAMEE Francis 422; George 463;
Moses 333, 470; Thomas 481
M'NEELY James 713; John 713; Letitia
713; Martha 713
M'NEIL John 212, 533
M'PHERSON & BRIEN's iron works 562
M'PHERSON & BRINN's Iron Works 451
M'PHERSON --- 101; Col. 66; John 3,
114; Jonas 284
MACALL Walter 444
MACATEE Ignatius 731
MACKALL --- 195; Walter 442
MACKENHEIMER Major 758; Miss 758
MACKEY Robert 269
MADTERT Jacob 806
MAGRUDER Alexander 12; Charles 250;
Edward 190, 250; George 197;
Patrick 748; Zachariah 269
MAHANY John 257
MAIN George 222, 788; John 222, 787
MAINE Adam 221
MAINS Philip 261, 299, 377, 532
MAJORS Elizabeth 271
MALAVAY Rev 257
MALLAVAY Rev 252
MALONE Thomas 462

MALOTT Benjamin 287; Daniel 273, 491;
Michael 273, 491; Peter 264, 273,
491
MALTZ Jacob 694
MANADIER Col. 169
MANN Mary 54
MANTZ Casper 732; Elizabeth 112; Ezra
53, 101, 110, 210; Francis 7, 16,
17, 65, 88, 112, 114, 240, 246,
636, 659, 806; Isaac 113, 259, 66;
John 113, 259, 666; Mary 636;
Peter 1
MANYDIER William M. 1
MANYWEATHER Nicholas 673
MARCHANT Charles 778
MARK James 210
MARKEL Jacob 87
MARKER George 710
MARKLE George 763
MARKLEY John 298; Susanna 298
MARKWERT Henry 691
MARKWORTH Elizabeth 701
MARMADUKE Presley 271, 336, 550
MARRIOT William Hammond 734
MARRIOTT Richard 6
MARSH Joel 73, 127
MARSHALL James 31; John 36; William
231, 622, 629, 651
MARSTELLER George 284
MARTIN Benjamin 496; Charles 696;
David 100, 148, 499, 807; Honore
59; Jacob 213; John 74, 680; Lenox
212, 533; Rev 590, 724; Samuel 337
MARTINI Elizabeth 432; George 432,
447
MASON Armistead T. 213; Jeremiah 350;
John 350; John T. 261, 273, 287,
314, 346, 347, 369, 373, 394, 473,
486, 532, 550; Thomas 131; W.T.T.
244; William T. 211; William T. T.
533
Mason's Mill 337
MASONER Frederick 15; George 15
MATHEWS Chudley 733
MATTHEWS Jesse 5, 579; Mill 591
MATZABAUGH Catharine 463
MAUCHLER Christian 355
MAUGHLER Christian 311
MAUTTER Valentine 527
MAXWELL Charles 320; Nancy 320;
Thomas 790
MAYBERRY Justinian 41

RHAUHAUSER Rev 533
RHODES George 800; Henry 653; Sarah 653
RICE George 579, 593; James 210, 683, 732; John 212, 533; William 683, 732
RICHARDS John 600; John C. 240; John Custis 247; Miss 74; Rev. 74
RICHARDSON David 140; Samuel P. 55
Richardson's tavern 232
RICHMOND Braddock 7; Christopher 1; John 96, 170, 190; Joseph 584
RIDDELL Mr. 316
RIDENOUR Amelia 340; Catharine 298; Charles 427; Conrad 298; George 324; Jacob 298, 348, 367, 371, 411; Mary 298; Matthias 312; Milley 298; Nicholas 491; Samuel 298, 319, 385; Sarah 298
RIDGE Cornelius 224
RIDGELEY Sarah 752; Westall 752
RIDGELY Charles 130, 256; Charles Sterett 673; Samuel 130; Samuel N. 256; William 256
RIDGLEY Samuel 1
RIDGWAY Lieut. 516
RIED John 221
RIGGS William 805
RIGHTER Charles G. 799; Peter 298
RIGNEY John 26, 745
RINEHART David 59; George 312, 321; Jacob 392; Thomas 490
RINGER John 271; Mathias 639
RINGGOLD & BOERSTLER 400, 409
RINGGOLD Col. S. 400; Mrs. 290; S. 274, 305, 335; Samuel 175, 267, 273, 287, 373, 408, 456, 475, 476, 479, 494, 532, 541, 550, 558; Tench 124, 218, 309, 313, 367, 401, 406, 541; Thomas 278
Ringgold's Mill 409
RINGLAND John 107, 604
RISE Jacob 236
RITCHIE Abner 44; Ann 44; Esther 324, 347; John 1, 22, 36, 61, 83, 90, 317, 324, 347, 606; Maria 101; Robert 642; William 101, 182
RITTER Adam 689; Jacob 311
Ritter's Ford 522
Ritter's Old Fording 410
RIZER George 212, 228, 533

ROBARDET James 320, 466
ROBERTS Ann 93; John 75; Richard 75; Sarah 75; William 93
ROBERTSON James 10, 16, 65, 580
ROBEY Susanna 375, 432
ROBINETT Moses 447
ROBINSON Charles 662, 663; Matthew 692; Samuel 692; William 673
ROBY Susanna 335
ROCHESTER & BEATTY 332
ROCHESTER Col. N. 273, 322; N. 262, 285, 287, 294, 309, 330, 353, 360, 362, 547; Nathan 341; Nathaniel 349, 468
ROCK George 544
ROCKHOLD Jesse 445
RODGERS Mr. 323; Susanna 317
RODWICK Abraham 745; Catharine 745
ROHR Jacon 65; Philip 6
ROHRBACK Catharine 475; John 475
ROHRER Frederick 328; Jacob 282, 289, 315, 334, 451; Magdalena 474; Martin 295, 324, 474; Samuel 458, 459, 474
Rohrer's Mill 282
ROOT Jacob 318, 354
RORER Elizabeth 731; Jacob 731
ROSS George G. 324, 444, 503; John 1; Samuel 395; William 10, 580, 734
ROTE Jacob 190
ROTROFF Rev 429, 442
ROUSER Abraham 622
ROUTZONG Benjamin 682
ROUZONG Jacob 165, 196
ROW Arthur 593; Frederick 593; George 593
ROWLAND David 282
ROWZAN Christian 700
RUCH Jacob 343, 389
RUCKET Margaret 393
RUDY Frederick 774; Peder 774
RULTON Robert 808
RUNNER Henry 635; William 295
RUSHER John 662, 776
RUSSELL John 238, 337, 384, 388, 401, 402, 410; Susanna 384, 388, 410
RUTH Henry 5
RUTTER George 396
RYLAND Rev 224; William 554

SACK Martin 622

SHAW Mr. 511; Thomas 115, 190, 217, 422; William 212, 533
SHEALY Andrew 747; Apolonia 747
SHEARER Thomas 483, 487
SHEETS Henry 273
SHELBY James 381
SHELHORN John 285
SHELL Charles 7
SHELLMAN Elizabeth 762, 783; Jacob 762, 783; John 154; Mr. 209; Susan 154
SHELMERDINE Eunice 163; Mrs. 169; Stephen 163, 169, 172, 200, 647
SHERBAN Philip 364
SHERER Jacob 379; John 471; Mr. 362
SHERT John 66
SHICK Lawrence 353
SHIMER Jacob 311, 467; John 274
SHINDLER Adam 657
SHIPLEY Rachel 77, 113; Sarah 768; Thomas 77, 244, 768; Thomas Chew 154
SHIRAS George 442
SHIRCLIFF William 387
SHIRTZ Philip 655
SHOEMAKER Elizabeth 745; Henry 745; Jacob 632; Peter 765
SHONK David 398
SHOOL Jacob 462
SHORT Jane 298, 307, 333, 404
SHOUN Daniel 803
SHOUP George 677
SHOUSE Philip 490
SHOVER Peter 161, 411
SHOW Samuel 176
SHOWMAN John 420
SHRADER John T. 321
SHRINER Elizabeth 687; Peter 113, 129, 145, 205, 638; Polly 145
SHRIOCK Emelia 639
SHRIVER Abraham 6, 10, 105, 114, 580, 766; Andrew 210; Elizabeth 630; Frederick W. 630; Frederick William 806; Jacob 83, 171, 806; Juliana 766
SHROEDER Henry 264; Mary 264
SHROYER Jacob 611
SHRUP Matthias 11
SHRYOCK George 354, 366
SHULTZ George 137; Henry 137
SHUMAN Sarah 361; Thomas 272, 343, 361, 403, 464, 573

SHUPE Daniel 374; Jonathan 421
SHYCAW William 282
SIBERT Jacob 399; John 269; Nancy 269
SILVESTER S. 122
SIM Anthony 4, 37
SIMKINS Mary 415; William 415
SIMMITT James 459
SIMMONS John 205; John H. 150, 211; Zachariah 184, 213, 647
SIMON Benjamin 615
SIMPSON Allen 240, 653; Benjamin 583; Charles 95; Sarah 240; Solomon 11
SINGLETON John 287
SINN Jacob 154, 165, 196
SIZE Hieronimus 653
SKILES Margaret 3
SKINNER James 594
SLAGLE John 287; Joseph 397
SLEIGH John 306, 313, 337, 490; Samuel 301, 306
SLICE John 591
SLICER James 79
SLIFER David 118; Ezra 488; Samuel 84; Stephen 293,332
SLONAKER John 636; Margaret 636
SLYDER Peter 757
SMITH Adam 165, 244; Catharine 91; Charles 207; Christian 107, 618; Conrad 467; Daniel 183, 197; David 250; Elizabeth 321; G. 501; General 750; George 328, 399, 432, 449, 472, 504, 532, 538, 552, 760; Gera 451; Henry 111; Isaac 509; Jacob 355, 472, 584, 760; Jacob G. 38; James 282, 321, 459; John 91, 207, 267, 420; John H. 210; John K. 27; Joseph 100, 111, 173, 216; Joseph S. 21, 743; Joseph Sim 54; Lewis 232, 236, 669; Louis Buchanan 750; Matthew 30; Matthias 269; Middleton 21, 210; Mr. 503; Nicholas 380; Peter 272, 320, 471, 492; Philip Charles 753; Reuben 244; Robert 354, 459, 532; Samuel 230, 280; Walter 631; Widow 199; William 203, 285, 629; William H. 558; William M. 749
SMOOT George C. 265, 269, 310, 345, 355, 408, 452
SNATCHEL George 214
SNAVELY Samuel 463
SNETHEN Nicholas 19

TRAXSEL Frederick 644
TRETT Peter 791
Trindle's mill 436
TRISLER George 115, 165, 193, 249,
  254, 672
TRIT Catharine 697; Paul 697
TROUTMAN George 410, 424; Peter 15
TROXALL Jacob 741; Mary 741
TROXEL John 230; Peter 448
TROXELL Jacob 734; Peter 420, 464
TRUNDLE Daniel 134, 207, 242; Ruth
  242
TUCKER Andrew 129, 805; Betsy 805;
  Elizabeth 129; Henry St. G 131;
  Meshach 146
TURBUTT Nicholas 227
TURLEY Charles 63
TURNER Edmund H. 529; Henry S. 63,
  248; Samuel 196; Thomas 196
TUTWILER David 477; Jacob 481, 495;
  Mr. 511
TYGART John 602
TYLER George G. 28; John 114, 115;
  William 238; William B. 198
TYSON Benjamin 518, 550, 552; Peggy
  518

ULRY Mary 290; Samuel 290
UMRICKHOUSE Margaret 465; Peter 282,
  337, 376, 465
UMSTATTD A. 676
UNDERWOOD William B. 783
UNKEFER Frederick 206, 210
UNKERFER Frederick 82

VALANDIGHAM William 259
VALENTINE Elizabeth 200; Esther 817;
  John 817
VAN BIBBER Abraham 1, 8, 268; Andrew
  8, 268; Washington 8, 268
VAN LEAR Matthew 368; William 365
VAN NESS John P. 165, 244
VAN SWEARINGEN Isaac 716; John 716;
  Thomas 716
VANCE Abigail 535; Mary 535
VANLEAR Col. 175; Eliza 518; M. 264;
  Matthew 511, 518
VARNER Anthony 486
VASS James 105
VEATCH Nathan T. 190
VINCENDIERE V. 2; Victoire (Mrs.) 652
VINCENT Samuel 388

WADE Lancelot 98, 233
WAGGONER Rev 625
WAGNER Daniel 4, 13, 16, 21, 26, 44,
  54, 56, 65, 67, 72; 100, 101, 123,
  145, 150, 203, 217, 227, 260, 604,
  646, 744, 769; Elizabeth 203, 712;
  George 5; John 808; Rev 173, 579,
  582, 586, 685, 689, 701, 704, 745,
  751, 754, 757, 772, 782, 799
WAGONER John 337; Rev 677, 706
WALKER George 337; James 124, 325,
  337; John 713; William 385;
  Zachariah 620
WALLING Col. 287; James 527; Mercy
  527
WALMSLEY Dr. T. 262
WALTER Daniel 697; Isaac 697; Michael
  772
WALTERS --- 320; Jacob 320
WALTZ Jacob 373; John 697
WAMPLER J. Lewis 3; John 210; Ludwick
  89
WARDS William 153
WARENFELS Jacob 792
WARFIELD Absalom 54, 94; Alexander
  210; Charles 210; H.R. 189;
  Hezekiah 764; Peregrine 177, 744;
  Thomas 54, 94
WARRING Edward 598
WASHABAUGH David 416
WASHINGTON Fairfax 194; Gen. 11;
  George C. 196; Lau. A. 484
WATERS Basil 184; Bazil 629; Joab
  667, 763; John 1; Joseph 654, 658;
  Sarah 1
WATKINS Edward 338
WATSON Mary 785
WATT James 15; John 315, 352
WATTERSON George 322, 355
WATTERSTON George 365
WATTS John 1
WAUGH A. M. 280, 446, 499; Archibald
  M. 305, 340, 346
WAYMAN John 134; Perry 671
WEAVER Christian 643, 782; David 176;
  Jacob 176; John 176, 232; Lewis
  230; Mary 785, 782; Mr. 352;
  Samuel 232; Sophia 689
WEBB John 298, 327, 357; William 298,
  301, 307, 310, 312, 327, 357
WEBER George 723
WEBSTER Philip L. 1

WOODCOCK John S. 341
WOODS William 1
WOOLF Frederick 404
WOOLGER George 591
WOOTTEN Richard 34
WORLAND Charles 318, 406, 460, 465
WORLEY John 383; Thomas 320
WORMAN Andrew 93; Henry 158; Jacob
    613; Mary 613; Noah 158, 613
WORTHINGTON I.W. 152; John 63;
    Matilda 63; Mr. 220; Nicholas 72,
    214; Thomas 63; William 101
WOUNTER Julianna 375
WRIGHT Edward 1; Gustavus W. T. 673;
    Henry 63; Jesse 210
WYANDT Yost 624
WYANT Yost 210
WYLIE Nathaniel 773

YAKLE Elizabeth 450; Henry 347, 450;
    Jacob 450, 460
YANDES Daniel 624; John 792
YANTZ Conrad 355
YATES William 282, 355, 474, 532, 550
YERGER Michael 392
YOAST Susannah 520
YOE Benjamin 550
YONDISS John 593
YOST George 338
YOUNG Adam 212; Conrad 681; Dr. 262;
    George 353; Jacob 411; John 142,
    281, 289, 309; John E. 212; John
    W. 98; Lodowick 337; Ludwick 293;
    Mr. 307; Mrs. 316; P. C. 281, 289,
    309, 316, 340, 341, 374; Samuel
    271, 309, 341, 465, 625
YOUST George 520

ZARLEY Jacob 285
ZEALER Adam 706
ZEIGLER Christopher 51, 72; Ludwick
    447
Zeigler's store 513
ZEILER Adam 72
ZELLER Jacob 332, 347, 363, 373, 399,
    412, 416, 418, 455; Mary 412
ZENTMOYER David 463
ZIGLER Frederick 395; William 398
ZIMMERMAN Benjamin 121, 618;
    Catharine 416, 618, 647; George
    708; Gotleib 462; John 568;
    Michael 220, 633

174